Signs of Deference, Signs of Demeanour

Signs of Deference, Signs of Demeanour

Interlocutor Reference
and Self-Other Relations across
Southeast Asian Speech Communities

Edited by
Dwi Noverini Djenar and Jack Sidnell

NUS PRESS
SINGAPORE

© 2023 Dwi Noverini Djenar and Jack Sidnell

Published by:
NUS Press
National University of Singapore
AS3-01-02, 3 Arts Link
Singapore 117569

Fax: (65) 6774-0652
E-mail: nusbooks@nus.edu.sg
Website: http://nuspress.nus.edu.sg

ISBN 978-981-325-184-7 (case)
ePDF ISBN 978-981-325-198-4

All rights reserved. This book, or parts thereof, may not be reproduced in any form or by any means, electronic or mechanical, including photocopying, recording or any information storage and retrieval system now known or to be invented, without written permission from the Publisher.

National Library Board, Singapore Cataloguing in Publication Data

Name(s): Djenar, Dwi Noverini, 1961- editor. | Sidnell, Jack, editor.
Title: Signs of Deference, Signs of Demeanour: Interlocutor Reference and Self-Other Relations across Southeast Asian Speech Communities / edited by Dwi Noverini Djenar and Jack Sidnell.
Description: Singapore: NUS Press, [2023]
Identifier(s): ISBN 978-981-325-184-7 (case)
Subject(s): LCSH: Sociolinguistics--Southeast Asia. | Forms of address--Social aspects--Southeast Asia. | Interpersonal relations--Southeast Asia.
Classification: DDC 306.440959--dc23

Cover image: "Neo Old II" by K.E. Djenar, acrylic on canvas

Typeset by: Ogma Solutions Pvt Ltd
Printed by: Integrated Books International

Contents

List of Illustrations		vii
Acknowledgements		ix
Chapter 1	Interlocutor Reference in Southeast Asian Speech Communities: Sociolinguistic Patterns and Interactional Dynamics *Dwi Noverini Djenar and Jack Sidnell*	1

Part 1: Systems

Chapter 2	Asymmetries in the System of Person Reference in Kri, a Language of Upland Laos *N.J. Enfield*	27
Chapter 3	Speaking of People in South-Central Java *Joseph Errington*	44

Part 2: Practices

Chapter 4	Vocatives in Javanese Conversation *Michael C. Ewing*	63
Chapter 5	New Patterns, New Practices: Exploring the Use of English Pronouns *I* and *you* in Asymmetrical Relations in Kuala Lumpur Malay Talk *Sarah Lee*	88

Part 3: Intimacies

Chapter 6	"Respect Those Above, Yield to Those Below": Civility and Social Hierarchy in Vietnamese Interlocutor Reference *Jack Sidnell*	111

Chapter 7   "Friends Who Don't Throw Each Other Away":
             Friendship, Pronouns and Relations on the Edge
             in Luang Prabang, Laos   138
             Charles H.P. Zuckerman

Chapter 8   Interlocutor Reference and Deferential Relations
             in Indonesian Political Interviews   160
             Dwi Noverini Djenar

Part 4: Theories

Chapter 9   Interlocutor Reference and the Complexity of East
             and Southeast Asian Honorific Registers   189
             Luke Fleming

List of Contributors   215
Bibliography   217
Index   243

List of Illustrations

Chapter 2

Figure 1	Kri kin relations and terms	32
Figure 2	A set of kin relations among Kri Mrkaa speakers, labelled by name	34
Table 1	Kri pronouns	29
Table 2	Kin relation categories	42

Chapter 3

Table 1	Changing uses of polite second-person pronouns	46
Table 2	Changing kin term use	47
Table 3	Complementary use of Javanese and Indonesian personal pronouns	55

Chapter 4

Table 1	Four conversations that make up the data analysed	67
Table 2	Frequency of vocatives in Cirebon Javanese conversation	73

Chapter 5

Table 1	Reciprocality of common first- and second-person singular forms in Malay	94
Table 2	Co-participant relations represented in the data	101

Chapter 6

Figure 1	Kin-terms used in reference to persons not genealogically related to speaker	113
Figure 2	Participants in VNR 05	113

Figure 3   Video stills for section of transcript (1)   115
Figure 4   Video stills for line 403 of transcript (10)   132
Table 1   Personal pronoun levels according to Thompson (1988)   130

Chapter 7

Figure 1   The image Muu sent to the group   139
Figure 2   Using "siaw1", Muu tells Dii not to rush during a card game   150
Figure 3   Muu and Khêêng pose with a crate of beer   153
Figure 4   Muu, Khêêng, and Muu's winnings   157
Table 1   Three levels of pronouns   147
Table 2   Two levels of prefixes   147

Chapter 9

Table 1   Paradigmatic patterning can be diagnostic of the indexical
             focus of a T/V system   201
Table 2   Pronouns in the Austronesian language, Sumbawa,
             spoken in Indonesia   203
Table 3   Vietnamese example of asymmetric address between
             housekeeper and house owners   207
Table 4   Old Javanese/Kawi pronouns   212

Acknowledgements

Most of the chapters in this volume grew from papers presented at the Workshop on Language and Social Hierarchy held at the University of Sydney in June 2019. We wish to acknowledge Sydney South East Asia Centre and the School of Languages and Cultures at the University of Sydney for their support. Sincere thanks to Nerida Jarkey for co-organising and contributing to the exchange of ideas that also included David Gil, Zane Goebel, John Hajek and Fakry Hamdani. Special thanks to Joe Errington and Chip Zuckerman for accepting our invitation to contribute to this volume. Many thanks also to two anonymous reviewers for generous comments and suggestions, Peter Schoppert from NUS Press for supporting this project and to Qua Lena for her assistance and patience in responding to our queries.

CHAPTER 1

Interlocutor Reference in Southeast Asian Speech Communities: Sociolinguistic Patterns and Interactional Dynamics

Dwi Noverini Djenar and Jack Sidnell

Delimiting the Domain of Interlocutor Reference

In the Jakarta suburb of Puri Kembangan in the early 2000s, neighbours Basori and Wijanarko, two Indonesian men from comparable socioeconomic backgrounds but different ethnic groups, would often spend the late afternoon chatting, sitting together on a bamboo bench in the common area of the housing complex where they both lived. On such occasions Basori, a Javanese in his forties, and Wijanarko, a Chinese Indonesian in his sixties, would talk to each other in a mixture of high and low *básá* (Errington 1998)—variants of the refined register of Javanese more commonly known as *krama*—employing the pronouns *kula* "I" in self-reference and *panjenengan* "you" (often shortened to *njenengan*) or the kin term *pak* (father) followed by the first syllable of their respective names (*Pak* Bas, *Pak* Wi) in addressee reference. When contextualised by a multitude of co-occurring signs—smiles, nods, a gentle tone of voice—this mutual exchange of *básá* and these terms of reference helped to build an interactional alignment that conveyed mutual respect and affection, an easily recognisable form of urban, multicultural and trans-ethnic civility. At the same time, when viewed from the perspective of a hypothetical observer—for example, an itinerant worker who happened to be in the area—this same conduct might be understood in quite other ways, not as marking an alignment between the conversationalists but rather as distinguishing them from others less skilled in the use of refined Javanese. It is this complex interrelationship between deference and demeanour, between signs in context and the ideologies in relation to which they are understood that the studies in this book seek to explicate.

By "interlocutor reference" we mean the various ways in which speakers (or writers, or signers) refer to themselves and to their addressees (see Sidnell 2019; Fleming and Sidnell 2020). In English, this is almost always accomplished by means of the pronouns *I* (or *me*) and *you*. In other European languages, reference to the addressee involves a choice between a "familiar" (for example, French *tu*) and a "formal" or "polite" form (for example, French *vous*). Questions about the sociolinguistic and interactional consequences of this selection have been at the centre of a research tradition which developed in the wake of a pioneering study by Roger Brown and Albert Gilman (1960) titled "The Pronouns of Power and Solidarity". Indeed, anthropologist Michael Silverstein (2003, 204) proposed that the study by Brown and Gilman "started a whole sociolinguistic industry". As a result of its enduring influence and because subsequent scholarship has likewise tended to focus on Indo-European languages, research in this area has emphasised reference to addressee as opposed to speaker, and reference by means of pronouns as opposed to other lexical classes. However, if we shift the empirical focus from Europe to Southeast Asia, such patterns of address are recast as but one half of a more encompassing domain of interlocutor reference.

Thus, to appreciate the significance of the contributions to this volume we must put together two disparate sets of ideas in the study of participant reference and situate both within an appropriately reflexive semiotic theory of language use. We must first begin with an initial sense of what is involved in address: the indexical modes of deference and demeanour by which self-other relations are mediated in both face-to-face interaction and in other forms of linguistic communication. Second, we have to take account of the ways in which speaker subjectivity is more proximately mediated by forms of self-reference. Consider, in this respect, that a child acquiring Vietnamese will have few opportunities to refer to herself by means of the first-person singular pronoun (although several are theoretically available). Rather, a child acquiring the language in a family setting will typically self-refer with *con* (offspring), *cháu* (niece/nephew/grandchild) or with an appropriately calibrated sibling/cousin term—for example, *anh* (elder brother), *chị* (elder sister), *em* (younger sibling). As such, if Benveniste (1966 [1958]) was correct in proposing that subjectivity is acquired in one's engagement with others in linguistic communication and through the assumption of a term of self-reference, then in the Vietnamese case the subject is constituted not as an autonomous monad (that is, as an "I") but as a node in a network of familial relations. Third, these strands of sociolinguistic thinking must be combined within an appropriately reflexive semiotic framework (Agha 2007). As we discuss below, object signs such as pronouns and kin terms are subject to multiple forms of construal by metasigns—discourses that serve to characterise the significance, distribution, organisation and so on of those object signs.

Sociolinguistics of Addressee-Reference

In "Pronouns of Power and Solidarity", Brown and Gilman considered the use of *T* and *V* forms (for example, French *tu* and *vous*) in a number of European languages including French, German and Italian, describing an historical shift from what they called a "power semantic" to a "solidarity semantic". They argue that, at some point in the past (at different times in different language communities) there was a stable pattern of usage such that:
(1) superiors addressed inferiors as *T* and received *V* in return;
(2) when the parties to an exchange were of equal status and they were familiar with one another, they would use *T*;
(3) when the parties to an exchange were of equal status and they were unfamiliar with one another, they would use *V*.

Brown and Gilman suggest that it is from this long enduring pattern of usage that "*T* derives its common definition as the pronoun of either condescension or intimacy and *V* its definition as the pronoun of reverence or formality" (1960, 258) and go on to propose that the notion of "solidarity" which originally applied only to talk between status equals, differentiating "familiars" from "strangers" etc., eventually spread to other kinds of relation. In other words, solidarity became a factor in selecting a pronoun even in interaction between status unequals: "The dimension of solidarity is potentially applicable to all persons addressed. Power superiors may be solidary (parents, elder siblings) or not solidary (officials whom one seldom sees). Power inferiors, similarly, may be as solidary as the old family retainer and as remote as the waiter in a strange restaurant" (1960, 258–9). This shift towards solidarity gave rise to tensions in which the power semantic suggested one alternative and the solidarity semantic another, and Brown and Gilman argue that in the contemporary period, across a wide range of languages, this tension has resolved in favour of solidarity. Thus, the customer in a French restaurant today addresses an unfamiliar waiter with *V* not with *T*.

While Brown and Gilman were thus able to elegantly account for an historical shift documented for European languages, problems arise when the framework is applied to languages with a wider repertoire of forms, the uses of which do not fit comfortably into such a framework. We note three such problems.

First, the focus on pronouns raises a question as to how lexical nouns, widely employed across Southeast and East Asian speech communities for both addressee and speaker reference, might be accommodated within this model. Note that while pronouns refer by virtue of an indexical connection to the transient facts of interactional role inhabitance—*I* refers to the speaker, *you* to the addressee (see Benveniste1966 [1958])—nouns such as kin terms and titles denote by identifying institutional roles such as "mother," "elder brother", "teacher/master" and so on.

Second, because in the national languages of Europe, speaker reference is almost always accomplished by means of the single available first-person pronoun (for example, English *I*, French *je*) the research tradition that emerged from Brown and Gilman's study focuses on addressee reference and there has been very little attention paid to the ways in which the practices of self and addressee reference combine to form a dynamic system of social meaning.

Third, this focus has likewise encouraged studies of "address" which tend to collapse distinctions between *address* as the act of identifying the recipient of an utterance ("Hey, you there!"), *address terms* being the forms sometimes used to accomplish this ("Excuse me, sir."), and *addressee reference* which involves reference to the addressee as a clausal argument of a verb (*Je t'accuse!* "I accuse you!").[1] For these reasons and others in this introduction and in the book as a whole we recentre the research focus around questions of interlocutor reference as a way to both incorporate and to extend important previous work specifically on address.

Structurally, interlocutor reference involves identification of an argument within a clause, while the vocative is a form of address positioned outside the clause. To take a Shakespearean example, when Lear says to Kent, *Dost thou know me, fellow*? *Thou* and *me* are instances of interlocutor reference, whereas *fellow* is a form of address. In English, kin terms and names are essentially limited to vocative use (*Look at it, Mum*), or third person reference (*Mum will look at it*). The exceptions to this include the highly marked practice of so-called *illeism* which involves a speaker referring to him- or herself by name (see Schegloff 1996) and the use of a kin term—typically *Mummy* or *Daddy*—to refer to the speaker in what Charles Ferguson (1964) described as baby-talk register (sometimes a noun is also used in reference to the child, for example *baby*). Note that in Vietnamese, Indonesian and many other languages of Southeast Asia, nouns such as mother and father as well as personal names are used in making reference to the speaker, the addressee or an absent third party without generating any such specialised inferences (e.g., that this is "baby-talk").

Our purpose in mentioning these problems is both to draw attention to the limitations of the approach that Brown and Gilman introduced and to offer an alternative perspective for conceptualising speaker and addressee reference in terms of the linguistic mediation of self-other relations. As Errington puts it: "[f]rom an interactional viewpoint, more may depend on acts that [...] identify persons, especially speech partners, than on any other aspect of linguistic style" (1988, 111). More specifically, we argue that Southeast Asian languages offer crucial empirical and theoretical opportunities for the study of this domain both in terms of the sociolinguistic dynamics of interaction and the larger social, cultural and ideological conceptualisation of self and personhood.

Indeed, anthropologists of the region have long gestured towards the domain of linguistic practice that forms the focus of this book. In the classic and theoretically groundbreaking *Political Systems of Highland Burma*, for instance, Edmund Leach (1964 [1954], 215) remarks that among the Shan the "*de facto* definition of the nobility is 'those people who can persuade their fellows to address them by title names such as *Sao, Hkun, Nang*, etc.'". (See also, appendix IV of that work on Jinghpaw kinship terminology which likewise concerns various aspects of interlocutor reference.) In *Buddhist Monk, Buddhist Layman: A Study of Urban Monastic Organization in Central Thailand*, the anthropologist Jane Bunnag (1973, 46; see also, the table on page 47) writes: "In the context of interaction between a member of the *Sangha* and a person belonging to the lay community the status superiority of the former over the latter is acknowledged by numerous linguistic usages; in such a situation both monks and laymen use special terms of address and self-reference to express their awareness of the spiritual disparity which exists between them." And, in his famous essay "Person, Time and Conduct in Bali", Clifford Geertz describes a wide array of forms used in reference to persons and many of his conclusions are straight-forward inferences from practices of interlocutor reference.[2] Thus, he (1973, 372) notes that kinship terms are almost never used vocatively and only rarely for reference to non-participants. Geertz explains that "[f]or relatives genealogically junior to oneself vocative forms do not even exist; for relatives senior they exist but, as with personal names, it is felt to demonstrate a lack of respect for one's elders to use them" (1973, 372). Such an avoidance of kinship terms is seen even in the talk of young children: "As soon as a child is old enough to be capable of doing so [...] he calls his mother and father by the same term — a teknonym, status group title, or public title—that everyone else who is acquainted with them uses toward them, and is called in turn *Wayan, Ktut*, or whatever, by them" (1973, 373; *Wayan* and *Ktut* are birth order names). On the basis of such observations, Geertz concludes that "the Balinese system of kinship terminology defines individuals in a primarily taxonomic, not a face-to-face idiom, as occupants of regions in a social field, not partners in social interaction" (1973, 373). This selection of a few examples from many possible indicates that anthropologists have long been attuned to the importance of interlocutor reference in Southeast Asia. Until now, however, there has been no attempt to provide a systematic account of the relevant practices or to assess the degree of variation across the region.

Before we discuss interlocutor reference practices in this linguistically diverse region, an elaboration on the three problems we have identified will serve to introduce some of the main themes of the book.

Pronouns, Lexical Nouns and Participant Roles

When used to refer to the interactional roles of speaker and addressee, lexical nouns such as kin terms, names and titles are sometimes called "pronoun substitutes" or "pronominal imposters" because, from the perspective of a language like English, they appear to stand in for pronouns, essentially "replacing" them at the surface of discourse.[3] But such implied characterisations are misleading insofar as they involve an attempt to fit non-pronominal elements into the universal paradigm of grammatical person, number and clusivity which typically define the set of pronouns in a language. The purpose of drawing a pronoun paradigm is to inventorise available pronominal forms, but the inclusion of the various lexical nouns used in interlocutor reference would undermine any such attempt. Although the number of kin terms available to a speech community may be finite (if extensive), and titles may be reduceable to a list of commonly used forms, the number of distinct names is limited, in principle at least, only by the number of people who bear them (and, of course, a single person may have multiple names). Unlike pronouns, then, lexical nouns can only be included as categories, not forms, which does not align with the purpose of a paradigm. Yet if lexical nouns are excluded entirely, this effectively obscures the fact that in many speech communities they are key resources for indexing interlocutor relations.[4] Even in communities in which pronouns *are* widely used, they not only denote interactional roles but also simultaneously index specific kin relations and deferential stances (see for example, Enfield, this volume; Kruspe and Burenhult 2019; Errington 1985b, 1988, 1998, also this volume).[5] Some pronouns are grammaticalised from forms of lexical nouns historically employed within contexts of deference (see below), while others are invented to fill a perceived gap in the language for a suitably deferential pronoun—for example, Indonesian *anda*, invented by taking the deferential suffix *-(a)nda* attached to kin terms *anakanda* ([your] dear child), *ayahanda* (dear father) and *ibunda* (dear mother) (see Sabirin 1957).

An additional issue is that a pronoun paradigm is essentially a listing of forms according to person, number and clusivity which link, through the morphological system of agreement, the grammatical subject of a finite clause to the main verb or predicate of that clause. While many languages of Europe and elsewhere encode person and number agreement, the relation is more variously expressed in the languages of Southeast Asia. Agreement is either completely absent or weakly elaborated in some languages while in others, roughly analogous relations are better understood in terms of voice, transitivity and cross-reference (see, for example, Himmelmann 2005 for typological characteristics of Austronesian languages).[6]

Because patterns of verbal agreement are very nearly definitional of "grammatical person" this raises a question about how this category is represented in the forms used for interlocutor reference in Southeast Asian languages.[7] In many of these languages, to say that some form is a "second-person pronoun" is merely to say that it is used in reference to the addressee. This is quite different, then, from describing an Italian form as "third person" since that does not preclude its use to refer to the addressee (Italian *lei* "3sg feminine" is also used as an addressee-referring *V* form). Or, to take things from the other direction, saying that illeism involves referring to oneself in the third person is meaningful precisely because this involves the conjugation of the verb—in speaking of oneself one says, "Jane walks" not "*Jane walk". Notice that in Vietnamese, Indonesian and many other languages of Southeast Asia, names are used in reference to speaker and addressee and, because verb agreement is not present, we see no corresponding pragmatic "person" effects as in English.[8] It is then necessary to distinguish speaker or addressee reference from "first person" or "second person" forms. More generally, in research on interlocutor reference in Southeast Asian languages, we must be careful not to unthinkingly import into the analysis categories—such as grammatical person and number—that come from the study of languages that differ substantially in their morphological and semantic profile.[9]

Lexical nouns used in interlocutor reference typically offer a rich characterisation of the social relationship between speaker and addressee. Kin terms, for instance, are two-place predicates which often encode information about relative age, generation and also gender. Moreover, by virtue of their association with the family, kin terms have an affective aspect, conjuring feelings of affection, intimacy, mutual obligation and so on, while at the same time fulfilling their referential function by identifying speaker or addressee. There are crucial differences between the way kin terms, names and titles are employed in languages such as English and French and in many Southeast Asian languages. As noted, the use of English *mummy* as self-reference is limited to parent-child interaction, and, in that context, appears to alternate quite freely with pronominal forms. By way of contrast, in Vietnamese, kin terms figure as the default means of interlocutor reference and thus a mother who self-refers using the pronoun *tao* in speaking to her own child will be heard as withholding the kin term for pragmatic effect (for example, to convey anger or to constitute the utterance as a reprimand). Moreover, an utterance containing a kin term may yield different interpretations depending on whether the person denoted by the term inhabits the role of speaker, addressee or a third person. In the example from colloquial Indonesian given as (1), the referents of *bunda* (mother) and *ayah* (father) remain the same in all instances, but the way they map onto the communicative situation differs according to transient facts of interactional role inhabitance (see also Luong 1990, 11–12 for an example from Vietnamese; also Enfield, this volume, for Kri).

(1) **Bunda** *pergi* *sama* **Ayah**.
    Mother go with father

    (a) "I'm going out with Dad."   (mother talking to child)
    (b) "Mum is going out with me."   (father talking to child)
    (c) "You're going out with me."   (father talking to mother)
    (d) "I'm going out with you."   (mother talking to father)
    (e) "You're going out with Dad."   (child talking to mother)
    (f) "Mum's going out with you."   (child talking to father)
    (g) "Mum's going out with Dad."   (child/other talking to person other than mother/father)

In comparison, English kin terms *mum* and *dad* are typically limited to third person reference, as indicated in the translation (notwithstanding the few exceptions already mentioned above).

It will be noted that in the various possible glosses of the Indonesian utterance above, while the referential value changes, the perspective remains the same. Specifically, the perspective is that of a child of the mother and father to whom reference is being made. If, as in case (b), the father is talking to the child, the speaker adopts the perspective of the addressee. If, as in case (d), the mother is talking to the father, the speaker adopts the perspective of someone (the child) who may or may not be present. Such shifts of referential perspective are quite common across the languages of the region and have been particularly well-described for Vietnamese (see Luong 1984, 1990; Luong and Sidnell 2020). In that language, any given occasion can be calibrated in a variety of ways depending on whose perspective is adopted by the speaker of an utterance. For instance, a man who is a few years younger than the speaker might be addressed as *em* (younger sibling, speaker's perspective) or as *chú* (father's younger brother, speaker's child's perspective) (see Sidnell, this volume). As Luong explains, as a result, terms used in interlocutor reference do not merely "designate" the speaker and addressee (1990, 7), or "describe a sociocultural reality," (1990, 15) they "also function to structure interactional situations".

In many Southeast Asian speech communities, multiple forms—including multiple pronouns—are available for self-reference, enabling speakers to convey different senses of self. For instance, Indonesian speakers use the pronoun *saya* "I" (from Sanskrit *sahāya* [companion, follower]), according to Englebretson (2007, 84), "to construct a public social and personal identity, to show deference, and to index social distance" and *aku* "I" to help relax "the prescribed norms of public language use" and to build social intimacy (2007, 84; see also, Errington, this volume).[10] Pronoun borrowing can provide a way for speakers to make even finer social distinctions or, on the other hand, as a means by which speakers attempt to avoid distinctions altogether. But while borrowed forms may potentially allow speakers to avoid some social implications (of for instance intergenerational hierarchy or age-determined seniority) they inevitably convey *other* meanings such as, for instance, the claimed cosmopolitanism of the speaker and so on (see Lee, this volume).[11]

Beyond the Sociolinguistics of Address

Within sociolinguistics, Brown and Gilman's (1960) account of T/V pronouns in European languages has enjoyed a longevity not generally characteristic of research in the social sciences, and its basic premises continue to inform the work of many sociolinguists, historical linguists and others working on address in European and other languages. The theory's influence extends also to studies that do not focus exclusively on address, such as, among many, Brown and Levinson's (1987) theory of politeness and Tannen's (1993) account of the "relativity" of discourse strategies.

Despite this influence, different aspects of the theory have been questioned. Kendall (1981, 237), for example, writes that:

> The model articulated in Brown and Gilman and extended in Brown and Ford does not just assume a systematic and consistent correspondence between behavior and ideas, it also assumes that this relationship is determinate. It incorporates a theory of meaning formulated without reference to speaker's intent or addressee's interpretation of speaker's intent, and it fails to consider the possibility of multiple meanings for the same form. Finally, it assumes that all variations in behavior are instances of deviations from, or violations of norms, or at any rate are indicators of some other anemic condition.

Kendall's argument involves casting Brown and Gilman as "determinists" whose theoretical "model" denies human agency. In other words, Kendall reads a kind of 1970s practice theory back into the essentially structural or structural functional account that Brown and Gilman proposed. Kendall's argument can be understood then as an attempt to reprioritise individual agency and intention in opposition to an account which is cast as overly "normative", "structural" or, even, "deterministic." A more recent, and more sophisticated, proposal along similar lines by Chase Raymond (2016) employs the methodological techniques of Conversation Analysis to explicate the way T/V alternations in various dialects of Spanish serve the accomplishment of social action in interaction. More specifically, Raymond argues that such "shifts contribute to the action of an utterance by mobilizing the semantic meaning of a pronominal form in order to recalibrate who the interactants project they are, and who they project they are to one another—not in general, but rather at that particular moment in the ongoing interaction" (2016, 636). The author emphasises the dynamic relations between token uses of the forms and the specific sequential contexts in which they occur to suggest that while

> the underlying semantics [sic] of *usted* and *tú* can indeed carry with them the notions of social distance and intimacy, [...] the ground-level pragmatic significance of invoking such distance or intimacy is no more automatic or predetermined than the identities of the interactants themselves. Rather, the interactional relevance of these pronominal options is conditioned by way of the moment-by-moment negotiation of identities in and through the ongoing talk. (2016, 651)[12]

Part of the issue here, it seems, is the characterisation of the forms themselves in terms of their "semantics". Specifically, Raymond's distinction between "semantics" and "ground-level pragmatic significance" merely relexicalises the Saussurean opposition of *langue* and *parole*, and thus fails to take account of the fact that many aspects of pragmatics—for example, deixis—are just as much a part of the linguistic system as are word meanings. As Silverstein (1976) long ago pointed out, the type-level meaning of an indexical sign—such as that of non-referential "deferential" *usted* or "familiar" *tú*, or that of referential second-person plural *usted* or second-person singular *tú*—cannot be adequately characterised by means of a decontextualised, metasemantic gloss (unlike, for instance, non-deictic words such as *juice* and *barber*). Rather, type-level definition must employ rules of use which specify pragmatic, that is, contextual, presuppositions and entailments (see also Luong 1990). At the same time, such non-referential indices are subject to construal by various and simultaneously circulating metadiscourses which characterise the significance or "meaning" of the object forms (see, *inter alia*, Morford 1997 on French; Paulston 1976 on Swedish). The point being that the precise meaning of any particular token will be ultimately indeterminate and variously construable after the fact. As such, it is impossible to say in so many words just what a speaker meant to convey by its use. As Raymond seems to have discovered through detailed conversation analytic study, this implies that these forms are the means to an indefinitely wide range of interactional ends.[13]

Michael Silverstein (1979, 2003) developed what is, for the contributors to this volume, the most important critique of Brown and Gilman. Not unlike Kendall, Silverstein begins by noting the way Brown and Gilman's account implies a psychologisation of what is fundamentally a social and interactional phenomenon. By reducing the problem of T/V alternation to the decision of a single individual, Brown and Gilman paved the way for the Geoghegan decision-trees used by later researchers (see for example, Ervin-Tripp 1972). A key point for Silverstein (2003, 205) is that

> the indexical sign-form whose meaning is at issue—is not, in fact, a single token occurrence of a discursive 'T' or a discursive 'V'; it can only be gauged over the interactional interval of two turns-at-talk, showing two forms of asymmetry of pair-part dyadic usage, first pair-part T followed by second pair-part V (T, V) or vice-versa (V, T), or revealing symmetry of usage, (T, T) or (V, V). [...] Such adjacency-pair-revealing textual fragments are the minimal signs of what is going on.

This either symmetrical or asymmetrical patterning across at least two utterances by alternate speakers is what Silverstein refers to as first order, deference indexicality. Such text-level patterns are subject to reanalysis via "strong ethno-metapragmatic understandings of the phenomenon" (Silverstein 2003, 210), resulting in second order indexicalities, perhaps most prominently in languages such as French, Spanish and Italian where a second-order honorific register in which individual token uses of *V* are treated as inherently "polite" or "formal" etc. (see also Agha 2007). Importantly, as we discuss below, such honorific registers become associated not only with addressees to whom talk is directed (as stereotypically appropriate targets of deference), but also with speakers (as stereotypically appropriate and entitled users of the register) and situations (as stereotypically appropriate occasions for its use).[14]

Object Signs and Metasigns

Studies within linguistic anthropology have shown that there is no simple correlation between social structure and language forms. Rather, the forms used to index speaker and addressee roles are always mediated by ideologies of language that, often tacitly, characterise their function and significance (Silverstein 1979, 2003; Irvine 1998, 52). At the same time, alternate forms—namely, those from different lexical classes such as nouns and pronouns—afford different kinds of construal by metasigns. Lexical nouns, for instance, provide richer semantic infrastructure for interpreting speaker-addressee relations than do pronouns which offer only the most minimal characterisation of the referent, such as "human", "singular", or "higher/lower than speaker". When nouns and pronouns are used in interlocutor reference, they are contextualised within a complex interplay between co-occurring signs on the one hand, and widely circulating metasemiotic discourses on the other. The social relations constituted through acts of interlocutor reference, in this sense, are best described not in terms of what is "encoded" in the forms themselves but rather as dialectical relations between object signs, co-occurring and contextualising signs and metasigns.

Lexical nouns and pronouns are caught up in macro-level discourses that construe their significance, and often, multiple discourses are circulating at any given time. For instance, until recently, the Indonesian pronoun *aku* "I" was rarely employed in public contexts, and when it was used it was often interpreted as a display of arrogance and self-interest—qualities perceived to run counter to public sensibility, but which were appreciated precisely by those who sought to set themselves apart from the crowd (Djenar 2008). These discourses circulated at the same time as other discourses which linked ideas about national development and modernity to new social identities and innovative language form(s). State efforts to modernise the nation were framed as efforts to achieve prosperity, and such prosperity could only be achieved when national unity was secured. Continuing secessionist movements in Indonesia at the time made it clear why national unity was presented as precondition for prosperity. Such discourses served to metasemiotically contextualise the meaning of *aku* as an index of an undesirable citizen identity.

Or take the example of Phan Khôi, one of the most prominent men of letters in late colonial Vietnam. In a series of writings in the 1930s, Phan Khôi argued that many aspects of Vietnamese needed to be updated and modernised so as to allow for participation in national and even international forms of public, mostly written, discourse. In particular, he suggested that Vietnamese compared unfavourably with languages such as French and modern Chinese which allowed for the use of what Phan Khôi described as "neutral" and "unanimous" pronouns. By this he meant pronouns that could be used by any addressor to any addressee, without social implication of, for instance, insolence or arrogance. While the traditional Vietnamese system in which lexical nouns and especially kin terms were regularly used instead of pronouns was sufficient for spoken, face-to-face interaction, Phan Khôi suggested its application to written communication was "inconvenient" and "troublesome". Here then, in adopting a comparative and historical point of view, this emergent metadiscourse of language reform cast practices of interlocutor reference as an obstacle to modernisation and the development of public life, linking them to an antiquated Confucian sensibility that Phan Khôi, and others, reckoned was at least partially responsible for the Vietnamese failure to resist French colonialism (see Marr 1981; Ho Tai 1992).

To take a more narrowly defined case, we may note that in Vietnamese (unlike Thai, see below), there are no dedicated pronouns for use with monks, but the question of how lay persons and monks should address one another (and self-refer) is a popular topic of discussion among Buddhists. One popular press article, for instance, begins by noting that many Buddhists who have been going to the temple for a long time still do not clearly understand the appropriate way to address and self-refer in this situation.[15] The author advises that a lay person should address the monk as *thầy* (master, teacher) and self-refer with *con* (child). The monk on the other hand, the author goes on to note, will often self-refer with *chúng tôi* (1PL EXC) leading many people to wonder why, "even though only one person is indicated," the monk nevertheless uses a plural term. The author explains, that, in this context, the first-person plural exclusive carries the meaning of self-effacement and self-extermination which is central to Buddhism. The discussion thus illustrates one way in which object signs and metasigns—in this case drawing upon a popular Buddhist theology—are brought into a mutually elaborative relation with one another.

Reference to speaker and addressee may be metasemiotically elaborated in indefinitely many ways. In a number of communities, for instance, some practices of interlocutor reference are understood as being uniquely appropriate for men or women. For instance, Chirasombutti and Diller (1999) observe that in modern Thai, there are distinctive pronouns for self-reference for men and for women speakers, *phom* and *dichan* respectively. However, these are not considered appropriate in the equivalent range of contextual situations. Whereas a male speaker's self-reference with *phom* is unremarkable across a broad range of everyday, urban contexts, women's use of *dichan* is much more constrained. The authors suggest that an essential difference lies in the fact that *phom* conveys "deferential politeness", while *dichan* shows little sign of "speaker-self-effacement." As a result, women "use a collection of different self-reference strategies including occupational terms, epithets such as *nu* 'rat,' kinship terms such as *phi* 'older sibling,' the deictic form *ni* 'this,' or the speaker's own nickname." (1999, 116). The authors conclude that, "Thai women are required by the prevailing linguistic system to 'place themselves' through self-reference selections in a more finely-determined social space than that required of male speakers" (1999, 117).

A somewhat similar gender asymmetry has also been described for Vietnamese. For instance, in a survey of speaker attitudes, Pham and Pham (2020) found that both men and women respondents considered non-deferential pronouns more acceptable when used by men talking to women than when used by women talking to men. The authors suggest that this reflects the continuing influence of Confucian teachings and ideas about the "traditional" Vietnamese family, which is idealised as patrilineal, male-oriented and in which women are often seen "as inferior by nature." However, the authors also point to alternative construals, exemplified, for instance, by a tabloid article titled "Use of *mày-tao* between husband and wife: When is it appropriate?"[16] While the author of this article reports that one "expert" ("who wishes to remain anonymous") proposes it is appropriate to use pronouns in the right circumstances such as when the couple is "having fun together" or "having sex", the general consensus is clearly that pronouns are best avoided. According to one psychologist, Đinh Đoàn, for instance, regardless of whether the couple quarrels and irrespective of who is right and who is wrong, husband and wife should not address each other as *mày-tao* as this will only make one or both feel disrespected and unloved, will promote conflict and cause hurt feelings.[17]

Deference and Demeanour

Erving Goffman (1956, 473) begins his classic article, "The Nature of Deference and Demeanour," by proposing that under the influence of Durkheim and Radcliffe Brown anthropologists have "learned to look for the symbolic meaning of any given social practice and for the contribution of the practice to the integrity and solidarity of the group that employs it." To this functional agenda, Goffman (473) proposes an addition, one that would focus on the individual as "representation of the social collectivity." According to Goffman (473) in "our urban secular world" the person is treated as a sacred object and this sacredness is displayed and confirmed by symbolic acts. In this way, Goffman linked the micro-sociology of social interaction to the larger theoretical project of structural functional anthropology. In other words, he sought to reveal the ways in which mundane and largely secular activities served both to constitute and to reproduce the social order of everyday life.

Deference and demeanour emerge in Goffman's writings as key terms in this micro-structural functionalist analysis of everyday symbolic acts constitutive of "ceremonial" life. Goffman defines deference as that "component of activity which functions as a symbolic means by which appreciation is regularly conveyed *to* a recipient *of* this recipient, or of something of which this recipient is taken as a symbol, extension, or agent" (1956, 477, *italics* in the original). Demeanour, on the other hand, Goffman describes as "that element of the individual's ceremonial behavior typically conveyed through deportment, dress, and bearing, which serves to express to those in his immediate presence that he is a person of certain desirable or undesirable qualities" (1956, 489). In the simplest terms, deference is appreciation directed toward another, while demeanour is that which the individual conveys about him- or herself. But while Goffman is at pains to emphasise that deference and demeanour are not the same, neither can they be easily separated and isolated from one another. When, for instance, an individual withholds or fails to convey the deference otherwise expected of another, they run the risk of being seen as rude, as failing to comport themselves with an appropriate demeanour. For this reason, Goffman suggests that the analytic relation between deference and demeanour is one of "complementarity, not identity."

In a typical example of Goffmanian argumentation, the individual is pictured as bound to others in a reciprocal pact: one's own self-image is secured at the cost of helping to maintain that of the others with whom one interacts. The self which the individual presents to the world is, in other words, a product of an active and collective collusion:

> Each individual is responsible for the demeanor image of himself and the deference image of others, so that for a complete man to be expressed, individuals must hold hands in a chain of ceremony, each giving deferentially with proper demeanor to the one on the right what will be received deferentially from the one on the left. While it may be true that the individual has a unique self all his own, evidence of this possession is thoroughly a product of joint ceremonial labor, the part expressed through the individual's demeanor being no more significant than the part conveyed by others through their deferential behavior toward him. (1956, 493)

While studies of address from Brown and Gilman onwards have, perhaps understandably, tended to emphasize the paying of deference (as "politeness" for instance), reframing this domain in terms of interlocutor reference encourages us to bring the complementary signs of demeanour back into focus. At the most obvious, when speakers select a term for self-reference they are, inevitably it would seem, conveying something about their own standing, even when it seems largely derivative of the relationship to the addressee. Consider for instance, so-called humiliative forms derived from a lexical noun meaning "servant" or "slave". But more subtle are the inferences about the speaker that are to be drawn from the way he or she addresses the other. Brown and Gilman noted such effects, remarking that the use of proportionally more *V* forms was widely treated as a sign of elegance and social elevation: "In later centuries Europeans became very conscious of the extensive use of *V* as a mark of elegance" (1960, 257).[18]

The emphasis on demeanour brings into focus the important ways in ways in which skill in the use of honorific registers, and registers of participant deixis in particular, are socially and hence unevenly distributed. This is perhaps most obvious in the case of Javanese where alternate styles "mediated hierarchy and interactional intimacy" through their principal ideological function of deference-to-addressee while at the same time serving as a mark of speaker mastery and thus social origins (Errington 1998, 41, citing Silverstein 1995, 283). As Errington, building on ideas from Pierre Bourdieu (1984, 255), puts it, fluency in these techniques is learned as "part of a broader range of social demeanors, and so 'cultivated' within a kind of 'natural sensibility'." As such, Errington notes, properly refined speech conveys "a sense of transparency between observable conduct and internal nature" evincing "that sense of 'relaxation within tension,' [...], which bespeaks the embodiment of a state, rather than the conscious application of learned technique."

In sum, while interlocutor reference has been understood largely in terms of politeness and deference to an addressee, such interactional meanings are inevitably linked to others which direct attention towards the speaker—addressing correctly, appropriately, eloquently and so on is treated as a mark of the speaker's own sophistication.

The Sociolinguistic Typology of Southeast Asia

In his book on the history of Southeast Asia, Anthony Reid (2015, xvii) describes this complex and culturally heterogeneous region as "a distinct place, but one of infinite variety". Historically, influences from two great civilisations—China and India—have contributed to the region's linguistic, social and material cultures. China's greatest contribution, according to Reid, is the diverse groups of people that moved south to escape imperial rule, bringing their languages, agricultural skills, cultural and literary traditions to the region (2015, 26; also see Wu 2009 on Chinese migration; Alves 2021 on Chinese linguistic influence in SEA). China's expansion to the south was limited by a tropical climate, which brought diseases, and terrains that were difficult to penetrate, including the mountainous region where modern China meets Southeast Asia, described by Scott (2009) as "Zomia." Moreover, China's relative disinterest in the sea prior to the 13th century also meant that stateless sea peoples, the Austronesians, could freely migrate from Taiwan to Madagascar, Easter Island and island Southeast Asia where contact occurred with non-Austronesian speaking peoples whose presence in this part of the region predates the arrival of the Austronesians. This part of the region was also strongly influenced by cultures from India in the west, through the spread of Hinduism and Buddhism. In fact, according to Reid, by the 15th century, Indian traditions were "vastly more influential" than Chinese except in Dai Viet—roughly, present day Vietnam (2015, 29).

The history of language contact in this region is complex, as typological studies of the different language families show (see for example, Adelaar and Himmelmann 2005; Enfield 2019; Klamer 2017; Palmer 2018; Schapper 2017).

Languages from at least five families are spoken in modern day Southeast Asia: Austronesian, Austroasiatic, Tai-Kadai, Hmong-Mien and Sino-Tibetan.[19] In addition, there are languages in the eastern part of Indonesia collectively known as Papuan (non-Austronesian) languages (see Palmer 2018, 5). Our goal in this volume is not to describe interlocutor reference practices across communities in all these families of languages; rather, we want to highlight the main patterns that tend to be at work across the speech communities.

In this respect, we have already pointed to the widespread use of lexical nouns for speaker and addressee reference in the region, particularly among speech communities in Mainland and the western part of Island Southeast Asia. Fleming and Sidnell (2020) call this "open class interlocutor reference" or OCIR. The use of nouns meaning "lord, master" and "servant, slave" is a widely attested feature of these languages that seems to have been borrowed (via calquing) from Classical Chinese—the same source that gave rise to OCIR in Japanese and Korean (Fleming and Sidnell 2020). As Fleming (this volume) emphasises, there is no simple correlation between patterns of interlocutor reference and social hierarchy. Although Sanskrit has been noted to have had enduring influence on western Indonesian languages (Gonda 1973; Hoogervorst 2021, also forthcoming), it is not likely the source of OCIR diffusion in this part of the region.[20]

Based on what we know so far, interlocutor reference in the languages of Southeast Asia tends to follow the three patterns below.

(1) Open Class Interlocutor Reference (OCIR): a name for a system of interlocutor reference characterised by the open class of nouns used in reference to speaker and addressee, and a weak expression or total absence of subject-verb agreement (Fleming and Sidnell 2020; also see Fleming this volume). OCIR is widely attested across the languages of the region but is more prominent in some than in others. For instance, in Vietnamese OCIR is the unmarked, default means of reference, accounting for upwards of 80 per cent of all acts of interlocutor reference in some contexts, while pronouns are generally avoided (see Sidnell, this volume). In other languages, Thai for instance, OCIR serves as an alternative strategy to pronominal reference used most often by certain categories of speakers (for example, women), in particular social settings and contexts (for example, urban, interactional with non-intimates) (see Chirasombutti and Diller 1999).

(2) "Pronominality": a historical, diachronic analysis reveals a recurrent, cyclical process in which lexical nouns are grammaticalized as quasi-pronouns, come into widespread use across a segment of the speech community, and are eventually replaced by newer, innovative forms. As nouns are more semantically specific than pronouns, they are lower in the scale of pronominality than pronouns (Sugamoto 1989). Grammaticalised nouns,

notably those meaning "lord/master-slave/servant" in Southeast Asian languages, are of this kind. In terms of their use in interlocutor reference, it is perhaps not surprising that the nominal meaning may still be apparent to language users, such as seen in metadiscourses surrounding their use. For example, in Vietnam some reformers objected to the use of *tôi* in the 1930s because it derived from a word meaning "servant" while others felt that these meanings had no bearing on its contemporary use. In Indonesian, the commonly held view that *saya* is a "polite" pronoun likely reflects the lexical meaning of its Sanskrit origin—companion, follower—via religious contexts. In terms of the analysis developed by Sugamoto, then, words like *tôi* and *saya* (and Javanese *kula* "I", from *kawula* "servant") are lower on the pronominality scale compared to English *I* or French *je*.

(3) Pronominal complexity: many pronominal systems of the languages in the region are complex. While distinctions of person (first, second, third), number and clusivity (singular-plural, inclusive-exclusive) are common, number distinctions are absent in some languages (for example, Javanese, Balinese, Madurese and some varieties of Malay) while in others, include dual, paucal, and even trial and quadral (see Adelaar and Hajek, forthcoming). Pronominal mutation (that is, forms mutating with syntactic contexts) is also attested (for example, in Nias; see Brown 2005), and animacy and kin-based "politeness" or "deference" additionally form the bases for pronominal distinction (see Enfield this volume; Fleming this volume; Kruspe and Buhrenhult 2019). Müller and Weymouth (2017) distinguish the reference systems of languages in the Greater Burma Zone (Myanmar and surrounds) into three categories: "grammatical", "hierarchical" and "mixed" systems, corresponding to languages that rely mainly on a small set of pronouns, those that make use of a larger set of forms historically linked to sometimes quite specific hierarchical relations (for example, a lay person speaking to a monk), and languages that have a mixture of both. However, as indicated above, the sociolinguistic typology of interlocutor reference (which must take into account OCIR as well as pronominal systems) in the Greater Burma Zone is considerably more complex than such a tripartite distinction suggests.[21]

Overview of the Volume

The studies presented in this volume all deal with the indexical relationship between forms used in interlocutor reference and social relations, taking a broadly semiotic approach to describing the ways in which practices for referring to speaker and addressee are intertwined with social structure, historical and sociopolitical changes, and interactional dynamics. We hope the volume will enrich future discussions on the topic and encourage further explorations in the study of interlocutor reference, particularly with regard to lesser-known languages in the region.

Following this introduction, in chapter 2, Nick Enfield's analysis of a whole system for referring to self and others in Kri, a Vietic language with a few hundred speakers, shows the way kinship is reflected in, and partly constituted by, practices of interlocutor reference. Enfield explains the complexity of the system by suggesting that it operates along two asymmetrical axes: "hierarchy" (up-down) based on sibling and generation order, and "inclusion" (inside-outside) based on consanguinity. People on the "inside", that is, those in blood relations, may use "bare pronouns" and names, and relative age provides the basis for determining which forms to use when and with whom. Enfield points out that hierarchical relations between siblings are reflected in the asymmetrical use of kin terms and pronouns, and this hierarchy is "transmitted" to the siblings' offspring, their offspring's offspring and extended to affinal relations.

The Javanese system of interlocutor reference is also complex, though less because of its elaborate pronominal system and more because of the existence of speech levels with associated sets of lexical items, and the fact that the language has several varieties. In chapter 3, Joseph Errington describes a series of transformations occurring since the early part of the twentieth century due to largescale social, political and demographic changes and continuing contact with Indonesian. Errington examines the use of kin terms and pronouns and accounts for shifts in terms of what he calls, after Friedl (1964), "lagging emulation", that is, the manner of adoption by a group of speakers of forms used by another group. Errington suggests that in the 1920s and the decades that followed, lagging emulation is evident in the way non-elite speakers of Javanese adopted prestige forms used by the elites as markers of deference within what was once a Javanese exemplary centre. As Indonesian became more widely adopted in the 1980s, patterns of lagging emulation persisted though, during this time, they were motivated less by distinctions between urban and rural or elite and commoner than by distinctions based upon educational background and orientation to the "regime of the standard", that is, authority that prescribes who should use which languages when and where. The Javanese case discussed by Errington illustrates the broader point that historical shifts in sociolinguistic patterning reflect changing dynamics between micro-level interactional contingencies and macrosocial contexts.

In chapter 4, Michael Ewing considers aspects of the Javanese interlocutor reference system through a study of conversational practices involving the vocative in *básá Cerbon*, a variety of Javanese spoken in Cirebon, West Java. Ewing points out that speakers of Cirebon Javanese rarely use overt addressee reference but frequently use the vocative in acts of address. The vocative is employed even when no overt reference is used, and particularly at those points in conversation in which the management of turns and topics, mitigation, engagement in humorous banter and shifts in participation framework are involved. Based on this finding, Ewing argues that speakers of Cirebon Javanese employ the vocative not merely to reinforce relationships, as has been noted for English conversation (see for example, Leech 1999, cited in Ewing), but moreover to render explicit the intersubjective connection between speech participants.

In chapter 5, Sarah Lee presents a study of innovative practices of interlocutor reference among ethnic Malays in Kuala Lumpur, Malaysia's main destination for mass urban migration and a centre of education and commercial development. Lee begins with the observation that ethnic Malay speakers frequently use the English pronouns *I* and *you* in conversation and from this suggests that this practice is indexically linked to values of modernity. Lee then makes the point that, although *I* and *you* are perceived to be status-neutral in contrast to Malay forms which implicate hierarchical distinctions, it is precisely by virtue of this contrast that the use of *I* and *you* become socially meaningful. Thus, far from being "neutral" signs, *I* and *you* are treated as indices of upward mobility, modern values and a cosmopolitan attitude.

The next three chapters explore linguistically mediated relations between social intimates in different settings. In chapter 6, Jack Sidnell examines a conversation among Vietnamese speakers of the same generation showing how they orient to the ethics of interpersonal relations captured in the expression meaning "respect those above, yield to those below", which casts relations between juniors and seniors as relations involving mutual expectations of entitlement and obligation. Sidnell suggests that speech participants orient to this ethics by evaluating the conduct of others in real and imagined situations (including scenarios in which the participants imagine themselves occupying hierarchical positions relative to each other), and in doing so, they reassure themselves of their own civility. This then leads to Sidnell's broader argument that the often-subtle ways the participants index asymmetrical relations suggests that hierarchy is not as a "brute fact" but a reflexive semiotic model of conduct within which the social significance of object signs (for example, the use of a pronoun rather than a kin term to address a friend) is construed through widely circulating metasemiotic discourses.

In chapter 7, Charles Zuckerman takes up the question of how persons manage their relation as equals within a hierarchical system by describing the ebb and flow of friendship among members of a male peer group in Laos. Zuckerman draws a parallel between ideologies surrounding the use of pronouns and ideas about friendship that the group members subscribe to, arguing that similar to "bare" pronouns, which are often described as having two separate uses, namely, to convey intimacy and express aggression, friendship is thought of and enacted as ties that are potentially enduring but also fragile. Zuckerman suggests that these seemingly contradictory sets of meanings associated with pronouns and friendship are not distinct constructs but constitute a relation of complementarity. Like the "bare" pronouns, which are associated with solidarity and masculine aggression, the perdurance of friendship is tested through conflict and violence.

The study in chapter 8 by Dwi Noverini Djenar examines interlocutor reference in Indonesian panel interviews to show how journalists and politicians orient to the audience by performing deferential acts involving the use of kin terms, names and pronouns. Djenar notes that deferential acts are distributed across the participant framework. Alternating between first-person pronouns to index personal and institutional roles, asking questions that are semantically vague or questions presented as a cascade, and referring to co-participants using differentiated gestures, are among deferential acts performed by interview participants to elicit response and signal alignment. Djenar concludes by suggesting that within this institutional setting, participant framework is sensitive to change.

In chapter 9, the final chapter of the book, Luke Fleming presents a theoretical sketch of the development of honorific systems in the languages of Southeast Asia. Fleming begins by offering a functional typology of honorification, pointing out that, although referent honorifics (that is, honorification targeting the discourse referent) are widely attested cross-linguistically, elaborated honorific registers are mainly found in the languages of East and Southeast Asia, and distinct lexical repertoires of addressee-targeting honorifics are primarily attested in Southeast Asia. Fleming argues that social pragmatics are crucial to the development of speech levels and humiliatives in the languages of this region, and that to understand typological differences, one must consider not only extant forms of social hierarchy but also language internal developments.

Notes

[1] Moreover, the term "reference" is sometimes used in sociolinguistic studies to mean "third-person reference" specifically and is opposed to "address".

[2] See also Errington's (1960; revised 1976) description of Javanese *priyayi* conceptions of self as these are articulated in *kebatinan* which he (1984, 278) defines as "the study of cultivation of a man's interior—his *batin*" (see also Smith-Hefner 1988). Berman (1998) similarly discusses practices of interlocutor reference in Javanese women's narratives, noting that tellers refer to themselves using expressions that orient outwardly to the addressee and place them as "a major player in the framing of a speaker's story". Berman argues that in so doing, the women permit their addressee a role in the telling (1998, 194).

[3] An early statement of this view comes from Benveniste (for more approaches, see the studies in the volume edited by Collins 2014, especially Kaufman's).

[4] See Luong (1990) for an extended treatment of this problem, i.e., how to identify a system composed of alternatives drawn from different lexical classes, as in Vietnamese.

[5] In many languages of the region—for example, Thai (see Bunnag 1973)—there are specialised pronominals for use in reference to a monk (whether as speaker or addressee) as well as restrictions on which form can be used in reference to a lay person with whom the monk interacts.

[6] Verbal agreement is found in some languages in the region, for example, Fataluku, a non-Austronesian language spoken in the eastern areas of Timor Leste, but this appears to be limited to certain verbs (Engelenhoven cited in Schapper 2017, 28; also see Klamer 2017).

[7] Siewierska (2004, 8) writes "the universality of person as a grammatical category is sometimes called into question. The issue of whether all languages display the grammatical category of person is inherently tied to the issue of whether all languages have the category of personal pronoun." However, it is not clear why the presence of a dedicated form for speaker, addressee or third-party reference implies a grammatical category of person. Here it is important to remember that person grammaticalises interactional roles a.k.a. speech act participants. A functional morpho-syntactic study of the degree to which such roles are in fact grammaticalised cross-linguistically has, as far as we know, never been attempted (see also Silverstein 1976).

[8] Conners et al. (2016) argue that, because zero is a common strategy for marking reference in Jakarta Indonesian, imposters can be used to minimise ambiguity. Unlike in pro-drop languages in which person is indicated through verb agreement, no such indicator is present in Indonesian and therefore the use of imposters helps the addressee identify the intended referent.

[9] In a study of Indonesian, Kaufman argues that "one type of argument is positioned differently in the overt syntax when functioning as an imposter" (2014, 91). Specifically, when used as patient-voiced agents, imposter references to speaker and hearer (what Kaufman calls "local" features) procliticise to the verb and so seem to replace the patient voice prefix *di-*. When referring to "third persons" however, they follow the verb. In this they follow exactly the pattern of pronominals. On the basis of this, Kaufman concludes that, "This syntactic parity between imposters and pronouns offers a striking confirmation of the syntactic relevance of person features, even when they are not overtly spelled out by dedicated pronouns. The difference between imposters and regular noun phrases can thus not be one of mere pragmatic construal. That is, imposters do not merely allude to first- and second-person pronouns in Indonesian but rather contain their syntactic features." (2014, 92).

[10] Until recently, *saya* was also used non-referentially when speaking to an older addressee (A: *Sehat-sehat toh?* "Are (you) well?"; B: *Sehat, saya.* "(I'm) well, yes.").

[11] In the late colonial period, use of French-derived, case-invariant pronouns represented in writing of the time as *moa* and *toa*, by members of the Vietnamese elite was often treated as an affectation to European manners and styles. Such usage was satirised by Vũ Trọng Phụng in his 1936 novel *Số Đỏ* (translated by Peter Zinoman and Nguyen Nguyet Cam as *Dumb Luck* 2003).

[12] The "semantics" of *usted* and *tú* would be something like "second-person plural" and "second-person singular" respectively. Their capacity to indicate "deference" (etc.) is not, strictly speaking, an aspect of their "semantics".

[13] Raymond writes that "In a particular dialect, *usted* may typically embody a sense of deference or distance between the interlocutors, while *tú* may convey sameness and social intimacy; nonetheless, as we have demonstrated, social distance or intimacy between coparticipants in interaction is not absolute (cf. Brown and Gilman 1960, 255), but rather can be transformed over the course of a stretch of talk, indexed grammatically through switches in recipient reference forms" (2016, 660). Needless to say, Brown and Gilman never use the word "absolute" and what

they write on page 255 (and elsewhere) provides no evidence of their holding the view that Raymond attributes to them.

[14] While studies such as Raymond (2016) and Oh (2007) examine interlocutor reference, most work on reference within Conversation Analysis has focused on "person reference," which centres on the task of getting the addressee to recognise who it is that is being referred to (see Enfield and Stivers 2007). This focus is an outcome of the fact that in referring to non-present persons, the range of possible referents is effectively infinite. In reference to addressee, the range of referents is limited to the present coparticipants (see Lerner 1996, 2003). In reference to speaker, the range of referents reduces to one, namely, the present speaker. However, in interlocutor reference, the focus is on the relation between self and other.

[15] Thích Như Điển, 2017 "Cách xưng hô trong chùa" (The way to address and self-refer in temple); https://phatgiao.org.vn/cach-xung-ho-trong-chua-d25587.html

[16] "Vợ chồng xưng hô mày tao: Khi nào thì 'được phép'?" might be more literally translated as "when is it 'permissible'?".

[17] For speakers of Vietnamese, the use of pronouns between husband and wife is marked in relation to the more common practice of using sibling terms (see Haas 1969).

[18] Later scholars such as Paulston (1976) observed that the rights of dispensation fell to the acknowledged superior member of a dyad (notwithstanding various complications).

[19] It is unfortunate that Hmong-Mien and Sino-Tibetan language families are not represented in the contributions to this book. For some discussion of interlocutor reference in Hmong-Mien languages see, for example, Ratliff (2010) and Taguchi (2021), for Sino-Tibetan languages see, for example, Manosuthikit (2013); Thurgood and LaPolla (2016). Also not discussed in the following pages are the national languages Thai (Kra-Dai) and Khmer (Austroasiatic). Aspects of interlocutor reference have been described for a number of smaller Southeast Asian languages. See for instance, Badenoch (2016) on Bit, a Palaungic spoken in northern Laos and Yunnan province by about 3,000 people. See also Benjamin (1983 [1978]) for a fascinating account of a "phonetically marked distinction between Self and Other which underlies the lexicon of person" as well as the morphology of verb inflection and discourse structure in the Temiar language (also see Benjamin 2013).

[20] Thanks to Luke Fleming and Tom Hoogervorst for pointing this out.

[21] As Luong (1990, 13) writes: "[...] common nouns, proper nouns, and personal pronouns in Vietnamese person reference [...] constitute integral parts of one single system of person reference."

PART 1

Systems

CHAPTER 2

Asymmetries in the System of Person Reference in Kri, a Language of Upland Laos

N.J. Enfield

Kri is a Vietic language spoken by about 500 people in upland Laos, just inside the Vietnam border around 300 km due East of the Lao capital, Vientiane (see Enfield and Diffloth 2009; Enfield 2009; Enfield 2018). The dialect of Kri discussed here is spoken in the Mrkaa cluster of villages. Kri Mrkaa is regarded by Kri speakers as "real Kri" (*karìi tàn*). Another dialect, known as Kri Phòòngq, is spoken at lower altitudes than the dialect described here, for example in the village of Pung, a few hours' walk downstream from Mrkaa on the Lao side (Zuckerman and Enfield 2020, 2021). (Note that in this chapter when I write of Kri I mean Kri Mrkaa exclusively; the statements made below are not all true of Kri Phòòngq.) The Kri language is spoken in the context of two other small-population indigenous languages: Bru, an Austroasiatic language of the Katuic subbranch, and Saek, a Tai language, both spoken in nearby villages. Most Kri speakers know these two languages to some extent, alongside Lao and Vietnamese, the national languages of Laos and Vietnam, respectively. Kri has clearly been shaped over centuries in part by Kri speakers' contact with these other languages and their predecessors.

Kri speakers form a small community. They number little over 500 in total (around 300 of whom speak the Kri Mrkaa variety). Each Kri-speaking individual personally knows every other individual and they know how everyone is related. Speakers of Kri have a complex and dynamic set of practices for referring to persons. By its nature, this system invokes meanings that are tied up with key features of social organisation and differentiation, including age, kin relatedness, social formality, and gender. In this chapter, I focus on some key features of this system. My goal is primarily descriptive. I will show that the system is organised with reference to two independent axes of asymmetry: *hierarchy* (up-down), grounded in sibling order, and *inclusion* (inside-outside), grounded in consanguinity.

Elements of Person Reference in Kri

As in any language, person reference in Kri draws on a number of distinct linguistic subsystems. The three basic subsystems for person reference are personal names, pronouns, and other reference terms.

Kri Personal Names

Kri speakers have single-word personal names. They do not have surnames. Sets of siblings are often given names that are phonologically similar to each other, in a pattern that I have observed in other mainland Southeast Asian languages. In one example, three Kri brothers are named Khwan, Khween and Khùàn. In another, three brothers are named Nun, Mun, and Môônq.

Titles are widely used as prefixes to personal names. One type of title derives from kin terms, used in situations where the kin term refers to a kin relation who is older than the self. A man named Nun might be referred to by certain others as "Uncle Nun" (though he may not necessarily be their actual uncle). By contrast with these kin-based title forms, some title forms are not derived from words with other meanings. The most widely used of these are *qôông* and *mooq*, for respected males and females, respectively (for example, *qôông nun* "Mr. Nun"), and *qaj* for non-respected or "lower" individuals; for example, children and younger kin. Nun's older relatives could refer to him as *qaj nun*. This system of titles closely resembles the system used in Lao (Enfield 2007a, 151–3).

Teknonymy is widely used in Kri. This is the practice of referring to a person using their firstborn child's name. When the man named Nun had a son, he named the boy Kham. From that time onwards, Nun was referred to by many community members as *pòòq kham* "father (of) Kham". In time, the explicit reference to his kin relation to Kham ("father of") could be dropped altogether, particularly when he reached old age. Then, Nun could be referred to as *qôông kham* (Mister Kham), as if his own name were Kham. After the birth of his first child, not all of Nun's consociates switch over to using the teknonym to refer to him: After Nun had his first child, some people in the community continued to use Nun's personal name, while others switched to the teknonym. Who switches and who doesn't is determined by certain kin-based rules, discussed below.

Pronouns

Kri has a system of shifters, that is, true pronouns whose reference shifts depending on who is speaking. The system of Kri pronouns is depicted in table 1. The system shows distinctions for person (first, second, and third), number (singular, dual and plural), an inclusive/exclusive distinction in both first-person dual and plural, and some gender and "politeness" distinctions which I will discuss below. I note that the words *mooq* and *qôông* (polite third person singular, female/male) are not pronouns, technically speaking. They can function as person classifiers and as name titles (see mentions of these terms elsewhere in the chapter), though unlike other terms with similar functions—such as *mêêq* (mother)—they do not occur as regular, stand-alone nouns. I include them in table 1 to reflect the fact that they occupy a functional place in the pronoun paradigm, being able to stand alone as third person-singular referring terms that mark gender, paradigmatically contrasting in "politeness" with *hanq*, on the one hand, and in number with *qaar* and *paa*, on the other. See below for further information.

Table 1. Kri pronouns

	SG		DU		PL	
	Bare	"Polite"	INCL	EXCL	INCL	EXCL
1	teeq/pààanq	koon/khoojq	saa	ñaar	cawq	caa
2	cak	mii/nôôq	maar		prii	
3	hanq	mooq qôông	qaar		paa	

Table 1 is a static depiction of a system that is in fact highly dynamic. The system cannot be understood without attention to Kri kinship practices and terminology. As we shall see, Kri kinship is central to person reference, and kinship relations are central to Kri speakers' lives.

Other Substantives

Other substantives can be used in place of pronouns (as *open class interlocutor reference* forms; see Luong 1990; Luong and Sidnell 2020; Fleming and Sidnell 2020), that is, as referring expressions that track speech act participants and others through discourse. For example, *mêêq* (mother) in *mêêq hôôm cơng*—literally, "mother not yet see"—could mean (1) "You haven't yet seen", (2) "I haven't yet seen" or (3) "She (your/my/their mother) hasn't yet seen".

People may also be referred to (in the third person) using any number of ad hoc descriptions. These are productive and context-specific uses of the general referential resources of the language. Examples would be "the people we passed on the bridge yesterday" and "the man who was selling cigarettes". I make no further mention of them here.

Kri Practices for Referring to Persons

I organise this section in terms of kin relations. For Kri speakers, kin relations are the basis of societal organisation. Practices of person reference are grounded in kin relations. Let us start with consanguineal relations.

Consanguineal Relations

The term *cìà-maangq* in Kri refers to the people to whom one is blood-related: parents, aunts, uncles, grandparents, siblings, cousins, sons, daughters, etc. This category accounts for one important form of asymmetry in social organisation. From any one person's perspective, every other person in the community is either inside this category or outside it. This fundamental distinction has major consequences for how people talk and refer to others in the Kri-speaking community.

Being somebody's *cìà-maangq* means two things for person reference. First, if A and B are *cìà-maangq*, they may use the bare pronouns (listed in table 1) for referring to each other. Second, they can use each other's personal names in reference (for both lower and higher kin, though a title will always be added to the name when the referent is higher kin). Below, we examine some affinal relation categories that contrast with *cìà-maangq*, thus setting up an inside/outside opposition in social relationships. But first, we review some consanguineal relationships, as laid out in figure 1.

Parents

The terms *mêêq* (mother) and *pòòq* (father) are used exclusively for the actual mother and father relations, not for parents' siblings. Sometimes the third person terms *mooq* and *qôông* are used as titles together with the kin terms for parents, as in *mooq mêêq* ([my] respected mother) and *qôông pòòq* ([my] respected father).

Parents' Siblings

Kri has distinct words for all eight logical distinctions that result from three independent two-way distinctions in (1) sex of referent (male vs. female), (2) sex of Ego's parent (Ego's father vs. Ego's mother), and (3) age of referent relative to Ego's parent (older vs younger), as follows:

FyZ - *qoo*
FyB - *pòòq*
MyB - *kùùq*
MyZ - *mɯ́ɯ́q*
FeZ - *jaa*
FeB - *puu*
MeZ - *naaj*
MeB - *taa*

These can be seen in figure 1.

Siblings (People with the Same Parents)

There are three sibling terms: *cììq* (older sister), *maangq* (older brother), and *qeem* (younger sibling). Relative age (to Ego) is always distinguished in sibling reference (*maangq* and *cììq* are older, *qeem* is younger), but gender is distinguished only in elder siblings. Sibling terminology is necessarily asymmetrical, grounded in the difference in birth order (even for twins): if A is B's *cììq* (older sister), then B is A's *qeem* (younger sibling).

This asymmetry is passed on to the next generation. First cousins—children of people who are siblings—describe each other using the sibling terms. Note that the labelling used among cousins is independent of their actual relative age. If A is B's older brother (A is *maangq*, B is *qeem*), then A's son will be *maangq* (older brother) to B's son, even if A's son was born after B's son.

For younger siblings, the affectionate terms *qeeng/naang* (dear boy/dear girl) may be used as terms of reference or address. (Note that Kri *naang* and Lao *naang2* "girl" are similar in form.) These terms can also be applied affectionately with reference to any younger *cìà-maangq* (nieces, nephews, grandchildren). Similarly, the non-respect title *qaj* may be used with personal names for these lower *cìà-maangq*. Thus, normally, a child named Kham would typically be referred to as *qaj kham*.

Second Cousins (People whose Grandparents are Siblings)

Terms for second cousins show a Crow/Omaha-style skewing, in which Ego and second cousin are labelled as if they were in different generations. The higher second cousin (the one whose grandparent is the older sibling) is labelled as an aunt/uncle and the lower second cousin is labelled as a younger sibling. Let me give some examples to show what I mean.

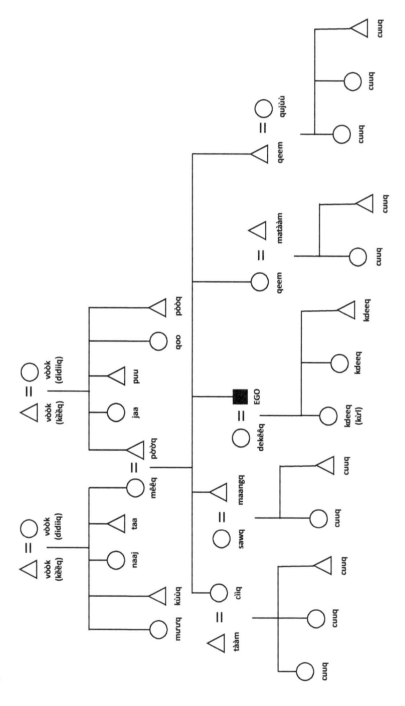

Figure 1. Kri kin relations and terms

Examples within Cìà-maangq

Consider the kin relations depicted in figure 2.

At the top of figure 2, to the left, we see that a man named Ting has a younger brother named Khààm. Ting describes Khààm as his *qeem* (younger sibling). In return, Khààm describes Ting as his *maangq*. They use *teeq/cak* pronouns and names reciprocally, but only Ting uses *qeeng* (dear boy) with (second or third person) reference to Khààm.

Ting's son (Thongdam) describes Khààm as his *pòòq* (father's younger brother). Khààm's son (Khaa) describes Ting as his *puu* (father's elder brother). Bare pronouns may be used when Thongdam or Khaa refer to each other, whether in third person reference or as speech act participants. Kin terms will often be used in place of pronouns, as open class interlocutor reference forms. So, Khààm might ask Ting: *puu qơớc quu mờờ* [FeB go loc which] "Where are you going?" (literally, "Where is father's older brother going?"). (This usage of *puu* "FeB" by Khààm could be interpreted as a recentring of the origo of reference to Khààm's own child; see Luong and Sidnell 2020 on the frequency of this pattern in kinterm interlocutor reference in Southeast Asia.)

Thongdam and Khaa are first cousins, and they use the same terminology that they would use if they were brothers. This means that they refer to each other in the same way that their parents refer to each other (for example, as just described for Ting and Khààm). In turn, the *children* of Khaa and Thongdam also refer to Khaa and Thongdam as if they were brothers. So, Khìàn—Khaa's first child—refers to Thongdam as *puu* (father's older brother) and Dùàng—Thongdam's first child—refers to Khaa as *pòòq* (father's younger brother).

All of the people referred to so far—Ting, Khààm, Khaa, Thongdam, Khìàn and Dùàng—are *cìà-maangq* to each other. As such, they may all use first names (with appropriate titles) and may use the bare pronouns *teeq/caa/saa/ñaar/maar/qaar/cak/prii* for address and reference to each other.

Dùàng and Khìàn are second cousins. Unlike their first-cousin parents, they do not refer to each other in the same way as siblings. Instead, there is a Crow-Omaha type of generational skewing. Going in one direction, looking down from Dùàng's high perspective, the sibling relation is maintained: Dùàng refers to Khìàn as *qeem* (younger sibling) and may use *naang* (dear girl) to address or refer to her. But in the other direction, looking up from Khìàn's low perspective, Khìàn refers to Dùàng as *qoo* (father's younger sister). This is the same reference to Dùàng that Khìàn's own children will use. Why does Khìàn do this? Kri speakers answer: "Because Dùàng is *qeem pòòq* of Khìàn", that is, Dùàng is Khìàn's "father's younger sister". This is not so much a claim about Dùàng individually, but rather about her membership in a category of people who are "below" Thongdam because of their lineal descent from a younger sibling of Thongdam's father.

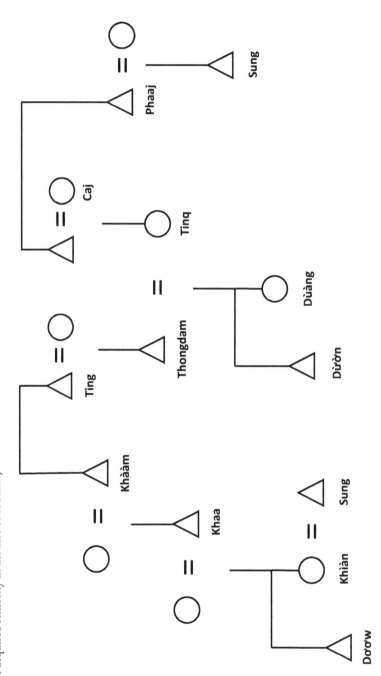

Figure 2. A set of kin relations among Kri Mrkaa speakers, labelled by name. (The vertical placement of individuals relative to each other in this diagram denotes their treatment of each other in linguistic practice as 'above' or 'below', either because of birth order in the case of siblings or acquired seniority in the case of cousins.)

Viewed as a kind of politeness strategy, there is a possible analogy with the "slave=I"/"lord=you" approach taken in many languages of Southeast Asia (including Lao; see Enfield 2007a). The logic is a metaphorical lowering of the self, combined with a raising of the other. In the Khìàn-Dùàng equation, Khìàn both lowers herself and raises Dùàng by means of the generational-skewing practice of casting oneself in a generation below the other.

Beyond Cìà-maangq: In-laws

So far, we have looked at relationships between *cìà-maangq*: people in the same bloodline. For people within this category, some linguistic practices of person reference are asymmetrical (generational skewing in kin term use, use of endearing appellatives, use of title with name), as determined by relative age (actual or acquired). Other linguistic practices of person reference are symmetrical/reciprocal (pronoun usage, name use). These symmetrical/reciprocal practices do not occur with affinal social relations.

Kri speakers describe their society as patrilineal but in practice both patrilineal and matrilineal descent occur. Each household has its own spirits, which are tended by the father of the household. A child is born under the spirits of the father of the house. But this does not mean that all children are born under their *own* father's spirits. This is because, in practice, Kri speakers have an informal practice of matrilocality in the early years of a partnership, when the first few children are born. In practice, formal marriage—that is, following prescribed Kri rituals customs and bridewealth payments—comes late, if at all. Typically, a partnership will be inaugurated by a pregnancy, and the couple will be regarded as married in all but name. In theory—that is, in the words of Kri Mrkaa speakers describing what *should* happen—a young man will immediately set up an independent household for his growing family. In practice, this is not what tends to happen. The usual first stage of marriage is called *loon suu*, where the groom takes up residence in the family home of the bride, under the spirits of his father-in-law. (This is widely practiced by other ethnic groups across Laos, including in the dominant Lao culture; it's possible that the Kri word *suu* here is cognate with a Lao word, *suu1*, which refers to an act of ritual giving, as in the *suu1 khwan3* ritual of "giving over the spirits".) This means that any children born during that time will come under the spirits of their maternal grandfather (and thus of their own mother). In time, the son-in-law will eventually set up his own house, with its own spirits, and only then will his own newborn children inherit their father's house spirits.

In Kri society, the son-in-law relationship is fraught. For a period of time after the son-in-law moves into the wife's parents' household, he occupies a menial position in that household and performs labour for it as a kind of marriage payment. He works hard, stays quiet, and keeps to those parts of the house reserved for women and girls of the family. He must remain in the "inner" and "lower" corner of the house (see Enfield 2009 on restrictions on the son-in-law's physical presence and movement in his father-in-law's house).

We now turn to the linguistic practices around being a son-in-law. (Note that the language described in this son-in-law example also holds, *mutatis mutandis*, for daughters-in-law.) Going back to the set of relations laid out in figure 2, recall that Khìàn is the first child of Khaa. Our example concerns the practices of person reference in relation to Khìàn's husband Sung.

Mree: In-laws above One's Spouse

The Kri word for son-in-law is *matààm*. (Daughter-in-law is *qujùù*.) In figure 2, Sung is *matààm* to his father-in-law Khaa, as well as to Khaa's brother Thongdam, and indeed to all the higher *cìà-maangq* of his wife Khìàn, including Khìàn's elder brothers and sisters. The collective term for the higher *cìà-maangq* of your spouse is *mree*.

The *mree* relation has special linguistic norms for person reference. An important constraint is that Sung's *mree* cannot say his name when addressing him or referring to him. Nor can Sung say the names of his *mree*. Instead, they use (extended) teknonymy, or appropriate kin terms or pronouns. The required pronoun usage follows norms that are distinct for this kin relation, which I now describe.

In relation to *mree*, dual pronouns are used with reference to singular speech act participants. A son-in-law will use *ñaar* "1du.excl" ("we two, not including you") for self-reference (="I") when speaking with a *mree* such as his father-in-law. In turn, a father-in-law or other *mree* will use *maar* "2du" ("you two") for second-person reference (="you") when speaking with a *matààm* "son-in-law" (or *qujùù* "daughter-in-law"). (See below for discussion of dual pronouns and their uses.)

Another special practice related to *mree* involves the dedicated first-person pronoun *pààng*. This pronoun means "I", but its only pragmatically unmarked use is by a *mree* when addressing a *matààm/qujùù*. While *pààng* is appropriate for this relationship, the pronoun is sometimes extended in usage with a strong pragmatic effect of arrogance or superiority (much as a bare first-person pronoun in a language like Lao, or a *T* form in certain European languages, might convey arrogance if used outside of its normally appropriate social relation). I can illustrate with an example from a recorded conversation between two adult Kri men. The two men are discussing the fact that I—the linguist/ethnographer—am learning the Kri language, a fact which they find strange, fascinating and funny. They imagine the scene when the recordings are played at my home base (in the Netherlands at the time the recording was done), where I would be the only person who could understand the language heard in the recordings. One of the speakers performs my imagined speech in this scene, in what I can only describe as a gruff voice: "You all don't understand it, but I understand it!" For the first-person singular reference here, he uses *pààng*. The usage is not plausibly linked to any literal kin relationship of parent-in-law to child-in-law in the imagined context. The pronoun is being appropriated for the specific pragmatic effect of framing a person who is flaunting their superiority. The use of *pààng* here also helps to build the humour of the moment (the talk is suffused with laughter). Combined with the gruff voice, the pronoun *pààng* conveys something along the lines of "You fools!".

It is worth noting that the word *pààng* is possibly cognate with one of the two first-person pronouns in Saek, a northern Tai language (not related to Kri historically) spoken in the next village downstream from the Mrkaa area. The Saek first-person pronoun in question is *phaan6* [pʰaːn?³²]. Most Kri speakers know some Saek, and many can speak it fluently. Kri and Saek have been in close contact for at least two hundred years.

Kmoon: In-laws below One's Spouse

The category label for the lower *cìà-maangq* of your spouse is *kmoon*. (Note the possible relation between the word *kmoon* and *koon*, an Austroasiatic root meaning "child"; see, for comparison, Vietnamese *con* [kɔːn] "child", and also the Kri word *knoon*, discussed below.) The rules for person reference regarding *kmoon* differ from those just described for *mree*. First, while Sung's *kmoon* (for example, Dǒǒw—Sung's wife's younger brother—in figure 2) may not use Sung's first name, Sung *may* use the names of his *kmoon* (who, unlike his *mree*, are below him), Second, Sung and his *kmoon* use dedicated first- and second-person pronouns for reference to each other: Dǒǒw would use *mii* (you) as second-person reference for Sung (the "higher" in-law), and first-person pronoun *koon*, which is reserved for just this relation: *koon* means "I" when spoken by a *kmoon* addressing a *tààm/sawq*. (This use of *koon* does not have any marked connotation analogous to the arrogance associated with *pààng*.)

Words for an In-law

Kri has special reference terms for affines: *matààm* (lower male-in-law), *qujùù* (lower female-in-law), *tààm* (higher male-in-law), and *sawq* (higher female-in-law). Immediately after Sung married Khìàn (or effectively married her; for example, when she became pregnant with their first child), Sung's *mree/kmoon* referred to him as *pǒǒq srooh* (man who is married but not yet with a child; father-to-be). Once Sung's first child was born (a boy named Khêên; not featured in figure 2), they referred to him as *pǒǒq knoon*, and can now do so ongoingly throughout his life. Also, once Sung's first child was born, Sung's *mree/kmoon* referred to Sung by teknonymy, initially as *pòòq khêên* (Khêên's father), and later potentially as *qôông khêên* (Mister Khêên) or later *vòòk khêên* (Grandpa Khêên). In practice, this means that everyone with children in Kri-speaking society comes to be known by two personal names: their own birth name and the name of their first-born child. This was a source of confusion to me in my early period of field research in the area, as it took time for me to realise that, for example, *vòòk nun* and *vòòk kham* were the same person (for example, the man named Nun whose first child is named Kham).

Sung calls his parents-in-law *vòòk*: *vòòk kèèq* (big *vòòk*) for the father-in-law and *vòòk didiiq* (little *vòòk*) for the mother-in-law. These terms refer specifically to male and female grandparents. Sung uses the same term for his parents-in-law as his own children do (his parents-in-law are his children's grandparents). Sung uses *vòòk* for other *mree* of the same generation, such as Thongdam (but does not use the modifiers *kèèq* or *didiiq* for people who are not actually his wife's parents). So, Sung calls Thongdam *vòòk dùàng* (Grandpa Duang), using teknonymy.

By the way, *vòòk* is one of the terms that is used when Kri speakers want to refer to people who are not members of Kri society. I am referred to by all Kri speakers as *vòòk nik* (Grandpa Nick). This usage appropriates the kinship system for a more generic function of expressing some kind of respect for seniority. *Vòòk* was the form that they chose for me. But this situation is unique. In general, for Lao people who they know, such as officials from the local district, they will use name reference and an appropriate Lao title. Kri speakers are acquainted with many Vietnamese, who pass through the area as hikers/traders. They refer to these men by name using the word *qunêêq*—which means "Vietnam"/"Vietnamese"—as a title form. So, the Vietnamese man named *thu* is referred to in Kri as *qunêêq thu*. For these outsiders, from both the Lao and Vietnamese sides, Kri speakers may convey formality/respect by using the forms *qôông* (for men) or *mooq* (for women), as stand-alone pronoun-like forms or as titles to personal names.

Kri speakers, in conversations with me about person reference practices, sometimes describe the relationship between a son-in-law and his *mree* as a *taa-ñaar* relationship, using the relevant paired linguistic markers as a metonym for the relationship. In this way, the compound phrase *taa-ñaar* [FeB-1 du.excl] can refer (in anyone's speech) to the relation between, say, a man and his younger brother's wife (or, conversely, a woman and her husband's older brother). It means "the pair of people for whom one is *taa* (father's older brother) and the other is *ñaar* (we two, not including you)".

Dual Pronouns for Lower In-laws

There are two special pronominal usages associated with the *mree* relation. The dual pronoun is used for the son/daughter-in-law, across all grammatical persons:

"I" (*ñaar* '1du.excl'), "you" (*maar* '2 du'), or "he/she" (*qaar* '3 du'). (Note how the presupposition that the referent of the pronoun is a son/daughter-in-law depends upon different participant role relationships for each of these usages: *ñaar* presupposes that the referent is a child-in-law with respect to the addressee of the utterance, while *maar* and *qaar* presupposes that the referent is a child-in-law with respect to the speaker of the utterance.) Sung will use the same terms that his own children use in referring to his siblings-in-law and cousins-in-law. For example, his wife's *qeem* (younger siblings) are his *mu'uq* (mother's younger sister) and *kùùq* (mother's younger brother). So here, there is a combination of two kinds of asymmetry: the up-down asymmetry of age-difference (as operates among *cìà-maangq*) and the inside-outside asymmetry of consanguineal versus affinal relations.

We may ask why the dual is appropriate for reference to a son/daughter-in-law. It is arguably an avoidance term. The dual reference has a highly restricted range of use (beyond its use as a pronoun when reference is simply to any two people together), being limited to just one (albeit salient) relationship type out of many across society. It does not express a general form of social respect or distance that a politeness function might imply. The relationship type in question—that between parent-in-law and child-in-law—is universally fraught. It attracts avoidance behaviour all over the world. In Kri society, the son- or daughter-in-law is both low and distant. (As noted to me by Jack Sidnell, this suggests that we can't simply equate "more in number" or "wider inclusion"—for example, plural/dual rather than singular—with "higher status", on the model of European *V* forms.) Through Kri language practices, parents-in-law treat this person as if they were two people. Why? Kri speakers say that the "two people" denoted by the dual are the son-/daughter-in-law and their spouse (who is *cìà-maangq* of the speaker; for example, the speaker's son or daughter). This usage of the dual is arguably a way to semiotically dilute the personhood of the referent individual, treating him or her as a representative of a larger unit rather than as an individual person. I don't refer to "you", but rather "you two" because I take you to be nothing more than a representative of the two-person unit which also includes your spouse, my *cìà-maang*. This usage can be compared to other "honorific" uses of the dual noted by Fleming (2017). Descriptions of avoidance behaviour in relation to in-laws show groupings of the referent and their spouse for the purpose of an avoidance rule. For example, in Mongolian, a married woman is forbidden to use the names, either in address or reference, of her *xadamud* (her husband's immediate senior male relatives: older brothers, father, father's brothers, grandfather), and this extends to "the names of the wives of close *xadamud*" (Humphrey 1993, 75). Humphrey suggests that the Mongolian daughter-in-law is subject to various taboos because she occupies an ambiguous position with respect to her loyalties and interests.

Is she part of her husband's family, and does she have her new nuclear family's interests primarily in mind? (Humphrey 1993, 90).

In Jahai, a language of the same family as Kri (Austroasiatic) but spoken in faraway peninsular Malaysia, non-singular pronoun forms are used with certain kin relations, including the third person dual *wih* for one's child-in-law (for both second- and third-person reference), and dual forms for second- and third-person reference to a sibling-in-law (Kruspe and Burenhult 2019, 294). And in Temiar, the second-person dual pronoun *kəʔan* is used reciprocally "with same-sex siblings-in-law who are younger than one's spouse" (Kruspe and Burenhult 2019, 306, citing Benjamin 1999, 13). From Kruspe and Burenhult (2019, 309):

> The use of dual distinctions in Jahai and Temiar is significant, since this is a cross-linguistically unusual phenomenon in both avoidance and honorific paradigms. Occasional reports hint at similar strategies elsewhere: Santali, a distantly related Austroasiatic (Munda) language of India, employs the second person dual for address between a parent-in-law and child-in-law (Ghosh 2008, 33 and 86–7; cf. McPhail 1953, 23). Further afield, Wuvulu (Austronesian, Papua New Guinea) is reported to use the second person dual for address between all affines (Hafford 2014, 60). Among honorific pronominal paradigms more generally, duals are put to use in languages like Kharia and Mundari (Peterson 2014, 102–5) as well as Tuvaluan (Besnier 2000, 388–9; cf. the typology of Head 1978, 157–8).

Fleming (2017) points out further cases of dual pronouns being used for affinal address. An example is Wa, a Palaungic language of northern Myanmar (Ma 2012, 43, n.8). Another is Yokuts, in which a son-in-law should refer to his mother-in-law in both second and third person with the dual (Newman 1944, 101). And in Kobon (a Papuan language), "skewing of dual number in singular pronominal reference is limited to same-sex in-laws (a man uses it for his brothers-in-law and father-in-law; a woman for her sisters-in-law and mother-in-law)" (Fleming 2017, 99, citing Davies 1991).

Fleming (personal communication) points out a contrast between the Kri case and the case of Santali. In both languages, dual pronouns are specifically used for singular persons in a son-in-law and parent-in-law relationship. In Santali, the dual is used in a wholly symmetrical and reciprocal manner as a sign of respect between son-in-law and parents-in-law (see Ghosh 2008; Choksi 2010; Fleming 2017). But in Kri it is only the child-in-law who is referred to using the dual. This creates an asymmetry in the relationship, which is also evidenced by the use by *mree* of the pronoun *pàànq* when addressing a child-in-law (a speaker-addressee-conditioned rule), and by other rules such as the constraints on where in the parents-in-law's house a child-in-law is allowed to be (Enfield 2009).

Finally, by what semiotic mechanism does a dual pronoun succeed in referring to a singular person? One possibility is that, as Fleming further suggests in personal communication, the dual is "skewed" and simply refers to a singular person. An alternative, which I suggested earlier in this section, is that, with the dual, a son-in-law is not treated as an individual at all, but as merely part of a paired person, as if he were nothing to his *mree* if not for his marriage, the one thing that makes him matter to them. (It may also reflect a "preference for association" in person reference; Stivers et al. 2007, 14.) I do not mean that when someone refers to a person in the dual—as when a man says to this son-in-law "You-two forgot your knife in the swidden"—he is saying that the man's wife also forgot the knife. What I mean is that the man is treating the son-in-law as part of a kind of corporate agent, comparable to when a man says "They wronged us" with reference to a feud between two families, rooted in a specific violent conflict by an individual family member in the past (Enfield 2017, 10): The man is not claiming that all members of the other family carried out the offending action, but that as members of the family they have some agency in an extended sense (for example, of being co-principals rather than authors or animators; Goffman 1981; Kockelman 2007; Enfield 2017).

Parents of Married Couples

A final special kin relationship to be noted here is the relationship between A and B where A's child is married to B's child. In this case, A and B are *sdoong*. They use dedicated pronouns for each other—*khoojq* "I" and *nôôq* "you"—which are used reciprocally. *Sdoong* may not use each other's personal names but will use teknonymy.

Note that the word *khoojq* "I" is a possible cognate with the Lao form *khòòj5* [kʰɔːj³¹], a polite first-person singular pronoun that derives etymologically from a word that means "slave". Similarly, note that *sdoong* may be cognate with the Lao word *dòòng3* [dɔːŋ¹³], which has the same meanings as the Kri term *sdoong*: (1) non-kin who are connected by virtue of the fact that their children have married, and (2) a wedding.

Table 2 is a summary of some of the points regarding different categories of kin relation in Kri discussed so far.

Clashes in the System

When a person gets married in Kri society, this often means that their kinship relation with certain people in their social world will change. In each case, they may have to change their linguistic practices of person reference with those people. This is referred to in Kri as *patooj* (alter, change, replace). Compare this to the

Table 2. Kin relation categories

Kin category of addressee	1st person pronoun	2nd person pronoun	Can use name?
1. *cìà-maangq* "kin of same descent group" (marriage not allowed)	*teeq* 1SG	*cak* 2SG	Yes
2. *mree* "'higher' *cìà-maangq* of your spouse"	*ñaar* 1DU.EXCL	kin term	No
3. *matàảm/qujùù* "so. married to your lower *cìà-maangq* (e.g., younger sib. or child)"	*pàảnq* 1SG	*maar* 2DU	No
4. *kmoon* "'lower' *cìà-maangq* of your spouse"	*koon* 1SG	*mii* 2SG	Yes
5. *tàảm/sawq* "someone married to your elder sibling"	*teeq* 1SG	kin term	No
6. *sdoong* "*mree* of your own child" (i.e. someone whose child you are *mree* to) [these pronouns used reciprocally]	*khoojq* 1SG	*nôôq* 2SG	No

practice of "dispensing" with formal *vous* and agreeing to *tutoyer* in French. The shift to reciprocal *tu* is a change made voluntarily between two people to mark a progression toward familiarity in their interpersonal relationship. By contrast, the practice of *patơớj* in Kri is a more consequential change in person reference, which has a broader array of impacts, not just affecting a pronoun, but also, for example, whether a person's name can (no longer) be used. Also, the process of *patơớj* is discussed and contested or negotiated in a broader circle of relationships. I observed a situation in which a woman announced that she did not intend to *patơớj* in the case of Sung's marriage to Khìàn, which led to extended family discussion about whether this was appropriate or not. It provided a locus for public stance-taking and gossip about the ethics of person reference. Typically, people who are "below" the person who is getting married will be expected to *patơớj*. Often people who are above them—and who have known the person in question since they were born—have the option not to *patơớj* (see, for comparison, Paulston 1976; Agha 2007, 33ff for discussion of differential rights to initiate dispensation depending on one's status).

Conclusion

We have seen that person reference in Kri is dynamic and complex. At the core of the system are two axes of asymmetry. The first is an above/below axis. This axis is anchored in the chronological birth order of siblings. Seniority within a sibling set is "transmitted" to the relations between their offspring, and to those offspring's own offspring. This axis is formally coded in kin term choice and in asymmetries of kin and pronoun usage in interlocutor reference. The second is an inside/outside axis. This axis distinguishes consanguineal and affinal relations. For insiders, basic pronouns and personal names are used symmetrically, but when outsiders are involved, there is asymmetrical use of names and pronouns, and special pronominal forms come into play. Of particular note is the use of dual pronouns for (first, second, and third person) reference to individual children-in-law.

The Kri system of person reference has not previously been documented. My aim here of getting some of the central facts straight is a prerequisite to any questions of broader comparative significance that may arise. In further research, we will need to better understand a number of issues in relation to the system if we are going to understand its implications. One issue is the system's historical development. Are its features inherited from an ancestor language? Have they developed internally in recent times? Are they borrowed from other language communities through social contact? Or is it a combination? And in turn, what will be the consequences for this system of the rapid and radical social change that Kri society is currently undergoing (Enfield 2018; Zuckerman and Enfield 2021)? And finally, what is the second-order native Kri understanding of the system, as captured in ideology and metalanguage about kinship and person reference practices? Why, for example, do my Kri language consultants giggle when I ask about dual reference for children-in-law but not when I ask about generational skewing with reference to second cousins?

While much more remains to be known, we have at least now established some fundamental points of reference for understanding the linguistic system of kinship-grounded relations that help to define the Kri social world. Through their dynamic and asymmetrical person reference system, each Kri community member places every other one at some point on the intersection of the two axes of asymmetry—above/below and inside/outside—through explicit markers of linguistic practice.

Acknowledgements

I am grateful to all participants in the workshop for feedback on the presentation, especially to Jack Sidnell and Luke Fleming for extremely useful comments and suggestions on written drafts.

CHAPTER 3

Speaking of People in South-Central Java*

Joseph Errington

When used to identify persons engaged with each other interactionally, kin terms and personal pronouns can have socially expressive as well as referential meanings. Those used in Javanese, as in many Asian languages, encode fine differences by marking or presupposing something about a speaker's relation to persons they speak about (their referents) and speak to (their addressees). They may key to differences of status or age, real or "fictive" kin ties, memberships in social groups, and so on. The social meanings of these acts of use change from context to context—relative to immediacies of place, topic, and biography—but also from era to era, relative to the shifting relevance of attributes which are broadly understood for gauging relations of status and intimacy.

This chapter sketches some of these patterned changes in use of kin terms and personal pronouns in Javanese, with a focus on their mediating role in the broad transition from a "traditional" Javanese to a "modern" Indonesian society. First, I sketch the political and cultural backdrop which supported and was expressed through use of linguistic hierarchies in south-central Java before the fall of the Dutch empire and the rise of the Indonesian nation in 1945. This is done by linking the doctrine of exemplary centres to use of Javanese kin terms and personal pronouns, and then their assimilation to distinctly national modes of interaction in the 1970s and 1980s. This broad sketch is organised around the ways that recurring patterns in talk—"micro" processes of social interaction— have aligned with the broader sociopolitical dynamics that have shaped changing senses of relations between Javanese persons as members of an ethnic community, and citizens of an ethnically heterogeneous nation.

44

Language use in an Exemplary Centre

Multiple styles of speech have long been commonplace in everyday life in south-central Java. When it was a region of the Netherlands East Indies it was divided into four royal principalities. All were politically and economically dependent on the Dutch empire, but legitimised by the supernatural and spiritual power attributed to the heads of each of these royal houses, defined as "places of rulers" (*kraton*). Two were located in Surakarta, which was distinct from and superordinate to its rural surrounds less because it was a governmental centre than the place of the king, and so an exemplary centre (Geertz 1976 [1960]; Moertono 1968).

Surakarta was distinguished also by its noble elites, *priyayi*, who were descendants and servants of the noble houses of Mangkunegara and Adiningrat. Status among these elites, and their ways of interacting with others, were shaped by finely calibrated evaluations of status along lines of descent, gender, seniority, marital status, occupation, and so on (Errington 1988). These factors directly shaped manners or styles of Javanese used between *priyayi*, and between *priyayi* and commoners. They involved knowledge of large, finely differentiated vocabularies, and the ability to deploy them appropriately (Poedjosoedarmo 1968; Errington 1985b, 1988).

In both respects fluency in these speech levels, as they are commonly known, was difficult to acquire outside the noble circles in which they were most widely used. Young persons coming of age in this fairly small, tightly knit community acquired knowledge of these levels along with practical senses of how they could be properly and creatively deployed.[1] Javanese who grew up outside those social circles, on the other hand, rarely acquired comparable fluency, and so an inability to speak in elevated or "polished" ways could serve as "natural" evidence of their less cultivated nature.

Unequal distribution of competences in the most polished styles could create interactional situations which presented commoners with a kind of double bind. In face-to-face dealings with elites, they were obliged to speak in styles of Javanese they rarely controlled. So, they displayed dysfluency in the presence of just those persons who had the competences they lacked, but who would never use those polished styles to them. In this way alignments between verbal abilities and group memberships created situations in which the concrete, "natural" superiority of *priyayi*, relative to commoners, was evident.

In commoner families, communities, and interaction, more limited linguistic expressions of politeness served to mark and presuppose less finely drawn distinctions of status, and senses of formality. The vocabularies of politesse they controlled, smaller than those used by *priyayi*, keyed most crucially to terms for persons: personal pronouns and kin terms. The stylistic differentiation of personal pronouns within the larger vocabularies of the Javanese speech levels indirectly reflected their importance or pragmatic salience (Errington 1988): *priyayi* at the turn of the twentieth century used three or four first-person pronouns, and as many second-person pronouns. Though commoners emulated them, they did so by choosing between two or perhaps three relatively polite forms.

Personal pronoun usage keyed to issues of social status in two ways. Choices between them served directly, and interactionally, to mediate a speaker's face-to-face relation with an addressee. Indirectly, such acts of use marked a speaker's broader social capacities and background. These double significances played out, over time, in sociolinguistic patterns of lagging emulation. As members of subordinate groups emulated their superiors, terms that had been "prestige symbol[s] for the high social group at an earlier period in its history, [became] obsolescent" (Friedl 1964, 569). Such changes in use patterns of personal pronouns—which could be prestigious because they were distinctively elite, and not just deferential—is summarised in table 1.[2]

Table 1. Changing uses of polite second-person pronouns

	Ca. 1920	Ca. 1960	Ca. 1980
Elite *priyayi*	*sampéyan*	*panjenengan*	*panjenengan*
Villager/commoner	*ndiká*	*sampéyan*	*sampéyan/panjenengan*

In the 1920s, *sampéyan* was the most commonly used by *priyayi* for polite and perhaps deferential reference to addressees; commoners, especially members of rural communities, more frequently used *ndiká*. By 1960 *sampéyan* was widely known and used in villages, having displaced *ndiká* as a means of expressing respect for an interlocutor (persons who had seniority or official status, more often than noble descent). In Surakarta, another polite personal pronoun, *panjenengan*, had by this time broadened in use beyond those of the highest rank, effectively displacing *sampéyan*. By the 1980s, in turn, young Javanese in rural communities were emulating city dwellers by using *panjenengan* rather than *sampéyan*, in order not to sound overfamiliar or "old fashioned".

This pattern of lagging emulation stemmed from a broad sense that uses of personal pronouns are among the most interactionally sensitive elements of verbal interaction. It rested also on awareness of links between traditional hierarchies and the kinds of polished speech associated with membership in an elite group. The unequal distribution of linguistic competences naturalised the political culture of the exemplary centre, and the strategy of territoriality used by city elites to "affect, influence, or control people, phenomena, and relationships by delimiting and asserting control over geographic areas". (Sack 1986, 19). These patterns can likewise be seen as examples of what Pierre Bourdieu calls class-based "integrative struggles". Rural Javanese were members of a what he calls a "dominated" class who emulated a dominant elite which innovated linguistically in ways that maintained the "constancy of the gap" between what came "naturally" to *priyayi* and commoners in verbal conduct. The status of elites licensed the linguistic innovations which ensured that non-elites were, in his words, "beaten before they start[ed]" (Bourdieu 1984, 165).

Kin terms, also interactionally crucial elements of linguistic etiquette, underwent similar patterns of lagging emulation, as can be seen in the top four rows of table 2. The same is true for the kin terms serving to identify a referent's status as a sibling of one's parent, in the left column of the bottom four rows. By 1980 *siwá*, *paman*, and *bibi* became less common among persons in villages, who adopted terms being used in the 1920s in cities. The "older" terms came into use to refer to and address older members of rural communities, unlike those identified with terms that had been in use in Surakarta two generations previously: *pak lik* and *pak dhé*, *bu lik* and *bu dhé*).[3]

Table 2. Changing kin term use

	Ca. 1920		Ca. 1980	
Gloss	Non-elite	Exemplary elite	Non-elite	Urban elite to kin
Mother	*(si)mbok, mak-(bi)yung*	*(i)bu*	*(i)bu-mbok*	*mami*
Father	*(ba)pak*	*(ba)pak* (+title)	*(ba)pak*	*papi*
Elder sister	*yu*	*mbak(yu)*	*mbak(yu), yu*	*mbak(yu)*
Elder brother	*(ka)kang*	*(ka)kang* (+title)	*(kang)mas, kang*	*(kang)mas*
Parent's older brother	*(si)wá*	*pak dhé*	*pak dhé*	*om*
Parent's younger brother	*(pa)man*	*pak lik*	*pak lik*	*om*
Parent's older sister	*(si)wá*	*bu dhé*	*bu dhé, mbok dhé*	*tante*
Parent's younger sister	*lik, bibi*	*bu lik*	*bu lik*	*tante*

The interactional significance of kin terms could be socially nuanced in multiple ways depending on the interplay between their "literal" meanings, glossed here into English, and the situations in which they were used. As means for speaking of a person being spoken to, their social meanings depended on issues of gender, relative age, birth order, and so on. When (as is common) those persons are not kin, use of kin terms presupposes a kind of "as if" trope of familial relations, expressing deference or intimacy, respect or social distance, and so on.

A person who is addressed with a term meaning "parent's elder sibling", for instance, can be identified by a speaker as relatively high status or senior, unlike the kind of intimacy that might be conveyed by a term meaning "parent's younger sibling". But use of either term tacitly identifies that speech partner as, or as if they were, a parent's sibling and so, as one person observed to me, like "real family". Unlike the more "neutral" terms glossable as "mother" and "father", discussed below, these referential meanings make them resources for expressing intimacy in an idiom of generational seniority and birth order.

Kin term use is also further nuanced by manner of pronunciation, either "full" and disyllabic or as a "short" monosyllable.[4] Parentheses in table 2 indicate which syllables can be elided to make less formal, perhaps more familiar, or condescending use of kin terms to refer to an addressee. Monosyllabic forms are also used vocatively to identify someone as an interlocutor, which means that scenarios of use for "full" referential and "short" vocative kin terms provides a useful illustration of their different social senses.

For example, see 1a (below), which transcribes a question that might be posed to a pedicab driver (low status, adult male), which identifies that person as addressee referentially with the kin term glossable as "father" (*bapak*). 1b transcribes another way of "saying the same thing", closing with the short form of that kin term (*pak*), used vocatively to affirm the identity of the person to whom the query is directed; this utterance could have the same referential meaning without that addition. These utterances differ socially in that 1b has a more casual feel which is more appropriate with intimates and persons of lower status. For this reason, older *priyayi* indicated to me it would be a more appropriate way to talk with a pedicab driver about paying a fare.

(1)   a.   *Bapak rak wis takgèki ta?*
           "*Bapak* [you] I've already paid, right?"

       b.   *Rak wis takgèki ta pak?*
           "Haven't I already paid [you] *pak*?"

A third technique for nuancing one's use of a kin term, less common in the national era, is to combine it with a title of noble rank or office. At the turn of the century, for instance, young males might be addressed with a form of the kin term meaning "elder male sibling" in combination with *mas*, then a title for persons distantly descended from a king. This "mixed" idiom of siblingship and descent could express respect for middling social status tempered by differences of age, or senses of familiarity. More formal combinations involve a term for a parent like *bapak* or *mbok* with a title of office like *ngabéhi*. But the felt formality of these combinations could be tempered, as noted earlier, with monosyllabic pronunciations of both elements, like *pak béhi*.

The last column of table 2 summarises patterns of kin term usage that became more common among members of Surakarta's educated middle-class residents after the New Order regime came to power in 1966. The New Order, set in place by factions of the military which deposed Indonesia's first president, Sukarno, established an authoritarian apparatus of oversight and control. That regime's elite was dominated by ethnic Javanese who reinvented elite *priyayi* traditions to legitimise their own power. But among the far-flung effects of their program of national development, including propagation of the Indonesian language, was a transformation of Surakarta from a distinctively exemplary centre to one of many urban centres found across Indonesian territory.

Spreading knowledge of Indonesian, the linguistic face of this massive program of development, led to new patterns of kin term use, a seemingly minor aspect of everyday life that fit into broader shifts in Surakartan society. More educated persons adopted innovative kin term usage—*mami, papi, om,* and *tante*—which were of Dutch provenance, but more associated with elites in Jakarta. This manner of speech marked a clear interactional break with the past because they were used only, and in the Western fashion, for persons who counted as members of "one's own" family. This preference became distinctive of persons who were members not of a traditional elite, but an educated, Indonesian speaking middle class.

Kin Terms, Ethnicity, and Nationality

Widely used kin terms for adult males and females can be sketched here as aspects of the dominant but shifting position of Javanese in the new politics and language of Indonesia. This shift can be traced to early stages of the nationalist movement, when Javanese *(ba)pak* (father) and *(i)bu* (mother) were adapted into the variety of Malay which was to be renamed Indonesian (publicly) in 1928. This began in 1922 when a founding figure in a progressive, anticolonial movement—a *priyayi* who had renounced his royal heritage—founded a school in Jogjakarta, south-central Java's other exemplary centre.

This was Ki Hadjar Dewantara, who established his Taman Siswa school to develop a "family-style" educational program that came to be emulated elsewhere in the Netherlands East Indies. To decouple those schools from traditional status hierarchies he instructed teachers in a new way of speaking of and to each other:

We used the terms "Bapak and "Ibu" because we considered that the terms of address currently in use, "Tuan" [Sir], "Njonjah" [Madam] and "Nonah" [Miss"] and the corresponding Dutch terms "Meneer," "Mevrouw," and "Juffrouw," and also the terms in use in Java, such as "Mas Behi," "Den Behi," and "Ndoro," which implied superiority and inferiority of status, should be abolished from Taman Siswa. We introduced the use of the terms "Bapak" and "Ibu" not only for when pupils spoke to teachers but also for when younger teachers spoke to older ones. We never once spelled this out as a "regulation" but this kind of appellation soon came to be used in educational institutions across Indonesia. (Tsuchiya 1987 quoted in Shiraishi 1992, 161–2)

Symmetric use of *ibu* and *bapak* among progressive colonial subjects offered a model for egalitarian conduct in circles that widened along with nationalist aspirations. It became commonplace among persons who learned to speak standard Indonesian as students in schools established by New Order across the nation.

This broad shift tacitly detached those kin terms from older differences in the kinds of status attributed to women and men. In Javanese, *(i)bu* had once differed from *mbok* as did the marital status of the persons properly addressed: the deferential *ibu* was reserved for the first, "official" wife (not concubines) of noble elite men (see Errington 1988). In Indonesian, on the other hand, it came to be used in accord with broader achieved statuses, presupposing a woman's distinctive educational accomplishments and occupations.

Traces of this shift across languages, and eras, could still be heard in everyday talk among rural Javanese in the 1980s. Women in villages were then still sometimes referred to and addressed as *(si)mbok*, that term paired with *bapak* for female and male parents respectively. This can be seen from example (2), in which their use for biological kin is marked by genitive suffix *-né*.

(2) *Nyusul mbokné karo bapakné, rak nang kana ndhisik.*
     "[He] followed his mother and father, [they] went there first."

Like other kin terms noted earlier, *(si)mbok* had short or full pronunciations and could combine with titles of office.

In the 1980s, young Javanese in rural regions learned a different, Indonesian use of *ibu*, which they addressed to educated woman (typically teachers, often using the monosyllabic form combined with the word meaning teacher: *bu guru*). This use at school did not carry over to their homes, where they addressed their own mothers, and others of her generation, as *(si)mbok*. One young villager told me of a male cousin who acquired non-Javanese habits of speech during a year in

Speaking of People in South-Central Java 51

Jakarta, and addressed his monolingual aunt (her own sixty-year-old mother) as *ibu* in Javanese. His expression of respect for an elder elicited from her the dubious reaction "Why, that's palace usage!" (*Lho rak cárá ningrat kuwi*).

Young persons in villages (and elsewhere) clearly recognise these shifting links between kin term and modes of social stratification, as can be seen from an excerpt of a conversation transcribed in (3). During rehearsal of a play a director from the city, named Surya (S), interrupted the young man playing Teja. He had just responded to the character of his mother (A) who had called to him with the short, vocative form of his name (Já). He acknowledged that vocative by responding with the short form *bu*. This elicited the discussion transcribed here, in Javanese (transcribed in *italics* typescript) and Indonesian (transcribed in ***boldface italics***).

(3) Preparing for a play
A: *Já! Tëjá! Cobá réné le.*
Já, Teja! Come here son.
C: *Ènten nápá bu?*
What is it, *bu*?
[Surya interrupts]
S: *Ha mbok ápá bu? Mbok ápá bu?*
Now [should he use] *mbok* or *bu*? *Mbok* or *bu*?
X: *Mbok waé.*
Mbok.
Y: *Mak, mak yá isá, mak.*
Mak, mak will do, *mak*.
Z: *Mbok aé.*
Mbok.
S: *Aksiné mbok.*
Mbok is good.
X: *"Mami" aé* [laughter]
"Mami!"
S: ***Mana yang lebih wajar pada keluarga mlarat, pada keluarga mlarat seorang anak terhadap ibunya memanggilnya** "mbok" **apa** "mak" **apa** "bu"?*
What's more natural in a poor family, in a poor family, [does] a child to his/her mother call her "*mbok*" or "*mak*" or "*bu*"?
X: "*Mbok*".
"*Mbok*."
D: ***Yang banyak itu** "mbok mak": **itu.***
What's common is "*mbok*" [or] "*mak*".
[C repeats the line]

C: *Ènten nápá tá mbok?*
What is it *mbok*?
[B interrupts]
B: *Nek "mboké"?*
What about "*mboké*"?
D: *"Mboké", ájá "mboké".*
'*Mboké*', don't '*mboké*'.
[The scene resumes]
A: *Já Tejá!*
Já, Tejá!
C: *Nggih mbok?*
Yes *mbok*?

C, playing the part of Tejá in this artificial performance/rehearsal context, might have used *bu* as he would at school. Responses to Surya's query identified this usage in broadly socioeconomic terms, including the joker who interjected the suggestion that Tejá use *mami*. The laughter this elicited rested on shared awareness that *mami* "belongs to" a class of persons too geographically and socially distant to be emulated.

Bapak, as Ki Hadjar Dewantara intended, is now similarly used for nonintimate adult males, and has largely displaced titles of office and descent. So too it became, like *ibu*, a more stylistically "flat" but not impolite mode of address.[5] But the different social trajectories of these two terms, still evident in the 1980s, keys to the absence of an urban/rural contrast between terms for males, unlike that between what now count as "modern" Indonesian *ibu* and "traditional" Javanese *mbok*.

Terms for "Elder Sibling"

Kin terms meaning "elder sibling" were affected by similar patterns of lagging emulation. At the turn of the twentieth century, *mbak(yu)* and *kangmas* were Javanese terms used in Surakarta to address, perhaps with some formality, adolescents and young adults. By the 1980s both were used in both Indonesian and Javanese, but in ways reflecting their different places in a broader integrative dynamic.

Mbakyu, the "full" form term glossable as "elder sister", derived from the phrase *mbok ayu* (lit. "pretty mother"). It contrasts referentially with two short forms that can combine with names or be used as vocatives (like *pak* and *bu*, mentioned above). In the 1980s use of *mbak* felt less formal but not necessarily less polite than *mbakyu*; use of *yu* was associated with older, rural Javanese speakers and persons spoken of. This expressive contrast between *mbakyu* and *yu* can be read from a chance remark made by one woman (A) about another (Tanem) during a casual conversation with a female friend (G):

(4) G: *Tanem ki sing ndi ta ya?*
 Which Tanem, huh?
 A: *Mbakyuné yu Daliyem kaé.*
 The mbakyu [elder sister] of *yu* Daliyem.

In her answer to G's query, A added the genitive marker *-né* to *mbakyu* in order to identify Tanem's kin, but combined *yu* (not *mbak*) with that person's name. This served as a relatively polite—but rural, from a city person's point of view—way of identifying Tanem's younger sister.

The contrast between *mbak* vs. *yu* can be seen here to contrast broadly as do *ibu* vs. *mbok*. Use of *mbak* or *ibu* can be polite but not necessarily deferential in either Javanese or Indonesian interaction; use of *mbok* and *yu* are associated with rural, distinctly Javanese, less educated ways of speaking. These terms for interlocutors can be seen in this way to align with territorial distinctions that apply widely in Indonesia, marking Surakarta now as one among scores of urban centres, rather than an exemplary centre.

Mas, previously a title of descent, was at one time combined with titles of office (like Ki Hadjar Dewantara's example: *mas béhi*). In the 1920s it commonly served to lend some respect to the use of *kakang* "elder male sibling", commonly pronounced as a monosyllabic *kang* in that combination. *Kangmas*, a combination of kin term and title of descent, was comparable in interactional feel with *mbakyu*, a combination of kin term and adjective. By the time of Indonesian independence, *kangmas* was commonly use outside *priyayi* circles, and entirely detached from considerations of royal descent. The shortening processes noted earlier made it possible to use *mas* as a short, informal alternative to *kangmas*, as *kang* could be used relative to *kakang*.

By the 1980s, *kangmas* and *mas* were common usage among young bilinguals in villages. *Kang* was used, as one middle aged villager put it to me, to and about "someone who must be kind of old, and someone I know fairly well". In the city, *kangmas* had already been largely displaced by *mas*, which came to serve as a kin term, not a title of descent. This occurred, for instance, when a mother speaking to her daughter identified her other child as *masmu* ("elder male sibling" with the second-person possessive suffix *-mu*).

These ongoing patterns of lagging emulation still join and differentiate the city and its rural surround, but in ways that reflect a new strategy of territoriality, and that presuppose different social categories. Social hierarchies and statuses are now more widely linked to educational and socioeconomic positions, and so indirectly to fluency in standard Indonesian. This dynamic, sustained but not uniform, can be inferred from the ways that the "entry" of *mas* in at least some rural locales preceded that of *mbak*. This broad pattern surfaced, for instance in the casual remark transcribed as (5), made by one middle-aged monolingual woman to another about a mutual acquaintance. She identified the male in a married couple with *mas* (*mas Kus*) on one hand, and the female with the more traditional or old-fashioned *yu* (*yu Tun*) on the other.

(5) *Lha kula ngertiku ndhèk mbèn Mas Kus niku bojoné yu Tun kaé.*
     "Well me, I know before *mas* Kus, the spouse of *yu* Tun."

This is a transient interactional reflex of ongoing patterns of lagging emulation, and a newer "integrative struggle" in Javanese Indonesia. It might also be taken as specific evidence that kin terms used for males were at the leading edge of this broader social shift.

Speaking of "Me" and "You"

Use of *bapak* and *ibu* in standard Indonesian is now commonplace all over Indonesia, and a minor example of Javanese influence on the national language. When other Javanese kin terms figure in spoken Indonesian, they can have the effect of blurring the interactional salience of a categorical difference between the two languages. Such use is enabled, in part, by Indonesian's status as a national lingua franca.

Structurally and historically, standard Indonesian counts as a variety of Malay. Politically and ideologically, it is a language acquired and used everywhere in the absence of native speakers.[6] This unusual condition leads some to see Indonesia as an "improbable" nation (Pisani 2014). But it enabled an instrument of imperial rule to become the common language of most of Indonesia's 270 million citizens.

For brevity's sake Indonesian can be described here as having its origins in actions taken by the Netherlands East Indies to standardise an administrative variety of Malay. It was this literate language that was pirated as the language of a nationalist movement in 1928 and then used in 1945 to declare Indonesia's independence. A generation later the New Order began to propagate what it called standard Indonesian "good and true"—*bahasa Indonesia yang baik dan benar*. This instrument and symbol of state oversight was key for its program of economic development, and categorically distinct from hundreds of native ethnic languages, including Malay and Javanese.

Standard Indonesian's distinctness rested on what Amy Liu calls the "regime of the standard" established by the New Order as an ostensibly neutral "third party" (2015, 4) to "delineate which languages can be used when and where", and so "counteract potentially ideological as well as economic effects of the country's heterogeneity" (2015, 13). This regime of the standard was both necessary, and possible, because it governed a language with no native speakers for others to emulate. Now standard Indonesian's forms are everywhere assimilated to native languages, which shape the way its sounds are pronounced, its use of grammar and intonation, and so on. It has also enabled the assimilation of Javanese modes of interactional engagement, including the personal pronouns used in each.

Javanese commonly observe that Indonesian is stylistically and expressively simple (I: *sederhana*), bland (I: *tawar*), or plain (I: *polos*). But there are style contrasts between Indonesian first- and second-person pronouns, displayed next to those in Javanese, in table 3.[7]

Table 3. Complementary use of Javanese and Indonesian personal pronouns

	Javanese	Indonesian
1st person	*aku/kulá (dalem)*	*(aku)/saya*
2nd person	*kowé/panjenengan (sampéyan)*	*kamu/(anda)*

First-person *aku*, cognate between these languages, contrasts stylistically with Javanese *kulá* and *saya* in Indonesian. The style difference between Javanese *kowé* and *panjenengan* touched on earlier similarly parallels that between Indonesian *kamu* and *anda*.

Similarities between interactional significances of use of all four pairs of terms broadly resemble those described for second-person pronouns in European languages by Roger Brown and Albert Gilman (1960). They identified different social meanings (or "semantics") for interactional relations keying to dimensions of power and solidarity. Persons who symmetrically exchange grammatically singular (T) or plural (V) pronouns, "giving what they get", presuppose one of two kinds of status comparability. Reciprocal use of singular terms expresses a sense of commonality or intimacy; reciprocal use of plural terms marks a sense of social distance or lack of familiarity. Asymmetric exchanges, on the other hand, key to relations of hierarchy or inequality between an inferior or junior, who "gives" the plural form to a superior or senior and receives the singular form in return.

Brown and Gilman described long term changes in these patterns and "semantics" as symmetric usage became more common in more egalitarian social formations. Their observations can be adapted to the grammatically equivalent, "purely" stylistic contrasts discussed here, insofar as Javanese generally use *aku* in relations of familiar equality, reserving symmetric use of Javanese *kulá* or Indonesian *saya* for relations that are more formal. Symmetric exchange of "familiar" *kamu* or "polite" *anda* in Indonesian presupposes an interactional contrast paralleling that for Javanese *kowé* or relatively polite *panjenengan*.[8]

These patterns of exchange, in situations very different from those described by Brown and Gilman, can be associated with shifting social meanings, or "semantics". They have developed because of an indirect but important difference between bilingual Javanese ways of speaking to each other in Indonesian, and reserving *aku* for talk in Javanese. They also use "formal" *anda* in very specific, narrow ways in otherwise Indonesian interaction.

The research I draw on here shows that educated Javanese speaking casual Indonesian during the 1980s showed a general preference for "polite" *saya* over *aku* when speaking of themselves. The latter figured almost exclusively in otherwise Javanese linguistic interaction. Simple illustrations of this difference are examples (6) and (7), drawn from points in casual conversation when young persons switched between Indonesian and Javanese in a single remark to create shifts in interactional footing (Goffman 1981). These were shifts also between Javanese *aku* and Indonesian *saya*. (Javanese verbiage is underscored, personal pronouns are in **boldface italics**.)[9]

(6) <u>Mbok aku dipikir nèk sekolahan káná, ya, ming,</u> kecuali saya rugi waktu, kesel.
"So I should be thought of in that school there, right, but, aside from losing time I get tired."

(7) <u>Ning</u> dalam pengalaman **saya** lho, **aku** <u>wis tahu nganti nyang Salatiga kono</u>.
"But in my experience, I've been to Salatiga there."

Anda, likewise more "polite" than *kamu*, was rarely used in Indonesian talk we recorded. Its rare use reflects its skewedness with interpersonal dimensions of language, and so its development as part of Indonesian. The technocrats who worked to "develop" standard Indonesian under the New Order sought to make it the language of a decisive break with status hierarchies rooted in the colonial and feudal (*féodal*) past. In the case of Javanese, that history was nowhere clearer than in the personal pronouns which were integral to the speech levels. This made them special objects of concern for those working to make Indonesian an "optimally efficient tool for the communicative needs of a modern society" (Grijns 1981, 7).

Anda was purposely coined to displace other second-person pronouns in a stylistically simpler, socially neutral language. But among Javanese it came into use not as a means for avoiding the obligation to mark aspects of relations with a speech partner, but to identify persons so identified as anonymous or absent relative to an act of use. That is why some align *anda* with the "language of advertising" (*bahasa iklan*) and use this pronoun to address virtual or hypothetical addressees.

Anda's impersonal character makes it available to temporarily adopt a kind of anonymous stance for one's words and the person one is speaking with by modelling speech (Errington 1998b) that might be addressed to someone else in another context.[10] Two examples occur in the exchange between two young men transcribed as example (8). Opining about the possibility of a trial, S used *anda* not to identify M as the referent in his hypothetical statement, but to model what someone else might say to the defendant (*"anda"*) in such a trial. M echoed and elaborated his statement using *anda* in the same way.

(8) S: *Ada kemungkinan malah anda tersangkut.*
 You might in fact become involved.
 M: *Ada kemungkinan malah anda ikut mendukung atau ikut melindungi terdakwa.*
 You might in fact have helped or protected the accused.

Polite reference to interlocutors is made in Indonesian more often by means of kin terms, titles, or combinations of the two discussed earlier. Recourse is commonly made also to elliptical grammatical constructions (typically passive) that need not include a linguistic element referring to an addressee.

Kamu, used in the same kind of hypothetical address as *anda* in example (8), can serve to model utterances directed to an anonymous or hypothetical addressee (rather like "you" in English phrases like "you never know"). During one discussion of affairs of the heart that I recorded, an older man used *kamu* as he offered a piece of general advice to his younger acquaintance, as transcribed in example (9). "Informal" *kamu* and "formal" *saya* were stylistically appropriate because they presuppose an impersonal stance skewed with the relation between these interlocutors.

(9) *Jadi cinta itu bukan hanya cinta saja* kamu *dengan* saya *saja.*
 So love is not only love between you and me.

Parentheses in table 3 serve to mark this interactional marginality of *aku* and *anda*, and what might be called the Javanese non-use of these terms in stylistically flat Indonesian interaction. This fairly narrow complementarity can be seen more generally as enabling different senses of interactional engagement between coethnics as citizens of the nation. Javanese, more stylistically elaborate, offers more resources for expressing senses of relationality between "you" and "me".

Personal pronouns in Indonesian enhance its interactional neutrality. This complementarity suggests that Javanese conversational practices have been modified, but survived, in complementary relations with Indonesian, a language only partly governed by a regime of the standard.

Conclusion

This sketch of talk among Javanese Indonesians who came of age before the fall of the New Order, in 1998, is something of a period piece. Accelerating political, economic, and infrastructural change have increasingly integrated rural regions with cities in the nation as a whole. New representations of ethnic identities, and their languages, now circulate through expanding digital and mass media (Goebel 2017). Elevated forms of "high" Javanese continue to lose relevance along with the images of the exemplary centre they helped legitimise.

Indonesian is not only spoken more widely across national territory, but in nonstandard ways that have gained visibility in new mediascapes. The interplay between standard and nonstandard varieties can be seen more clearly now as part of what the cultural critic Goenawan Mohamad (2008) called the valuable paradox (*paradoks yang sangat berharga*) of Indonesian, a language that is both emblematic of national unity and enabling of its diversity.[11]

The narrower purpose of this review is to provide examples of the interplay between "macro" and "micro" aspects of sociolinguistic change. A focus on terms used to and for persons in interaction helps do this because personal pronouns and kin terms are closely tied to language codes, but also conspicuously expressive of subjective states in interpersonal conduct.

As parts of different languages, these terms can align with different political cultures which those languages can legitimise, reproduce, and help to change. I framed these here as strategies of territoriality tied to different kinds of hierarchies and class stratification. Terms for persons were shown to change along with images or stereotypes of speakership: noble versus commoner, urban versus rural dweller, national versus ethnic, educated versus uneducated, and so on.

As linguistic marks of social types, kin terms and personal pronouns have changed along with the "social personae or models of social action" (Agha 2007, 55). their uses can presuppose. These are the situated values of "micro" social dynamics in which persons mediate, affirm, and modify their relations to each other. Though their expressive significances may pass with the interactional moment, they partake of and pattern with durable social categories of person. They figure, then, as revealing points of interface between social systems and interactional lifeworlds.

Notes

* This chapter draws on research done in 1978–80 in Surakarta, and in 1985–86 northwest of that city in the Sragen Regency of Central Java. Thanks for financial support for the first research period are due to the Social Science Research Council and the National Science Foundation. I thank both organisations, and the Wenner-Gren foundation, for financial help during the second research period as well. I am grateful also for institutional support from the Indonesian Academy of Sciences (Lembaga Ilmu Pengetahuan Indonesia) as well as Gajah Mada University during the earlier research period and Santa Dharma University during the latter.

[1] The simplest, most commonly used distinction for these styles is between *ngoko* and *básá*. *Ngoko* is developmentally a "first" language and most natural medium of internal thought and feeling. Varieties of *básá* were acquired later in life in the process of becoming competent in polite demeanors appropriate in the presence of others.

[2] Standard orthographies of Javanese and Indonesian are used mostly to transcribe both languages with a few diacritics added to mark distinctive vowel sounds. The character *á* transcribes the Javanese vowel pronounced low and back in the oral cavity, roughly like the first vowel in English "ought." The character *é* transcribes the Javanese vowel pronounced roughly like that in English "hay." The character *e* without the accent marker is pronounced either as schwa (like the second syllable of English "sofa") or a mid-front vowel like that in English "pet." The symbol *k* is used to transcribe voiceless velar and glottal stops, which vary allophonically.

[3] These terms can be analysed as combining short forms of the kin terms glossable as father and mother on one hand, and on the other adjectives meaning "big" (*dhé*, from *gedhé*) and "small" (*lik*, from *cilik*).

[4] For more on the effect of fast speech processes on personal pronouns and kin terms see Errington (1988).

[5] During the New Order era, broadly paternalist styles of rule were often referred to as *bapakism*, reflecting the referentially indefinite use of *bapak* to identify authority figures, especially in official contexts.

[6] This remark keys not to developmental but ideological dimensions of the native speaker identity, that is, not the time of life when a linguistic competence is acquired, but the social category of persons who are recognised to be natural exemplars of its standard forms. Vernacular varieties of Indonesian have millions of native speakers in the former sense, but the standard language has no speakers in the latter sense. For further discussion see Kozok (2006), and Errington (2022).

[7] In the interests of brevity, I do not discuss here the more polite Javanese first-person pronoun, *(a)dalem*, or the shortened second-person pronoun *njenengan*. For more details see Errington (1988).

[8] The same holds for use of Malay/Indonesian *engkau*, a dialectal variant that is cognate with Javanese *kowé*.

[9] In recordings collected during research only six of some two thousand occasions of use of *aku* could be seen as integral to Indonesian usage; four of these were in speech of non-native Javanese, and other two appear to be parts of other code switching. On the other hand, that same corpus contains some 370 occasions of self-reference with Indonesian *saya*, by and to persons who otherwise exchange *ngoko* (with *aku*).

[10] For discussions and examples of speech modelling as a Javanese conversational practice see Errington (1998, 117–38).

[11] More on complex relations between Javanese and Indonesian in contemporary Central Java can be found in Goebel (2010), Tamtomo (2016, 2017, 2018), and Zentz (2014, 2017). More discussion of nonstandard Indonesians, and Goenawan's paradox, is in Errington (2022).

PART 2

Practices

CHAPTER 4

Vocatives in Javanese Conversation
Michael C. Ewing

Javanese speakers frequently mention their interlocutors in conversation through use of names, kinship terms and other vocative expressions. Vocatives are of course not unique to Javanese, but they have been long noted as being an extremely important resource for Javanese speakers (Keeler 1975; Errington 1988; Wolff and Poedjosoedarmo1982). In this study I explore how Javanese speakers use vocatives in informal face-to-face interaction, and I place these small but crucial items in the wider context of Javanese address and reference practices. I suggest that the overarching role vocatives play is in recognising and highlighting intersubjective impact, thus making intersubjective contact within interaction explicit in an ongoing fashion, rather than simply assumed. They do this by overtly indexing the social relationship that holds between speaker and addressee through choice of vocative form (for example name or kinship term). At the same time, vocatives are part of the interactional moment in which they are expressed, pragmatically linked to the utterance in which they occur. They do not just name a perduring relationship but also participate in the management of turns, topics, stances and participation frameworks in moment-to-moment interaction.

Background

Vocatives are one of several ways that speakers recognise their addressees, or in grammatical terms, second persons. In this section I will first review the distinction between address and reference, which helps us understand how vocatives fit into wider practices of recognising intended recipients. I then provide background on vocatives by reviewing findings from some of the key work in the field.

Address and Reference

Although many researchers use the notion "terms of address" to cover all ways speakers can explicitly mention the addressee, including by means of nouns and pronouns (see Braun 1998; Leech 1999), I will follow Lerner (1996, 2003) in making a distinction between address and reference as two ways that a speaker can recognise an intended recipient in interaction. Addressing designates the intended recipient, while referring implicates someone (in this case also intended recipient) in what is being said.

Designating the intended recipient is generally not problematic in two-person conversation, but it can be an issue in multiparty interaction. Addressing may be done either explicitly with linguistic forms such as terms of address, or nonverbally as with gaze or body position. Addressing may also be accomplished implicitly, for example, when the topic of an utterance implies that one person and not another is the appropriate recipient of what is being said. Vocatives are explicit forms of address, usually in the form of a noun phrase, often a name, kinship term or sometimes a title, occupational designation or a term of endearment or familiarity. For some languages, "vocative" refers to a specific case which is associated with address. For languages like Javanese and English that do not mark case on the noun phrase vocatives are generally unmarked nominals that function as address terms.[1] Even if not declined for case, vocatives are still grammatically recognisable in that they are not syntactically integrated into an utterance. In Braun's (1988) terms, they are free forms that stand outside of grammatical constructions. Thus, in example (1), *dad* is a kinship term that functions as a vocative, addressing the intended recipient of the utterance *Last time you did that, it washed halfway down the drain*. The vocative *dad* is integrated intonationally, coming in final position of the first of two intonation units that make up the utterance, but it does not have any grammatical role in either of the two clauses uttered.

(1)   *dad* as a vocative (Du Bois et al. 2000, SBC013)

KEVIN: Last time you did that dad,
         it washed halfway down the drai=n.

In contrast to vocatives, referring expressions are bound forms that are integrated into the grammatical structure of utterances. They may serve as agents, patients or themes of verbs, as objects of prepositions, as possessives, or in other roles that link them as constituents within syntactic constructions. In

English, reference to the addressee is almost always done with some form of the second-person pronoun *you*. This is illustrated above, where *you* is a grammatical constituent of the utterance in (1), serving as the subject of the predicate *did that*. Both *you* and *dad* refer to the same person in the interaction—in this instance the recipient of Kevin's utterance whom we can additionally take to be his father—but they do so in different ways for different purposes.

Vocatives

Vocatives take a number of different forms. Biber et al. (1999) identify the following vocative types for English: terms of endearment, kinship terms, familiarisers, full first names, familiarised first names, titles with surname, honorifics, nicknames, elaborate nominal structures and impersonal terms. When we investigate languages other than English, we find that not all of these types will be relevant, while others may overlap or will be realised in very different ways than they typically are in English. Nonetheless, this list serves as good basis for thinking about the various forms that vocatives can take. Many researchers have been particularly interested in familiarisers, for example, dedicated vocative forms used to mark solidarity and intimacy (Kleinknecht and Souza 2017), such as *dude* in American English (Kiesling 2004), *mate* in Australian English (Rendle-Short, 2010), *blood* in British English (Palacios Martínez 2018), *güey* in Mexican Spanish (Bucholtz 2009; Kleinknecht 2013) and *siaw1* in Lao (Zuckerman, this volume). Other work has compared the relative social indexicality of different vocative types (see Hook 1984; Jaworski 1992; Wood and Kroger 1991).

Much research has explored the pragmatic functions associated with vocatives. Leech (1999) identifies three broad functional domains of vocatives: summoning attention, addressee identification and establishing or maintaining social relationships. McCarthy and O'Keefe (2003) make more fine-grained distinctions among functions. These include summons, turn management, topic management, relational work, mitigating work and badinage. They group the first three functions into a larger category of organisational vocatives and the latter three as interpersonal vocatives. At first brush, the core function of a vocative may seem to be to call someone's attention by summoning, but in fact studies have repeatedly found the more pervasive work of vocatives is to "identify participant roles and modulate politeness and positioning within the discourse" (Axelson 2007, 101) and "to define the interpersonal space between [speaker and addressee]" (Jaworski and Galasiński 2000, 79).

Research such as that cited above often groups vocatives categorically according to their perceived function. In the analysis presented below, I will discuss Javanese vocatives in terms of several of the functional domains mentioned above, but I will avoid categorising them. First, this is because multiple functional domains can often be seen to operate in the context of any given instance of vocative use, and so attempts at neat categorising quickly become messy. More importantly, the functional domains in which vocatives occur—such as turn management or mitigation of face-threatening acts—often involve multiple contributing factors such that it is difficult to tease apart the contribution of the vocative. As a result, it is difficult to claim that vocatives themselves have the function of managing topics or mitigating. The present study does not attempt to tease apart exactly what aspects of interaction contribute to which pragmatic functions or social actions undertaken by participants. While that would be a worthwhile endeavour, it would need to include a detailed of analysis of when vocatives do *not* occur as well as when they do, and as such goes beyond the scope of the current study. Nonetheless, the repeated occurrence of vocatives in particular functional domains across different languages suggests speakers find them useful at such points in interaction.

The investigation of vocatives in Javanese presented here asks what these domains have in common and suggests that a recurring aspect of the points in interaction where vocatives most frequently occur is their intersubjective impact. Intersubjectivity in interaction involves interlocutors' joint construction of alignment (or disalignment) based on the continued updating of common ground between them (Linell 2009). Intersubjectivity is prerequisite for successful interaction to take place, but it does not simply form the backdrop for interaction. Rather, intersubjectivity is something that interlocutors must continuously work to maintain and develop (Djenar et al. 2018). As Du Bois points out, "[a]lthough the role of intersubjectivity in language usually remains implicit or is subtly expressed (e.g., via prosody or sequential placement), sometimes it is realized overtly" (2007, 168), for example with discourse particles or in the case of the present study, with vocatives.

Data

The data used in this study are in the Cirebon variety of Javanese (Ewing 2005b). This is a regional variety spoken in West Java, bordering the Sundanese speaking area. There is a long history of contact in the Cirebon region between Javanese, Sundanese and Malay,[2] and Cirebon Javanese is distinct from the more extensively studied standard variety of Javanese associated with the cultural centres of Yogyakarta and Surakarta. It has become an emblem of local identity and pride, and thus, while from a linguistic perspective it can be considered a variety of Javanese, local language ideology regards it as a separate language, usually called basa Cerbon or basa Cerbon-Dermayu "the language of Cirebon (and Indramayu)".

Standard Javanese is well known for its extensive use of social registers that index differing degrees of respect for one's interlocutor through complex lexical and grammatical distinctions (Errington 1988). These registers are particularly intricate in regions surrounding the tradition royal courts of Surakarta and Yogyakarta. Social registers exist in Cirebon Javanese but are less elaborated than those of central Java. The data used in the present study involve speakers who are friends and family members and the language they use is in the common social register without honorific content.

The analysis of vocatives presented here is based primarily on four recordings of naturally occurring, informal conversations. These recordings were made by Cirebon Javanese-speaking research assistants who left recording devices with family and friends. All recordings were made in the 1990s in neighbourhoods on the outskirts of the city of Cirebon. The recordings were transcribed following the conventions of Du Bois et al. (1993). Detailed analysis was conducted on segments of 1,000 intonation units from each of the four transcripts. Explicit second-person mentions were identified and classified as free, vocative address terms or as bound, referring forms. All the conversations in the database involve family members or close friends, with the addition of a food seller in one conversation, who, although not a personal friend as such, is well known to the family. The interactions are informal and easy going, often with a lot of joking and teasing. Table 1 provides a brief summary of participants and context for each conversation in the data, while more specific details are provided for examples as relevant.

Table 1. Four conversations that make up the data analysed. (Example (16) is from a fifth conversation, 111 *Used Goods*, which was not included in the analysis. It involves four unrelated men talking about problems with business, women and motorcycles.)

Transcript	Speech participants, setting and topics
108 *Bi Nani*	A female food seller chats with members of a family on their front veranda in the afternoon. The family includes a man and two women who are siblings, two young daughters of one of the sisters and the husband of the other sister. Topics include food, joking with the children and gossip about acquaintances.
114 *Control Oneself*	Conversation between two male friends in their early twenties chatting in the home of one of them about university, hobbies, jobs, and relationships.
140 *Obscene Talk*	Five male friends in their twenties and thirties sitting on a veranda late at night, talking about their exploits with women, black magic and various colourful characters they know.
151 *In the Kitchen*	The mother in a household cooking in the late morning with her two adult daughters, accompanied by the older daughter's two young children. They discuss cooking, household issues and encounters with various neighbours.

Vocatives in Cirebon Javanese

The importance of vocatives for Javanese speakers has been highlighted by several researchers. Wolff and Poedjosoedarmo (1982) note that choice of address terms, whether used as vocatives or for reference, is crucial for expressing the relationship that speakers feel holds between themselves and their interlocutor. Such terms "place all Javanese speakers in real or fictive kinship relations" (Keeler 1975, 94) and help build social relationships by "provid[ing] the way for each member [of society] to express formality, familiarity and affection" (Norwanto 2016, 85). Errington (1988) and Manns (2015) have explored how Javanese speakers regularly use Javanese address terms when they are speaking Indonesian, providing further evidence of how important this practice is for speakers.

The work cited above has focused on the social meanings indexed by various terms of address, showing how the choice of term can reflect perduring social relationships and can also (re)constitute relationships in the moment of interaction. They also explore the role of vocatives in the discursive construction of identity. Kartomihardjo (1981) gives a particularly detailed discussion of factors influencing choice of address terms in East Java, including social relationship, situational context and ethnic background of speakers. The indexing of perduring social relationships through choice of address terms sets the scene for the present study. However, the main focus goes beyond this to identifying the interactional contexts in which vocatives are regularly used in order to provide further insight into why vocatives are so pervasive in Javanese. From this perspective, I will show the importance of vocatives for establishing and reworking participation framework and I will explore the question of why overt address with vocatives is so prevalent when overt reference to the addressee in argument position is so rare in Javanese.

Vocative Forms

The Javanese family-and-friends data examined here include names, kinship terms, kinship term plus name, and familiarisers as vocatives. Names are usually personal names and often have longer and shorter forms,[3] both of which can be used as vocatives as exemplified in (2).

(2) Lina addressed by her mother and her uncle (separate lines extracted from *Bi Nani*)[4]

197	O'OM:	... *Aci ta **Lina**?*
		(Do you want) a cassava snack, Lina?
571	ARI:	... *Pedes ta **Lin**?*
		(Is it) spicy, Lin?

Kinship terms are used in Javanese for both consanguineal and affinal kin. They are also used for "metaphoric kin" (Agha 2007, 26), that is non-kin in a similar age and status relationship to that named by the kin term. In Javanese, their use also extends to people who are not obviously in a relationship similar to that named by the kin term. For example, an older person might call someone younger *ibu* (mother) if her social position warrants that level of respect, for example a teacher (Kartomihardjo 1981, 89–93). Because of the complex ways in which ostensible kin terms are used in Javanese, Uhlenbeck (1978) and Wolff and Poedjosoedarmo (1982, 41) have noted that they need to be understood beyond a simple metaphor of consanguineal relations. Two examples of kin terms as vocatives are given in (3). The kin terms are kept in their Javanese form in free translations in order to avoid a sense of false equivalence. For example, translating *ang* (older sibling) as English "sister" in example (3) would carry a marked pragmatic connotation not equivalent to Javanese usage. It would also erase the fact that *ang* is gender neutral in Cirebon Javanese, something that distinguishes it from standard Javanese, which makes a gender distinction in terms for older sibling: *mbak* (older sister) and *mas* (older brother).

(3) Tuti addresses her sister as *ang* (older sibling) and her mother as *mak*, short form of *emak* (mother) (separate lines extracted from *In the Kitchen*)

156 TUTI: *Gede-gede beli sih **ang**.*
 (Are they too) big or not, *ang*.
643 TUTI: *Tuku ning endi sih **mak**.*
 Where (did you) buy (them), *mak*.

The combination of kinship term plus name is also commonly used, and like stand-alone kinship terms, can apply to both family members, metaphoric kin and others. Many instances appear later, including for example, *Ang Ari* and *Bi* (aunt) *Nani*.

Familiarisers occur exclusively in the transcript *Obscene Talk*. This is not surprising as the speakers are all young men. Work on other languages has shown that familiarisers such as *dude* or *güey* are particularly popular among young men and often index specific styles of masculinity. The familiarisers used by the men in *Obscene Talk* include *ca* (child), which, when used by these adult speakers is similar to English *man* as seen in (4). Another is *blog*, probably from *goblog* (stupid, moron). *Blog* appears several times in (5). Familiarisers were explained by a research assistant (in Indonesian) as "*expresi untuk keakraban*" ("expressions of closeness/friendliness").

(4) The familiariser *ca* (*Obscene Talk*)

221 MANSUR: *La mati **ca**,*
 Gosh (you'd be) dead, man,
222 *sampenan.*
 in the end.

(5) The familiariser *blog* (*Obscene Talk*)

184 DENDI: *Beli apapa **blog**.*
 (It) doesn't matter, *blog*.
185 *Wong nganu rangda ku **blog**,*
 Someone who gets with a widow/divorcée, *blog*,
186 *Sunnahe Nabi **blog**.*
 (is in) the Tradition of the Prophet, *blog*.

Vocatives and Addressee Reference

As has been outlined, vocatives are address terms and as unbound forms they are not linked into the syntactic structures of utterances. They complement referring terms, which are bound forms linked in some way to the syntactic structure of utterances, whether as arguments of verbs, possessives, objects of prepositions, answers to questions or any number of other bound structural points at which they may occur. With only a few pragmatically marked exceptions, English makes a fairly clear distinction between the use of nominal forms for addressing interlocutors and the use of pronouns for referring to interlocutors. The correspondence between form and function is not as clear cut for Javanese and so deserves some exploration.

But before reviewing Javanese reference terms, it is important to note that often no overt form is used for referring. Subjects in Javanese (like many other languages of the region) are often not explicitly expressed (Arps et al. 2000; Ewing 2001; Keeler 1984; Robson 1992). Ewing (2014) shows that in Cirebon Javanese conversation first- and second-person subjects are explicitly mentioned in a minority of cases. Using the same data discussed in the present study it was shown that of first-person subjects, only 33 per cent are explicit; the remaining 67 per cent are unexpressed. For second-person subjects even fewer are explicit: 17 per cent compared to 83 per cent unexpressed second-person subjects. We can say that alluding to (possible) core arguments, rather than explicitly stating them, is in fact the default in Javanese. I will refer to this phenomenon as allusive reference (for Indonesian, see discussion in Djenar et al. 2018, 112–30).

Returning to overt expression of first and second persons, the next thing to note is that Javanese, like many languages of East and Southeast Asia, has an open pronominal system. Two characteristics of open pronominal systems are that pronominal forms can be brought into the system (for example, through borrowing) and that non-pronominal forms are often used for speaker and addressee reference (Enfield 2007b; Thomason and Everett 2005). In the case of Cirebon Javanese, the older pronouns for speech participants are *isun* "I" and *sira* or *ira* "you".[5] Forms that are more popular in urban areas are *kita* "I", which is likely a Malay borrowing, although it also has cognates in other varieties of Javanese, and *ente* "you", borrowed from Betawi Malay and ultimately derived from Arabic. In addition, speakers regularly use names and kinship terms for bound addressee reference.

From an analytical point of view that takes pronouns to be the default form of reference to speech participants, such practices are sometimes called pronoun substitution (see, for example, Sneddon et al. 2010, 166–8) or imposters (see Conners et al. 2016). From the interactional linguistic perspective taken here, nominal forms used to refer to self and other are seen as alternatives equal to, rather than substitutes for, pronouns. These forms are generally considered by speakers to be more personal than pronouns. As such they are capable of showing degrees of respect that cannot be indicated by pronouns when speaking in the common social register. Pronouns, names and kinship terms as bound addressee reference forms are given in extracts (6)–(8). Note that because these forms are used in structures that would normally require pronouns in English, using names and kinship terms in the free translation would sound stilted and would not give the correct sense of the original. I therefore use pronouns in the translation, but when a name or kinship term is used in the original text, it is provided in brackets in the translation.

(6) Pronoun for addressee reference (*Obscene Talk*)

968 DENDI: *Sadurunge **ira** bari Madadi kawin nu.*
Before you and Madadi get married.

(7) Name for addressee reference (*Used Goods*)

437 TATA: *Milike **Nunung** deweke.*
(It's) your (Nunung's) own possession. (Tata reassuring Nunung that he is the rightful owner of a contested motorcycle).

(8) Kinship term for addressee reference (*In the Kitchen*)

966	FITRI:	@@ *Ira je,*
		((laughing)) "You" (she) said,
967		*rayae durung ngirim Kang Tanto.*
		"haven't sent anything to *Kang* (older brother) Tanto for the holiday."
968	TUTI:	... *Dadi* **mak** *apan ngirim.*
		So you (*mak*, mum) will send something.
969	FITRI:	*He'em.*
		Uh-huh.

The open system of second-person terms in Javanese means that (unlike English, for example) referring and addressing terms are often the same. In (9) the combination of kinship term and name, *Bi Nani* (literally "Aunt Nani"), is used as a possessive referring term in line 274 and as a vocative address term in 275.

(9) Kinship + Name for reference and address (*Bi Nani*)

274	ARI:	... *Ari umahe* **Bi Nani** *ku,*
		As for your (*Bi Nani*'s) house,
275		... *sebelah mendi* **Bi Nani**.
		where is (it), Bi Nani.

Frequency

Vocatives vary in function and import both across and within languages, and one of the ways vocative usage varies is in terms of frequency. Kleinknecht observes that "there are languages whose speakers make extensive use of a large number of vocatives, while in other languages, these elements are used far more sparsely" (2013, 235). Even within one language there can be differences. American English speakers are observed to use vocatives more often than British English speakers (Leech 1999), and young people have often been shown to use vocatives more frequently than adults (Jørgensen 2013; Palacios Martínez 2018).

So how frequent are vocatives in Javanese? As previously mentioned, most work on Javanese vocatives has focused on motivations of choosing one form over another and although the importance of vocatives is stressed, none of this work provides frequency counts.[6] Regarding vocative use in other languages, several studies that do provide frequencies have looked specifically at familiarisers rather than vocatives more generally (see, for example, Palacios Martinez 2018; Quaglio 2009; Urichuk and Loureiro-Rodríguez 2019). Leech (1999) provides total vocatives (408) and total words (99,566) in the corpus he used for his study of English. This calculates as a rate of 4.1 vocatives per 1,000 words. I tallied vocatives used in a selection of transcripts from the Santa Barbara Corpus of Spoken American English (Du Bois et al. 2000) and found a similar average frequency of 4.6 vocatives per 1,000 words.

The contrast with Javanese is striking. The frequency of vocatives was calculated for each of the transcripts used in the current study and results are provided in table 2. The average across the transcripts is 35.2 vocatives per 1,000 words—roughly seven times more frequent in Javanese than in English. While these data for Javanese vocatives may be slightly inflated by the unusually high rate in the conversation *Bi Nani* (due to the nature of that particular interaction, see for example extract (11)), even the lowest rate of any of the transcripts is almost five times more frequent than English. This is further evidence of the importance of vocatives in Javanese, and the relevance of their study for expanding our understanding of vocative use cross-linguistically.

Table 2. Frequency of vocatives in Cirebon Javanese conversation

Transcript	Vocative frequency
108 *Bi Nani*	56.6 vocatives / 1000 words
111 *Control Oneself*	28.9 vocatives / 1000 words
140 *Obscene Talk*	25.5 vocatives / 1000 words
151 *In the Kitchen*	29.8 vocatives / 1000 words
Average across the four transcripts	**35.2 vocatives / 1000 words**

Vocatives in Interaction

This section illustrates vocative use by examining a number of excerpts from the conversational data base. The discussion explores the functional domains in which Javanese vocatives occur, identifying several that have also been mentioned in the literature on vocatives across various languages and showing that these functions can overlap in particular instances. Vocatives are shown to be part of the "structure of address" (Sidnell 2009, 148) that Javanese speakers use to establish and manipulate participation frameworks. Finally, in the section that follows I argue that what is common across the interactional environments in which vocatives occur is intersubjective impact and I suggest that this is a key factor in what makes vocatives so important for Javanese speakers.

Vocatives can aid the management of turns, topics and discourse structure. Lerner (2003) points out that in English, utterance initial vocatives may be used to signal that the utterance is addressed to that person when there may be some issue with recipiency. Such utterance initial vocatives are a type of attention getting device or "alerter" (Alba-Juez 2009, 179). This can be heard as a kind of summons. Summonses can initiate an interaction and can also occur during ongoing interaction (Schegloff 2007). A summons not only calls attention but also typically indicates a disjuncture. It implies "new business to which those summoned should attend" (Moerman 1988, 74) and is often followed by a sequence initiation, such as a question or request, to which the addressee is expected to respond. Utterance initial vocatives in the Javanese data regularly serve as alerters and initiate new business as illustrated in line 155 of extract (10).

(10) Vocatives as alerters and initiating new business (*In the Kitchen*)

151	FITRI:	*Bayem.*
		"Spinach."
152		*Bibit bayem 'e.*
		"Spinach seedlings," (he) asked.
153		*Masih.*
		"(I) still (have some," I said).
154		... *Cukul [ta beli=je].*
		"(Will they) grow or not," (he) asked.
155	TUTI:	[**Ang**.
		Ang.
156		*Gede-gede beli] sih **ang**.*
		(Are these) too big, *ang*.
157		[2 *Semono* 2].
		That size.
158	MITA:	[2 *Beli* 2].
		No.
159		*Wis lah semono.*
		(They're) ok that size.

In (10) Fitri is chatting with her two adult daughters as they cook together. The extract begins with Fitri in the middle of a story she is telling about someone who came to buy some spinach seedlings from her. Tuti initiates a new topic directed to her older sister, Mita, addressing her as *ang* (older sibling) without using her name. Tuti uses this kin term as vocative and a summons to get Mita's attention and to indicate that Mita is the intended recipient of what she is about say. Tuti then immediately introduces a new topic via a question, asking whether she is cutting the vegetables the right size, and again uses the vocative *ang* in line 156. This sequence of vocatives involves both topic management by introducing the topic of cutting vegetables and turn management by alerting Mita to the fact that she is now the addressee and nominated next speaker when Tuti asks the question. In this way these vocatives work to initiate a change in overall participation framework (Goffman 1981). The new participant configuration no longer directly involves Fitri and her story about an earlier event, but now involves Tuti and Mita focusing on the task at hand. Repetition of vocatives as seen in (10) has also been observed in Indonesian (Ewing and Djenar 2019), where it is often used in contexts of strong exhortation. While Tuti is not exhorting Mita to do something in (10), the double address structure does give a certain insistent quality to the question, pressing the addressee to pay attention.

The management of turns and topics is also illustrated in extract (11). Here a family is sitting on the veranda eating snacks sold by a traveling food seller. Several participants are asking Bi Nani questions one after another. The family have been trying to find out how old Bi Nani is. Bi Nani says she's a similar age to their mother then subtly shifts the topic by asking how many children their mother has. O'om's response is not clear, but Ari brings the topic back to Bi Nani's age, using a vocative in his question, which spans lines 429 and 421. Here the vocative is not utterance initial, but rather intonation unit final.[7] In this position the vocative is not a summons, but it does play a role in turn management, similar to that of *ang* in line 156 of Extract (10). Budi simultaneously asks Bi Nani for a cracker with chili sauce, using a vocative in line 432 as a summons to get Bi Nani's attention. O'om now aligns with Ari by rephrasing essentially the same question, lines 434–5, again with a vocative. (The Japanese Period refers to the Japanese occupation of Indonesia during World War II).

(11) Topic shift (*Bi Nani*)

426	NANI:	*Ibu ka,*
		(Your) mother,
427		*anake pirang-pirang ka=.*
		how many children does she have.
428	O'OM:	X
		X
429	ARI:	... *Jaman Jepang wis ya **Bi Nani**.*
		During the Japanese Period (you had been) already, right *Bi* Nani.
430	BUDI:	... *Krupuk,*
		A cracker,
431	ARI:	*Wis lahir?*
		Already born?

432	BUDI:	***Bi Nani.***
		<u>Bi</u> <u>Nani</u>.
433		... *Sambel.*
		Chili sauce.
434	O'OM:	... *Perang ka,*
		During the war,
435		*lair durung **Bi Nani**?*
		(you'd been) born or not, <u>Bi</u> <u>Nani</u>?

Extract (11) is from a multiparty conversation, thus the identity of an intended recipient of a given utterance may not be clear and vocatives can be useful for indicating who an utterance is addressed to. At the same time, the vocatives used by Ari and O'om do not only implicate Bi Nani as the addressee, but also as the topic of their questions. These speakers are changing the topic from their mother back to the question of Bi Nani's age, and the use of vocative helps to highlight this shift. Note also that the entire interaction has a sort of free-for-all feeling, with everyone eating and talking at the same time. In this context, the vocatives are doing more than signalling intended recipient of talk. While these vocatives do specify one addressee out of many possible addressees, they also identify one speaker out of several possible speakers at any given moment. By addressing Bi Nani, speakers are not only saying "you (rather than the others) are my addressee", they are also saying, "I want you to attend to me (rather than others)", as speakers vie for her attention. Multi-party interactions display a many-to-many relationship between speakers and addressees and address terms augment other cues to help identify both sides of this relationship.

The importance of vocatives for managing turns and topics can also be seen in their use within narratives, where they can aid the audience in keeping track of which character is speaking to whom and what their relationships are. Excerpts (12) and (13) are from two different narratives, both told by Fitri. In both cases she is reporting something that someone said to her. She carefully uses the vocative that these characters would be expected to use with her. In (12) her interlocutor is an acquaintance of equal age and status and he is reported addressing her by her short name, *Fit* (line 143). Note that she models Man Mahmud's summons, calling out to her with the lengthened vowel in her name. In (13) Fitri is talking about a different conversation and models herself being addressed as *mak* (mum) (line 450). Despite Fitri's efforts, her daughter Tuti is not sure who the purported speaker is—there are many people who call her *mak*, not only her children, but also her grandchildren—and so she asks for clarification. The reported speaker turns out to be Fitri's other daughter, Mita. Given that vocatives are pervasive in Javanese conversation, it is not surprising that they also make an appearance in the conversations that are constructed as part of narrative. This practice provides additional evidence both for the importance of vocatives in Javanese interaction and the awareness that Javanese speakers have of the role vocatives play in their speech.

(12) Vocatives in narrated conversation (*In the Kitchen*)

142	FITRI:	... *Ari jare Man Mahmud lu,*
		So *Man* ("uncle") Mahmud said,
143		... ***Fi=t.***
		"<u>Fit</u>."
144		*Lagi macul.*
		(He) was digging (his field).
145		*Man Mahmude.*
		Man Mahmud was.
146		... *Anu je.*
		"Um," (he) said.
147		*Ira masih duwe= anu ta je.*
		"Do you have what-do-you-call-it," (he) asked.

(13) Vocatives in narrated conversation (*In the Kitchen*)

448	FITRI:	... *Iya.*
		Yeah.
449		... *Ku je,*
		"There," (she) said.
450		***Mak 'e.***
		"*Mak* ('mum')," (she) said.
451		... *Dau dirasani ku je=,*
		"(you) were talking about someone," (she) said.
452		*tek=a je.*
		"(and they) showed up," (she) said.
453		... *Munie nu,*
		That's what (she) said.
454		*mengkonon.*
		like that.
455	TUTI:	*Jare sapae?*
		Who said?
456	FITRI:	... *Jare Mitae nu.*
		Mita said.

Actions which make a demand on the addressee, such as requests, offers and corrections are often sites of vocative use. A simple request with vocative is shown in (14).

(14) Request (*Bi Nani*)

359 ARI: *Krupuk maning Bi Nani.*
            (I'll have) another cracker, Bi Nani.

Extract (15) is an example of an offer. While eating Bi Nani's snacks on the front veranda, Eni calls out to her husband Budi and offers him something to eat. Eni begins with a summoning vocative in line 183, using Budi's short name. She indicates the amount she is offering in line 184 and then in line 185 says he should have more if it is not enough. Each of these is marked by another instance of the vocative. This is another example of the multiple vocative marking mentioned in relation to extract (10), and it illustrates the more strongly hortative function discussed by Ewing and Djenar (2019).

(15)   Summons and offer (*Bi Nani*)

183 ENI: ... ***Bud***.
            Bud.
184   *Kuene seket **Bud**.*
            Here's fifty (rupiah's worth), Bud.
185   *Baka ... kurang nambah **Bud**.*
            If (it's) not enough take more, Bud.

The explicit construction of the offer in line 184 of (15) is structurally the same as the request in (14); they each contain an NP referring to a snack, followed by a vocative. They have neither verbs nor other explicit indications of the actions being performed. The conversation in *Bi Nani* is a complex multiparty interaction focused on food. In this context simply stating a type of food could create ambiguity around the speaker's intention. The vocatives supply important contextualising information that aids in the inferencing process. By explicitly naming the addressee, the speaker is also evoking certain rights, responsibilities and expectations that hold between the speaker and the addressee and this helps bring into focus the action intended by stating the name of a snack. In (14), Ari is a customer and Bi Nani the seller and so the vocative makes clear that this is a request to buy something. In (15), the wife, Eni, who is sitting with the group eating, is calling to her husband who is physically outside the group and so her mention of food that is physically proximate to her can be heard as an offer.

Vocatives frequently occur at points when participants are negotiating (dis)alignment. Alignment (with disalignment) here refers to a scale of commensurability between interactants as they converge (or diverge) in their affective and epistemological stances towards what they are saying and towards each other (Du Bois 2007; Du Bois and Kärkkäinen 2012). Extract (16) is an example of negotiated alignment. Wawan has asked Mardi what kind of music he's playing these days. While Mardi used to play *dangdut*, a type of Indian influenced Indonesian pop (Weintraub 2010), he says he now prefers western pop. Mardi hedges this point, repeating *mungkin* (maybe) three times as he says it. Wawan aligns with Mardi's hesitation by repeating *mungkin*, but then offers an explanation: this new interest is appropriate because Mardi is majoring in English at university. Wawan thus accepts the point Mardi had been hedging and indicates he understands why Mardi's tastes have changed. Wawan uses a vocative as he introduces this explanation (line 157) and again as he concludes it (line 162). Mardi then agrees with Wawan's point, also using a vocative (line 163). This mutual use of vocatives as they negotiate the point highlights the intersubjective nature of the alignment that is being produced.

(16) Alignment (*Controlling Oneself*)

152	MARDI:	*Mungkin=,*
		Maybe,
153		*... dadie lagu barat kang= taksenengi pisan koe dadie.*
		I've ended up really liking western songs.
154		*Mungkin,*
		Maybe,
155		[*mungkin ku nu*].
		Maybe that's it.
156	WAWAN:	[*Mungkin*].
		Maybe.
157		*... Karena anu **Di**,*
		Because you know, Di,
158		*Ya beli maidoni ya,*
		Yeah (you) don't go all over,
159		*karena ente mempelajari lagu,*
		because you are studying songs,
160		*.. anu maksude bahasa .. asing,*
		I mean a foreign language,

161		*dadi,*
		so,
162		*.. ente ku harus ngapal-ngapalnang lagu mengkonon **Di**.*
		you have to learn those kinds of songs, <u>Di</u>.
163	MARDI:	*.. Iya konon diantare kitae kepengene **Wan**.*
		Yes that's among (the reasons) I like them, <u>Wan</u>.

In extract (17) vocatives accompany displays of disalignment with one speaker, at the same time alignment is achieved between two others. These shifting alignments are a kind of reconfiguration of participation framework among the speakers. In the excerpt, Dendi suggests it would be good to record someone named Ahmed because he is a particularly unusual character. Asuri incorrectly thinks he means someone from Cemeng. Both Dendi and Mansur correct Asuri clarifying they mean Ahmed from Kemlaka. They each go on to explain why Ahmed would be good to record and they each use a vocative when doing so. In this case the vocative is not actually used at the point of disagreement (line 691) or correction (lines 692–695). Rather they use vocatives when they are explaining to Asuri why Ahmed would be a good person to record; that is, at the point they attempt to mitigate any damage to face by explaining the positive reasons for their suggestion. It is also interesting that both Mansur and Dendi use the vocative *Ang As* (*ang* 'older sibling' plus As, short name for Asuri) in structurally similar constructions (adjective plus vocative). This dialogic resonance of this repeated structure (Du Bois and Giora 2014) highlights the alignment between Dendi and Mansur and accentuates the fact that they are in agreement with the recommendation they are making to Asuri.

(17) Making a case and participant framework (*Obscene Talk*)

685	DENDI:	*A- kudue ngrekam kenen gu,*
		A- need to make this kind of recording,
686		*.. ngingu Ahmed na.*
		ask Ahmed.
687		*.. kang antik ku.*
		the unusual one.
688	ERIK:	*... Udud-udude [XXX],*
		The cigarettes ((unclear)),
689	ASURI:	*[Panitia] Cemeng.*
		(From) the Cemeng committee.
690		@@
		((laughing))

691	DENDI:	.. *Dudu.*
		No.
692		[*Ahmed*].
		Ahmed.
693	MANSUR:	[*Ahmed*].
		Ahmed.
694		.. *wong Kemlaka.*
		from Kemlaka.
695	DENDI:	[*Ahmed wong Kemlaka*].
		Ahmed from Kemlaka.
696	MANSUR:	[*aneh maning **Ang**] **As**.*
		(He's) even more unusual, Ang As.
697	X:	.. ((SNIFF))
		((sniff))
698		.. *Hm.*
		Hm.
699	DENDI:	.. *Enak **Ang As**.*
		(It would be) nice, Ang As.
700		.. *Lamun nggawa kaen ka ya.*
		If (you) brought that (recording device) there you know.

McCarthy and O'Keeffe (2003) point out that vocatives often occur during humorous segments of interaction. The example of badinage in (18) uses two familiarisers as vocatives, rather than the names and kinship terms we have primarily seen in examples up to now. This is from the transcript *Obscene Talk*, which has by far the most familiarisers of the interactions in the dataset. This is not surprising as familiarisers are cross-linguistically associated with youth language and particularly (although not exclusively) masculine interaction. Prior to the excerpt, the men have been discussing a particular woman, trying to work out where she lives. This topic winds down as Dendi says her house is to the south and west of the house of someone else they know (129–31).

In line 134, Asuri takes the discussion in a new, although clearly related, direction: beautiful women in general. He does so with two familiarisers, *ira* 'you' and *ca* 'kid'. These can draw the attention of any or all listeners as they do not name any specific addressee. Asuri is known as something of a womaniser and his comment is seen as humorous, eliciting laughter from Mansur and Erik. Dendi however does not respond to Asuri and begins his own new topic, a story about a practical joke he played on a woman named Yati. Throughout this recording the men are joking, teasing and trying to one-up each other. Often they break into small informal factions as we saw with Dendi and Mansur joining together to correct Asuri in (17). At other times there is a kind of competition between speakers, or participants split into parallel conversations.

Throughout the recording Asuri and Dendi each seem to be asserting dominance. During the first half of the recording Asuri is the dominant speaker and tells many stories, while Dendi's attempts at storytelling often fall flat. Later in the recording Dendi gains more control and spends much more time speaking while Asuri drops to the background. It is therefore not surprising to see Dendi ignore Asuri's new topic in (18) and begin his own story. Asuri similarly ignores Dendi and continues talking about how much he loves beautiful women. As Asuri continues with his topic in lines 140–2, he uses a name as vocative, rather than familiariser, to direct his contribution to a specific addressee, Ari, highlighting the potential for a split in the conversation.

This example again shows how vocatives can be used to manipulate the participation framework. They help signal shifts in participants' roles as speakers, addressees, overhearers or co-conspirators. Sidnell (2009, 148) points out that "structures of address" can be defined by judicial use of pronouns and other reference forms. In this example (and others), vocatives stand out as making important contributions to such structures, in lieu of pronouns, which are rarely used in Javanese. As vocatives aid the organisation of participants into particular roles, they touch directly on the intersubjective connections that participants have to each other and also on the stances they hold towards their interlocutors and towards what they are talking about.

(18) Badinage (*Obscene Talk*)

129	DENDI:	*Iya.*
		Yeah,
130		*kulone.*
		To the west.
131		*kidule.*
		To the south.
132	MANSUR:	... *Oh= iya.*
		Oh yeah.
133		.. [*Ya mbu*].
		I don't know.
134	ASURI:	[*Gembleng*] ***ira ca.***
		Beautiful (women), <u>man</u>.
135	MANSUR & ERIK:	@@@@@ @@@@
		((laughing))
136	DENDI:	*Anu sih,*
		You know,

137		*Yati ka.*
		Yati.
138		*Boko istirahat,*
		When (she) was taking a break,
139		[*ya tak-*] –
		yeah I –
140	ASURI:	[*Kita nu*],
		As for me,
141		*boko ning wong gembleng,*
		when (I'm) with a beautiful woman,
142		*.. paling seneng **Ar***
		(I'm) the happiest <u>Ar</u>.

Excerpt (19) provides another example of badinage and the competition between Asuri and Dendi, and demonstrates the subtle ways that vocatives can be used to alter participation frameworks. Asuri has been telling a story about difficulties he has had with a woman he is interested in. Problems have arisen because he has visited her house and got to know her family (lines 394–8) and he says it would have been better to get to know her away from the family by meeting at a show (399–400). Asuri has been telling the story to the entire group. Dendi responds, also apparently speaking to the entire group to provide an analogy: that a fighting cock should be tested before being put into the fighting ring. It is clear that Asuri's situation is the target of the analogy, and the meaning is also clear: Asuri should have made sure he had a better grasp of the situation before getting involved with the family, just as a fighting cock should not enter the ring untested.

Dendi also connects the two by playing on the double meaning of *manjing kalangan* "enter the circle/ring", where *kalangan* can mean a social circle, in this case the woman's family (line 395), or a sporting arena, such as the cock fighting ring (line 403). He ends his analogy with a vocative which makes explicit that the analogy is directed at Asuri (line 405). Here the vocative indicates Asuri is the recipient of the critique, but not necessarily nominated as next speaker. Whereas Asuri had been addressing the entire group and Dendi could have been heard as doing the same when he began to speak, his use of a vocative shifts the participation framework and he is now heard to be essentially lecturing Asuri, with the other members of the group positioned as ratified overhearers for whom Dendi is performing. Ari and Erik respond appropriately for such a role (lines 406–7) and Dendi continues to develop his analogy for several more lines after the section excerpted here. The others then begin to make jokes about different kinds of fighting cocks, shifting the participation framework yet again and eventually Asuri responds some twenty-five lines later.

(19) Shifting participation framework (*Obscene Talk*)

394	ASURI:	*Kita salae siji,*
		My one mistake,
395		*manjing kalangan.*
		was getting involved with the family.
396		*titik.*
		full stop.
397		*W- sampai wani ning umae kita.*
		I even went to her house.
398		... *Kesalaane ning kono gu.*
		That was the mistake.
399		(H) ... *Namun toh= kita kenalane ning=,*
		If only we'd gotten to know each other at,
400		... *tontonan-ton*[*tonan*],
		the shows,
401	DENDI:	[*Ya wis*].
		Alright.
402		*Sabenere lamun jago keding,*
		Actually as for a fighting cock,
403		*kang ari apan manjing kalangan,*
		that's going to enter the fighting ring,
404		*benere ku,*
		(it) should in fact,
405		*dicacak dikit **Ang As**.*
		be tested first, <u>Ang As</u>.
406	ARI:	... @[@@]
		((laughing))
407	ERIK:	[*Hm'mh*].
		Uh-huh.

Discussion and Concluding Comments

In his discussion of vocatives in English, Leech states that "vocatives are not used among close associates where neither their addressee-identifying role nor their relationship-maintenance role is felt to be necessary—often, presumably, because the participants in a conversation are totally sure of their mutual relationship" (1999, 117), and he points out that many of the samples he analyses include long conversations with no vocatives at all. It would be safe to say that, quite unlike English, a conversation in Javanese with no vocatives would be virtually impossible. In the sample of data used in the present study there is variation in frequency of vocatives—some conversations have a higher rate of vocative use than others—but all display a much higher frequency than English conversation. And so, while we have seen that the moment-to-moment appearance of vocatives in the Javanese data are found in functional domains similar to those for vocatives in English and other languages, their extremely high frequency relative to some other languages suggests that vocatives make an especially indispensable contribution to Javanese interaction.

Vocatives provide an overt indication of intersubjective connection between interlocutors. In one sense the intersubjectivity of vocatives arises simply by their expression. They explicitly name, and so reinforce, the social relationship that holds between interlocutors. But the intersubjectivity of vocatives goes well beyond this. If overt articulation of the particular relationship that holds between interactants is all there was to it, vocatives could occur at any time and they would still fulfil this function. That is, we might expect vocatives to occur evenly or randomly dispersed through interaction. What we see instead is that vocatives are clustered at certain points in interaction, such as those illustrated above, including points of topic and turn management, mitigation, badinage and shifts in participation frameworks. These patterns suggest that vocative usage is closely linked to moments of intersubjective prominence. Actions like agreeing or disagreeing, making requests or offers or bringing speaker and addressee into new roles within the participation framework are all moments when "the subjective stances of two participants collide within a dialogic exchange" (Du Bois 2007, 159). Using the metaphor of "collision", or less violently, "impact", we can say that Javanese speakers regularly use vocatives at moments of heightened intersubjective impact. And here "impact" can be read with both of the meanings it suggests: "making contact" and "having an effect".

Because address and reference are interconnected, it is worth returning here to allusive reference—the practice of alluding to referents through interactional context, introduced earlier. Researchers of Javanese have noted the association between allusive reference and politeness. Wolff and Poejosoedarmo note avoidance of reference to one's interlocutor, and in most of their conversational data there is "no word for 'you'" (1982, 44). They claim the reason for this is to avoid highlighting the distance or intimacy that is expressed through second-person pronoun choice. Berman similarly suggests that for Javanese speakers "[b]ecause of the specific ways in which pronouns index relative location in terms of status, consciousness of self, or agency, the vast majority of conversations use no direct reference" (1992, 9–10). Use of addressee reference is considered potentially face threatening and so best avoided.

Yet in the data I have examined here, where people know each other well and do in fact use familiar pronouns from time to time, the default in the majority of cases is still to *allude* to a referent rather than use explicit reference. The frequency of allusive reference in the familiar conversational exchanges suggests it is not fundamentally motivated by politeness. Rather, because allusive reference is so common in interactions of all types, speakers are easily afforded the opportunity to avoid explicit reference for purposes of politeness when needed, without it standing out as a marked strategy. The analysis briefly presented here (and in more detail in Ewing 2014) is consistent with findings by Wolfowitz (1991), who in fact characterises allusive reference (or ellipsis in her terms) as a sign of familiarity, in contrast to "programmatic redundancy" (1991, 38) in formal Javanese which includes explicit reference to self and other.

The question that follows is, why does the overt mention of recipient tend to occur as free terms of address in vocative position, but not as bound terms of reference in argument position, that is, within the grammatical structure of an utterance? There seems to be a paradox in observations that Javanese speakers use address terms in order highlight their social relationships (Keeler 1984; Norwanto 2016; Wolff and Poedjosoedarmo 1982), yet they avoid referring to recipients in argument position in order avoid highlighting social relationships (Berman 1992; Wolff and Poedjosoedarmo 1982). Recalling Lerner's (1996) distinction between address and reference, addressing involves designating who the recipient of talk is, while referring implicates someone in what is being said. It is precisely that implication in what is being said that can be heard as making claims about the recipient's actions or state of being, and thus could be heard as the speaker asserting some sort of authority over the recipient. Berman alludes to this when she mentions that pronouns can index agency (1992). By avoiding the overt indexing of agency, allusion may often be more appropriate than explicit assertion.

Vocatives stand outside the grammatical structure of utterances and so do not make direct claims on addressee's agency. Instead, vocatives assert relatedness between speaker and addressee. They do this at points of intersubjective impact and implicate both speaker and recipient together in intersubjective contact, jointly positioned within participation frameworks. And they make these claims to relationship without making direct claims about each other's agency. Any possible imposition on the interlocutor's agency, for example with the request and offer in extracts (14) and (15), are implicit rather than direct.

A key point is that in Javanese interaction, engagement between interlocutors is being explicitly and continuously reinforced through *address*, even (and especially) when no explicit *reference* to the addressee is being made. Keeler (1975) points out that (at least in mid-twentieth century Central Java) relationships are "strictly binary", by which he means that each utterance a person produces in Javanese needs to be tailored to a particular recipient because of the way relationships are indexed in the language. While the speakers in the data examined here are not using elaborated speech levels to indicate relative status with their interlocutors, the use of vocatives does stand out as a clear case of tailoring utterances to one-on-one interaction. A vocative indicates the specific social relationship and relative social status between a pair of interlocutors at the same time it creates the interactional relationship of speaker and addressee, connected intersubjectively. In so doing, vocatives highlight and manipulate the participation framework that envelops these two interlocuters, and potentially any other participants in the interaction. The crucial role of vocatives in interaction is the explicit acknowledgement (rather than simple assumption) of relationship between speaker, addressee and discourse through intersubjective contact.

Notes

[1] Both Javanese and English do mark case on pronouns in some contexts, but full NPs and proper nouns are generally unmarked for case, including when used as vocatives.

[2] Malay is spoken in many varieties and has long been a lingua franca in the Indonesian archipelago. It was used as the administrative language of the Dutch colonial government and became indigenised as Betawi Malay, spoken by inhabitants of Batavia, the Dutch colonial capital, now Jakarta. With Indonesian independence the national language, standard Indonesian, itself a variety of Malay, has had an increasing influence an all varieties of Javanese, as has the colloquial variety of Indonesian that is now spoken in Jakarta.

[3] The English concept of surname is not applicable to Javanese. People may have only one name and if they have more than one name, this is simply a series of names, none of which is a family name. For example, the current president of Indonesia, Joko Widodo, simply has those two names and Widodo is in no sense a surname (each of his parents have different names). Additionally, he is most commonly known by his familiarised name, which combines his first name and the first syllable of his second name: Jokowi.

[4] Following Du Bois et al. (1993), punctuation indicates prosodic features within the transcript. In the free translation however, punctuation is used with the conventional written function of indicating structural segmentation to aid the readability of the English.

[5] Cirebon Javanese polite forms (which are used to show respect to the addressee) include *kula* "I (polite)" and *sampeyan* or *panjenengan* "you (polite)". As mentioned in Section 3, all data in this study are in the common social register of the language and do not use any of the polite social register forms.

[6] Norwanto (2016) provides counts for use of kinship terms as titles, but he does not differentiate between address and reference, so it is not possible to tell how many of these are vocatives.

[7] I would argue that the vocative in extract (11) line 429 is also turn construction unit final. It occurs at the end of an intonation unit with a final intonation contour which on its own could be heard as complete turn construction unit. In line 431, Ari incrementally extends his turn with an elaboration to clarify what he is asking in line 431, but at the moment that line 429 is uttered, it can be heard of complete.

CHAPTER 5

New Patterns, New Practices: Exploring the Use of English Pronouns *I* and *you* in Asymmetrical Relations in Kuala Lumpur Malay Talk

Sarah Lee

In any exchange, "[t]he partners in conversation have the possibility to orientate themselves socially because of the forms of address" (Adler 1978, 201). Address forms tap into conventionalised ways to perform acts of linguistic politeness, help establish or maintain social bonds, and serve to strengthen solidarity and control social distance. Like many other address practices throughout Southeast Asia (Enfield 2007b; Cooke 1968), practices in Malaysian Malay[1] involve the observance of certain asymmetrical social relations, most importantly, differences in participant age and social status, which places an obligation on the junior party to demonstrate respect or deference to their senior by selecting forms that express the unequal relation (Asmah Haji Omar 1983). Such address practices contrast with other practices in which relational differences are much less ritualised or orderly, such as the trend in contemporary English where the default preference is for what has been called democratic, neutral or egalitarian solutions, principally the reciprocal use of reference forms that uniquely refer to the addressee such as first names[2] and denote speaker and addressee roles, such as pronouns.

Malay speakers index social relations by selecting appropriate forms, forms often thought of as constituting an open class since they include lexical nouns such as kin terms and honorific titles in addition to pronouns. In fact, for speakers of unequal status, the choice of pronominal forms, especially the second person,

88

is constrained by norms of politeness—a person of a lower status is prevented from selecting reference forms reserved for those of a higher status, and a lexical noun that elevates the addressee has to be used (Zulkifley Hamid and Naidatul Zamrizam Abu 2013; Baetens Beardsmore 1982, 65). Pronouns denoting speaker and addressee roles are more evolved to express contrasting or niche aspects of "social distance" between equal parties, and they are often characterised in terms of intimacy, formality, familiarity, and so on (Asmah Haji Omar 1983; Donohue and Smith 1998, 68; Djenar 2008). Usage patterns indicate that the alternative forms are not entirely socially stratified since selection also depends on a range of additional factors such as social, interactional or even idiolectal ones (Ewing and Djenar 2019; Yoong 2011; Djenar 2008, 2015; Englebretson 2007). Such dynamism can be reconciled by supposing that each form is a projection of a particular social deictic range or trajectory based on its history of use, pressures from authority and competing valorisations (Goebel et al. 2019, 3).

Another observation from previous research is that Malay is relatively open to new borrowing, including pronouns, introduced either through institutional channels or through more spontaneous contact (Donohue and Smith 1998; Thomason and Everett 2005). Efforts to modernise and transform Standard Malay, for instance, led Malaysia's national language agency to identify two second-person forms *anda* and *awak* as standard pronouns. In Betawi Malay (spoken in Jakarta) and Jakarta Indonesian, pronoun borrowing includes *gua* and *lu*, first- and second-person singular pronouns from Chinese Southern Min (Hokkien). Whereas these forms express person deixis only in the language of origin, they have acquired social values in these varieties of Malay, with values that range from being an index of place to associations with informality, coolness, cosmopolitanism (Sneddon 2006; Thomason and Everett 2005) and "assertive, humorous or even arrogant stance" (Ewing and Djenar 2019, 257).[3] Apart from this, Donohue and Smith (1998, 82) note that the English borrowing *yu* has appeared in "the formal speech of educated people in many regions", and Surjaman (1968, 91) long ago noted that the Dutch polite second-person singular *u* was being used by foreigners when speaking Indonesian. In the Malaysian context, the same Hokkien forms (*gua/lu*) are found in *Pasar* (Bazaar) Malay, reflecting time-spaces in which Malay and Chinese were or are in direct contact (Thurgood 1998; Pakir 1986). *Lu* on its own has also been found to mark the addressee as Chinese in some social settings (Nur Salawati and Hanita 2013).[4] As Thomason and Everett (2005, 301) stress, pronoun borrowing occurs because of "appropriate social circumstances" rather than random language mixing (Auer 1999).

A relatively recent (within the last five decades) contact-induced practice is the use of English pronouns *I* and *you* in Malay talk. Asmah Haji Omar (2012), while not mentioning *I/you* in particular, suggests that Malay-English bilinguals may prefer English forms because they are "cognitively lighter" than navigating the social complexities of Malay address. Others explain the preference for English pronouns by attributing it to common social criteria such as concentration of such speakers in in urban areas (Mansor 2019; Mansor et al. 2018; Othman 2006), their high educational level (Othman 2006; Mansor 2019), female predominance (Othman 2006; Mansor 2019), and informality (Othman 2006). Nur Salawati and Hanita (2013, 113) find some evidence that Chinese speakers prefer *you* to Malay addressee forms. In addition, while equals engage in symmetrical practice, it has been claimed that the use of English pronouns is overwhelmingly unidirectional, that is, they are used by speakers of a higher status to speak to those of lower status (see, for example, Othman 2006, 8), thus conforming to Malay norms. However, Mansor et al. (2018) mention a case of *you* being used by a child to a parent in a fictional context, suggesting an opening that circumvents the limits of Malay pronominal use. In addition, Othman (2006) suggests that certain inequalities of power relations between males and females in Malay culture may have contributed to the gendered patterns. Despite these findings, the use of *I/you* for indexing social relations in interaction remains under-explored.

In this preliminary ethnographic study, I explore the meaning-making potential of English *I* and *you* in what shall be called "Kuala Lumpur Malay" (see Bakar 2009), the largely English-Malay contact register spoken in the Greater Kuala Lumpur area. This area, which includes the capital city, serves as the primary commercial centre and is the preeminent site of ethnic Malay urbanisation in the country. I focus my analysis on instances in the data where the English pronouns are used by speakers of lower status. The following research questions guide this study:

> 1. How are *I/you* positioned relative to Malay address norms, in particular, observance of hierarchical structure and the limits on symmetrical use of pronouns?
> 2. To what extent can it be claimed that the English pronouns are gaining stable social meanings in Kuala Lumpur Malay?

It is proposed that insights into *I/you* usage patterns can be gained by examining the sociolinguistics of contact between Malay address culture and Malay(sian) conceptions of modernity. Social practices of indexing modernity are common in postcolonial states such as Malaysia but the way they are indexed, interpreted and valued, is unique to a particular community and its social history; therefore, exploring the English forms necessitates the examination of interactional structures (Auer 1998; Gumperz 2008), language ideology (Woolard 1998) and sociohistorical relevances (Ochs and Schieffelin 2011). It is argued that the enregisterment (Agha 2007) of the English language as representing modernity

(Pennycook 2007) in a multilingual setting has produced a rich semiotic pathway through which English forms can be used to index values associated with such a setting. Malay-English talk in general exhibits the tension and interplay between two powerful hegemonies in operation, values of modernity, on the one hand, and those of Malay ethnolinguistic identity on the other. Reconceptualising linguistic forms enable speakers to come up with new strategies to cope with emergent social identities, re-evaluate old ones, and test systemic borders. By using English pronouns to refer to the self and the addressee when speaking in Malay, speakers can enact new ways of demonstrating respect and deference, thus disrupting and maintaining the traditional norms at the same time.

Data for this study consist of audio-recorded naturally occurring conversations between long-time Kuala Lumpur residents who live in the older areas of the city, recorded as they went about their normal daily activities. Relevant background details of the participants were obtained during informal chats after the conversations were recorded. These conversations were collected between 2011 and 2012 as part of my PhD research. To complement the conversation data, an extract from the 2016 television series *7 Hari Mencintaiku* is added. Note that although *I/you* may be used by speakers residing in other urban areas of the country, the decision to focus on Greater Kuala Lumpur was based on the area's recognised role in defining postcolonial ethnic Malay urbanism (see Wiryomarto 2020; Bunnell 2002).

Sociolinguistics of Malay-English Contact in Kuala Lumpur

The Malay talk analysed in this study can be considered as contact talk, a type of talk that has emerged in a contact situation (Goebel 2019; Goebel et al. 2019). Contact talk analysis provides an account of the "... multiple semiotic resources used to make meaning in face-to-face talk in contact situations and their connection with resources from other chronotopes" (Goebel 2019, 332). In this section I discuss Malay talk as semiotically bound to a particular segment of the community, ethnic Malays. This contact register does not appear in other Kuala Lumpur contact registers that involve Chinese languages, Tamil or even Malaysian English. Instances in which *I/you* are used are hypothesised as hybrid social acts that make use of access to two languages, English and Malay. As Goebel et al. (2019, 2) write, "what counts as 'a language' is itself constructed through discourse, what comes into contact in a language contact situation is not so much the rapprochement of different languages, but the coming together of multiple discourses about what a language is, who speaks it to whom, when, how, and why." In a postcolonial Malaysia that is largely ruled by the "hegemony of race" (Leow 2015), the three main ethnic identities (Malay, Chinese and Indian) used for social organisation during the British colonisation period (1786–1957), are now constitutionally enshrined in ways that elevate ethnic Malays and identity symbols of Malayness (religion, culture and language) as central to defining Malaysian nationality (Chin et al. 2015). At the same time, certain citizenship rights and identity symbols and practices of the two non-Malay races, including their languages, are institutionally supported to some degree (Daniels 2005). Significant named languages—those shaped by "institutionally authorised commentaries that (re) create boundaries around [them] and the communities that are imagined to speak them" (Goebel 2019, 335)—with the exception of English, are thus monolingual idealisations linked to the three main ethnic identities: Malay with the politically and numerically dominant ethnic Malays, various Sinitic languages (Cantonese in Kuala Lumpur and Mandarin in national education) with ethnic Chinese, and South Asian languages, primarily Tamil, with ethnic Indians. Practices and repertoires are highly varied but forms from respective languages are often used to discursively construct social borders in typical plurilingual speech of Malaysians, especially in urban areas. Which linguistic resources are accessed differs from speaker to speaker, reflecting social and attitudinal configurations that depend on a range of factors such as actual lived experiences, educational and family backgrounds and personal choices (Asmah Haji Omar 1998).

In postcolonial Malaysia, there is a strong tendency to define Malay as only those linguistic varieties used by ethnic Malays (Collins 1989), thereby linking the language to Malayness. So while Malay is used by all citizens for intergroup communication, only ethnic Malay speakers and institutions are viewed as legitimate owners and shapers of the language (Leow 2015). Without entering into this debate and limiting commentary only to the forms used in interlocutor reference, it is fair to claim that Malay forms and address conventions are almost all indexed to ethnic Malays, with the forms constituting a store of linguistic signs associated with social identities, roles and relations that have relevance to ethnic Malay culture. Semiotic resources linked to other languages therefore tend to be used to signal membership in a non-Malay category, as in the case of the use of Hokkien second-person pronoun *lu* in Malay talk. In addition, in the Kuala Lumpur context, it is not typical for non-Malays to use Malay with each other, again supporting the position that they are not usually primary contributors to shaping socially sensitive forms.

Within the Malay world, modernity, as associated with education, commerce, science and technology, and Western culture, has emerged as a powerful force, which in some contexts is viewed as competing with the prioritised Malayness (Pennycook 2007). The ability to speak English and use English resources, which has long been identified as a marker of elite social status in the country, is also evaluated as modern, and modernity has also been held as the rationale for official Malay language modernisation efforts. Since the use of English is largely confined to urban areas where the language functions as "one primary language of social interaction" (Asmah Haji Omar 2012), large-scale contact between English and ethnic Malay speakers beyond the main urban centres is a relatively recent phenomenon, a consequence of the programs to mass-urbanise the Malays since the 1970s. The urbanisation efforts not only increased contact with non-Malay ethnic groups, but also gave rise to conceptions of new social categories and interactional identities, such as modern professionals linked to modern workplaces, and the official endorsement of a new non-rural Malay identity, the "modern Malay" or "new Malay" as a desired social category during the 1990s (Shamsul 2005). Valorisation and the value of English as social capital has undoubtedly resulted in Malay-English bilingualism or at least the inclusion of English in Malay talk. However, acceptance by the Malays of modernity values, including those linked to English, has been patchy. Some, including officials in government institutions, view such contact effects as a threat to Malayness that is capable of disrupting traditional hierarchies of power. For this reason, they are also discouraged in some official discourses, especially those connected to Islamic revivalism.

As an urban centre founded during the colonial period, Kuala Lumpur has been a high contact site from the beginning, with the three ethnic groups interacting with each other and with the British. Typical of urban areas until recently, Kuala Lumpur was Chinese dominated, with Malays mostly residing in rural areas. In postcolonial Malaysia (1957 onwards), the city's status was elevated when it was made the capital city and a centre of economic activities. It is also the location of the most visible nation-building projects and efforts to modernise (Bunnell 2002). Internal mass migration to the centre, especially of ethnic Malays, has steadily changed the city's demographics. Since 2010, Malays have become the largest ethnic group (44.7 per cent) in the area, while both the Chinese (43.2 per cent) and Indian (8 per cent) populations continue to decline. Meanwhile, the number of foreign residents is sizeable (13.8 per cent). In this new configuration, as Bakar (2009) remarks, contact effects with English are noticeable in the speech of Kuala Lumpur Malays.

The "Problem" with Second-Person Singular in Malay

The linguistic norms that guide the selection of Malay referent forms and their relationship to cultural norms have been discussed in many studies so they will not be elaborated here. Instead, in the following I focus on what Surjaman (1968, 90) calls "the problem of personal pronouns" (in Indonesian, as inherited from its Malay roots), particularly second-person singular. As mentioned, the meaning potential of the various available pronouns have semantic pathways associated with social distance or speech levels. Some of the more common ones appearing in Malay grammar and reference books and also encountered in Kuala Lumpur are listed in table 1. This list is by no means exhaustive, as the intention is only to demonstrate the principle that forms available for second-person singular are limited for a speaker of lower status speaking to a higher status addressee.

Table 1. Reciprocality of common first- and second-person singular forms in Malay (from Asmah Haji Omar 1986)

Social level	First-person singular	Second-person singular
	aku (informal, intimate, familiar); *saya* (formal, polite)	*(eng)kau; kamu, awak* (informal, intimate, familiar)
Higher to lower	*aku; saya*	*(eng)kau; kamu, awak*
Lower to higher	*saya*	*anda*
Neutral	–	–

The terms "democratic" and "neutral" have been used in different ways to describe pronouns in Malay (and in other languages). In relation to Malay, "democratic" describes a form that can be used across the three social levels (Zainal-Abidin 1950, 53) without distinguishing them, the only such candidate in this case being the first-person pronouns *saya*. The idea of neutrality relates to remoteness from social levels, and is applied to the one form, *anda*, which has been officially introduced. Exposure to this pronoun is almost always through public announcements, advertisements and formal education. (High status) foreigners are taught that this is the second-person form to use. In a sense, unlike *saya*, the usage patterns of *anda* emerged largely from rarefied social contexts such as these, with the effect that the addressee is positioned outside the Malay social world. Unlike *saya*, *anda* appears very infrequently if at all in colloquial speech. Defining "democratic" and "neutral" in these ways, a form borrowed from another language can arguably be considered as democratic and neutral. The Hokkien forms *gua/lu*, for example, insofar as they are perceived or used by Malays to index Chinese ethnicity, remain outside the Malay world and cannot be linked to the social levels given in table 1. Their social value if any is likely to stem from the social status of the group in the community that uses them.

The other second-person forms are neither democratic nor neutral. To reiterate, in asymmetrical relationships in the Malay system, the party of a lower status is obligated to choose forms that explicitly acknowledge the hierarchical difference while both pronouns and lexical nouns are available to the higher status party. One way of framing this is through the lens of politeness: "the more polite second-person forms successively raise the conceived status of the addressee, while the more polite first-person forms successively lower the conceived status of the speaker" (Brown and Levinson 1987 in Enfield 2007b, 102). Within the family for instance, kinship terms unsurprisingly are favoured as they not only convey relational information but also closeness; however, an older speaker can use a second-person pronoun instead of a kin term when speaking to a younger addressee (McGinn 1991). Outside the family, metaphoric kinship is also a common strategy for indexing social relations. A person in a lower social role may for instance address or refer to his or her boss as *bapak* (father) or *pakcik* (uncle), or use an honorific title equivalent to an English title. While a person of a higher status can also use kinship terms or titles in reference to an addressee of a lower status, they are not obligated to do so, and can use an appropriate second-person pronoun. The use of a second-person pronominal form from lower to higher is noticed, as example (1) indicates. Here, the reported problem centres on the use of *kamu* by a child in speaking to her friend's mother. Manom, an Indian woman in her forties, is speaking to her Malay friend. Her comment emerged during a discussion about interethnic rudeness.

(1) The use of *kamu* as reference to an older addressee

MANOM   *Whenever we go to the Indian house, enter to the culture. That's the way we are respect each other. But no **kamu**. Whenever she talk on the phone, "Er Aunty ah", she will call me Aunty first, "**kamu** ada rumah ke? Saya nak ambil buku dengan **kamu**. Saya dekat rumah **kamu**." So I don't know whether I'm her friend or my daughter's friend.*
Whenever we go to the Indian house, enter to the culture. That's the way we are respect each other. But no *kamu*. Whenever she talk on the phone, "Er Aunty ah", she will call me Aunty first, "Are you at home? I want to bring a book to you. I am at your house." So I don't know whether I'm her friend or my daughter's friend.

Other parts of their conversation make it clear that Manom believes showing respect in the Malaysian context includes orienting to politeness expectations of those from the other ethnicities. Here, she singles out her 11-year-old daughter's Chinese schoolmate as disrespectful for using an inappropriate form when speaking to her in Malay.[5] She reports that the girl begins by addressing her with *Aunty*. As mentioned below, this English term now serves as the default polite address term for women of one's mother's generation, especially for non-Malays.

While this initial address is respectful, the problem arises because *kamu* is used as addressee reference for Manom. Manom's evaluative statement *"So I don't know whether I'm her friend or my daughter's friend"* is somewhat facetious because she of course knows the girl is her daughter's friend. However, she is offended because *kamu* is not deferential and by using it in reference to her, her daughter's friend positions her as an equal. Preferred strategies include continuing with *Aunty* in all instances where *kamu* was used or to simply rephrase the utterance to omit the referent (zero anaphora). Even *awak*, which is considered a more polite form, would not have been appropriate as it is commonly used by equals or by someone higher to an addressee of a perceived lower status (Zainal-Abidin 1950, 53).

Effects of Contact with English

In the Malaysian context, there are two trends in practices of addressee reference that result from contact with English and which are perceived as modern: (i) extension of reciprocal direct referent forms, especially in unequal relations, and (ii) enlisting English forms. An example of (i) is the use of First Names (FN). It has been noted that within English-speaking cultures, reciprocal FN rather than more formal strategies such as Title + Last Name for instance has been increasing (Brown and Ford 1961; Dickey 1997; Murray 2002). The eventual result of this strategy to social deixis is a change to conventions in the system. Appropriateness of this strategy in Malaysian contact depends on other social factors such as the cultural orientation of the parties involved, for example, those who are English-educated, and is more likely to appear in settings indexed to modernity, for example, modern workplaces such as offices. The spread of the other trend, the enlisting English forms, appears to rely on the social indexicality of the form itself to some set of modernity values. Examples include giving oneself or one's child an English name (particularly prevalent among the Chinese) and the use of equivalent English lexemes once reconceptualised as indexing modernity, for example, kinship terms such as *aunty* or *uncle*. The latter provides respectful alternatives to terms from other local languages, which themselves are re-indexed to traditional (pre-modern) culture (Lee and Shanmuganathan 2019).

Modernity-affiliated address strategies are visible in Kuala Lumpur and are accepted if not outrightly favoured. Even so, there are still sizeable numbers of residents with traditional practices, so appropriateness needs to be regulated. Modernity/Western practices also vary across the three ethnicities, due partly to ideological positions and general levels of urbanism. For instance, while *aunty* is now a default older term for non-Malay older females, when the addressee is Malay, the addresser has to decide whether the former seems more inclined towards (Western) modernity or Malayness, in which case the Malay form *makcik* may be more suitable. The latter strategy also recognises the sensitivity of Malayness towards the perceived threat of Western values and the watering down of the Malay language through mixing (Asmah Haji Omar 1998).

Comparison between English first- and second-person pronominal conventions and Malay, especially the second-person limit, was undoubtedly a major motivation to re-examine the limits of Malay pronominal use, a particular interest to update "the chaotic, undemocratic and inefficient pronominal system" (Kridalaksana 1974 in McGinn 1991, 4; see also Surjaman 1968) by way of introducing new Malay forms suited for modernity settings and social relations. The neutral *anda* was perhaps supposed to address non-reciprocality in unequal relations but its semiotic trajectory positions addresser and addressee at such distance that it is unsuitable for most daily encounters, with use largely reserved for impersonal or the public second person, for example, in formal written genres, public announcements and advertisements (Mansor 2019). *Awak*, a pre-existing second-person form re-defined in Standard Malay as the polite second person operating in a dyad with *saya*, provides the means to address a wider range of workmates more politely but has not succeeded in providing a democratic solution for lower to higher parties. Zulkifley Hamid and Naidatul Zamrizam (2013), in a study of student to teacher address states outright that pronouns, even *awak*, cannot be used by the lower party. A survey on *awak*'s suitability by a business representative to a potential customer based on a real-world exchange in a WhatsApp text messages concludes that even in this setting, usage is potentially contentious (Raja Rozina 2017). Again, no pronoun was deemed acceptable, and *Puan __*, the equivalent of "Mrs __" was mentioned by the referent as the suitable alternative.

In summary, the difficulty of finding a reciprocable pronoun is at heart not a linguistic issue. Malay cultural norms rely on regulating politeness through socially indexed forms to mediate distance and to signal deference to higher social roles and identities. Successful extensions of fictive kinship for instance depend on there being no such violations. The widespread adoption of *abang* (older brother) as an intimate term by wives to husbands but never the reverse, *kakak* (older sister), accords with cultural definitions of family relations between males and females (Mansor et al. 2018; Banks 1974, 58). Selecting a Malay direct reference form, even a polite one levels co-participants, and can therefore be seen as lowering the higher status party without social compensation. A strategy of introducing or adapting pre-existing Malay pronouns for "democratisation" may not currently be successful for a number of reasons, least of all because (i) true bidirectional usage violates systemic conventions itself, and (ii) the nominated form(s) do not have a usage history that is bidirectional.

In the next section, it will be shown that *I* and *you* in Malay can be used bidirectionally in unequal relations. As borrowed forms, they follow an already present practice of enlisting English forms, and as evidenced in and by such practices, usage is socially licenced by the hegemony of modernity values in urban life. It is hypothesised that "being modern" is of such high status that it is able to accommodate the departure from the established power structures of the Malay system, and in some interactional environments, even preferred or fashionable.

I/you in Kuala Lumpur Malay

The usage patterns of *I/you* (2)–(3) in non-initial referent positions in Malay talk demonstrate that they are disentangled from source English grammatical conventions. In example (2), line 1, *you* and *I* are used in subject position, while in line 3, *I* is used in object position.

(2) Conversation between Zifal (male, 27 years old) to girlfriend Rosliana (female, 30 years old)

ZIFAL: *Oh aje ...* you *tolong cakap kat dia* I *busy gila babi a?*
Tak sempat nak reply pun dia punya ini ... apa ... message.
Dia ada ding I *dekat Facebook tadi.*
Oh can you please tell her I am crazy busy?
Didn't have time even to reply to her message.
She dinged me on Facebook just now.

(3) Conversation between Rosliana (female, 30 years old), Saniah (female, 60 years old)

SANIAH: *Kalau* you *tidur dengan contact lens, memang mata* you *kena affected.*
If you sleep with a contact lens, of course your eyes will get affected.

In source English, singular personal pronoun forms change to reflect predicate position whereas in Kuala Lumpur Malay, only the subject forms, *I* and *you*, are ever used. (2) and (3) provide examples in subject position but as can be seen in line 3 of (2) and in (3), there is no form change to reflect object (patient) and possessive. As well for the latter, NP modifying elements such as the possessor follows the possessed nominal, reflecting Malay rather than English word order conventions. It is notable that for third-person singular and first/second plural referents, Malay forms continue to be used. These patterns are consistent across the data set, suggesting that it is solely the lexical items *I* and *you* that have been enlisted to directly reference addresser and addressee.

Social Indexicality to Modernity

That the English forms express particular social values when in contact with Malay is highlighted in (3)–(4), excerpts from the most watched television series in 2016, *7 Hari Mencintaiku* (Seven days of love), adapted from a novel. While the dialogues are fictional creations, it is quite typical of contemporary fiction to "have a didactic orientation" (Goddard 2000, 90). The story is clearly situated in a complete ethno-Malay context: the actors and characters are all ethnic Malays, the settings contrast rural Malay village and Malay urban life (multicultural, multilingual characters and other signs are almost completely absent), and the medium used is monolingual Malay. The major theme centres almost completely on moral character, constructed through pitting Muslim-Malay values against external ones, with (Western) modernity clearly one major source of corruption.

The appearance of *I/you* in address acts is one of the very few aberrations from the monolingual Malay script, selected only by characters that are urbanised and have questionable moral dispositions. (4) is from an early scene, so the two main characters, Mia, a spoilt, rich, young, urbane lawyer, and her soon-to-be husband, introduced as a simple, humble goat farmer, Khuzairi (Ri), are still being revealed to the audience. At this point, Mia and Ri do not know each other well, having only briefly crossed paths after Ri almost ran her over in the parking lot when she stepped out without looking. Despite being at fault, Mia blames him, and in this chance meeting that takes place shortly after the near accident, Ri's steady and polite manner contrasts with Mia's direct "confrontation talk".

(4)   *7 Hari Mencintaiku* – Episode 1 (33.16-33.45);

RI: Cik Mia *(1.0) saya nak minta maaf dengan apa yang terjadi tadi.*
            Miss Mia, I want to apologise for what happened earlier.

MIA: *You two should be glad yang **I** tak apa-apa tau. Kalau **I** cedera tadi **you** jual kereta **you** pun belum tentu boleh cover claim hospital **I**. So lain kali kalau rasa dah tak berduit tu janganlah berhutang ya. Hidup je dengan apa yang ada. Kalau miskin buat je lah cara miskin, hmm?*
            You two should be glad that I'm fine, you know. If I was hurt earlier, even if you sold your car, it is not clear it could cover my

hospital claim. So next time, if you feel you don't have money, don't make a debt, okay. Just live with what you have. If (you're) poor, just live the poor way, hmm?

The contrasting verbal behaviours of Mia and Ri, who can be interpreted as unfamiliar equals, are meant to be noticed. Ri's conduct categorises him as *halus* (refined), in accordance with good social behaviours expected of Malays (Tham 1970; Goddard 2000). He opens by offering an apology (line 1), a speech act that attempts to dispel tension and highlights his concern for Mia's feelings. Further, beginning with the vocative *Cik Mia* (Miss Mia) followed by the polite first-person pronoun *saya* appropriately signals the unfamiliarity. Mia in return offers a dispreferred response and violates Malay social norms in a number of ways. She begins with no vocative address, let alone a respectful one, but simply reorientates their relationship as an unequal one, with her in a self-appointed higher position. This is signalled by the use of English pronouns. Notably, she begins with "*You two*", talking down to Ri and his friend, which is particularly insulting since Ri is not even acknowledged as an individual. Enlisting English forms adds further insult, since it ignores Ri's Malay preference and appears as arrogant. She continues with *I* and *you* in what turns out to be a lengthy lecture, dominating the floor and completely disregarding the polite framework Ri tried to establish. The neutrality of the English pronouns in terms of social distance and the bringing in of forms indexed to modernity when the addressee is clearly not modern (as judged by Mia) adds to the directness of Mia's approach. She is constructed as being *kasar* (rough), through her angry tone and directness, both negative characteristics by Malay standards.

Arguably, the audience is not supposed to interpret Mia's use of *I/you* as simply inappropriate interlocutor reference forms. Ri's doing the right thing through Malay and Mia's doing the wrong thing through English exploits the real-world tension between Malayness and (Western) modernity, which is also evident in other signs that contrast the two. Mia is dressed in a Western style and wears no head covering. Mia's aggression and directness are associated with Western behaviour and counter to Malay propriety (Zainal-Abidin 1950). Mia's mention of Ri's modest locally made car brings its brand and model into focus, and her insinuation that he would not be able to pay her private hospital claim if she had been injured exploits shared knowledge that foreign car models and affording private hospitals are symbols of status (and Western-type consumption) in urban areas. She is clearly high status by urban (modernity) standards, and he is cast as a rural identity, stereotyped as poor and unsophisticated by comparison, although of good character through the lens of traditional culture. Notably the only characters who shift to English pronouns in the entire 16 episodes are similarly urban and/or are of bad character. These contrasting essentialisations clearly present morality in terms of rural and urban Malays, categories that emerged in postcolonial Malaysia (Tham 1982).

The construction of themes in fictional works rely on shared sociocultural schemas in order to be successfully interpreted by the viewer/reader. What is exploited in this scene is the indexicality of English forms to modernity values as well as associated properties, such as being democratic or neutral. In English, such properties do not inherently express any social deixis but within the Malay system, they are socially meaningful. In this example, English pronouns are enlisted to support the creation of urban social identities cast as immoral characters who are out of alignment with their Malay roots.

Hierarchical Reciprocal use of I/you

In everyday exchanges, most *I/you* usages are not negative. Similar to Othman (2006), uptake by participants in equal social relations, for example, amongst friends and in relationships, was represented in the conversational data. However, whereas Othman's study does not include examples of directional use from lower to higher status parties, such instances of use were found in the present data. (Note that social relationships were not deliberately targeted during data collection, so these examples represent a limited sampling of co-participants' normal address patterns.) Table 2 provides the list of co-participants in unequal relationships and the contexts they appear in. By normal Malay standards based on age or social status differences, the lower participant should not be using a second-person pronoun.

Table 2. Co-participant relations represented in the data

	Participant 1 (lower)	Participant 2 (higher)	Context
1	Rosliana, preschool teacher, Malay (30 years old)	Saniah, preschool owner, Malay (61 years old)	Conversation between two professionals in the same industry who are on friendly terms
2	Ariff, passenger, Malay (25 years old)	Siow, taxi-driver, Chinese (72 years old)	Ariff, a student, is the passenger in Siaw's taxi.
3	Office worker, Malay (25 years old)	Boss, Chinese (48 years old)	Conversation in a small business office
4	Domestic helper, Indonesian (30 years old)	Lady of the house, Chinese (48 years old)	Conversation in the home
5	Adult child (in his twenties), Malay	Saniah, mother, Malay (61 years old)	Reported conversation between mother and son

The exchange between Rosliana and Saniah, both Malay, is the most extensive (approximately two hours) example. Topics discussed were not structured and ranged from their work lives, families, differences between urban and rural life, navigating between modern (Western) and Malay cultures, and their views on various subjects. Malay normativities would expect explicit show of deference by Rosliana, who is 30+ years younger and certainly much less accomplished in her career. While both grew up in rural regions, they are long-time residents of Kuala Lumpur, and, importantly, express urban views on such things as education and are open to viewpoints on a number of issues, including those that are known to cause tensions in the Malay world. Saniah is also married to a European man, has held managerial positions in corporations and government, and has lived overseas. Rosliana is aspirational, in the midst of being college educated, and seeks to make something of herself. Under the class categories used by Mansor (2019), Saniah would fall under "upper-middle social class" and Rosliana, "middle class". (Mansor found in her survey that the use of *you* by women in reference to their husbands increased significantly with class, with 56 per cent of instances of use found among speakers of upper-middle class and 30 per cent of middle class, with no instances found among working-class speakers.)

The medium of exchange varies from Malay or English only to a mix of Malay-English. *I* and *you* are used by both Saniah and Rosliana from the outset, which is interpreted here as two familiar parties (re-)establishing their social identities as two professionals in the same industry. The English forms are the most frequently occurring in the conversation, including *you* by Rosliana to Saniah, suggesting that it is unnoticed (accepted) by the latter.

That the English pronouns are regulated through Malay address conventions is supported by shifts to other forms by both women throughout the conversation. Such changes have been noted to regularly occur in Malay talk for a range of reasons (see for example, Djenar 2007). It is proposed that the switches provide evidence of the semiotic pathway of Malaysian modernity and the values to which the forms are indexed.

Topics related to family and those close or associated to family members motivate use of relational forms and *aku* and *(eng)kau*, the Malay pronouns that most reflects intimacy. For instance, Saniah uses *Aunty* for self-reference when depicting herself as a caring motherly figure, to be closer to Rosliana, or to take stances. As (5) shows, until Saniah uses *Aunty*, *I/you* are selected by both women as they discuss their experiences of using social media. Saniah's switch emphasises the improper, disrespectful responses by her son's friends when she commented on one of her son's posts. Because they did not know who she was and assumed she was just another friend, they started joking around with her son about "this Saniah". With Saniah self-referring with Aunty, it is understood that they would have acted differently based on her higher status.

(5) ROSLIANA: *Oh*, you *pun ada Facebook?*
So you also have Facebook?
SANIAH: *Ah lama dah. Yang Facebook tu lagi best. Er dulu menyamar dengan gambar bunga je tau. So my son ni dia kawan-kawan dia orang tau tulis tau la merapu-rapu kat dalam Facebook tu. So one day **I** commented lah. Er but **I** respond in German you see. So yang kawan dia tak tahu that was* Aunty *you see.*
Yes for a long time already. Facebook is the best. Er last time (I) used to disguise (myself) with just a picture of a flower, you know. So my son, his friends, they write all sorts of nonsense on things in Facebook. So one day I commented. But I responded in German you see. So his friends didn't know that was <u>me</u> (Aunty), you see.

In (6), Saniah again switches to self-refer with *Aunty*, this time when elaborating on her motherliness to Malay students in Germany. These instances co-occur with *I/you*, providing orderly frame shifts between her current interactional identity (the independent individual in the absolute sense supplied by the English forms' neutrality) and that of a caring motherly person (tied to others through the relational form).

(6) SANIAH: *Because er **I** have so many of the students in Germany, they come to* my *Hari Raya every year to the house kan, so yang banyak yang in- integrate dengan* Aunty *semua budak-budak tu la, student student itu.*
Because er I have so many of the students in Germany, they come to my Hari Raya (Malay festival) every year to the house right, so many integrate with Aunty (me), all the young people, those students.

Dia orang seronok tau <laughter> *Because **I**, **I** treat myself like a mother to them (.) so tiap-tiap tahun dia menunggu je. Kalau* you *tengok gambar-gambar dia orang penuh dengan makan-makan rumah **Aunty Saniah**, you know. Kadang-kadang* Aunty *jemput dia orang datang just for makan, that kind of thing.*
They have fun you know. Because I treat myself like a mother to them so every year they wait (for this). If you look at their photos, all with food at Aunty Saniah's (my) house, you know. Sometimes Aunty (I) invite them to come just to eat, that kind of thing.

(7) occurs when the women are discussing some difficulties of teaching. First, Saniah positions Rosliana's problems as the latter's, using *you*. Then she uses *kita*, the inclusive first-person plural to provide a sense of a shared problem. Finally, when offering Rosliana some words of wisdom, she switches to *Aunty* for first person, abandoning their professional independent roles to a shared intimate one, in which she is sympathetic as a more experienced elder in relation to her addressee. An added effect is to show Rosliana that she is on her side.

(7) SANIAH: *You know* you *teach macam mana pun memang tak boleh... tapi* kita *kena lah belajar adjust ourselves. Kadang-kadang, macam* Aunty *sendiri pun nak [XX] tak tahan tau [laughter] kadang-kadang geram sangat-sangat.*
You know you cannot teach in whatever way... but we have to learn to adjust ourselves. Sometimes, like Aunty herself (I myself) can't stand it you know [laughter], sometimes (I'm) very, very angry.

Finally, in (8), Saniah constructs a link with Rosliana by referring to herself as *Aunty*, contrasting with reciprocal *I/you* between her son and her in reported speech. The latter is contrary to expectations since a kinship term is being used between non-related addresser and addressee and *I* and *you* between mother and son. Furthermore, her son addressing his mother as *you*, violates Malay norms. It may be that her son, educated overseas and Eurasian, is Westernised, and the English forms are used in their household. However, in other parts of the exchange, Saniah uses Malay pronouns *aku* and *engkau* to report speech between her sons and her, suggesting that her choices of forms in reported speech take into consideration interactional factors (Tannen 1995). Arguably, using forms that index modernity values makes it clearer to the hearer that the context of the exchange is "being modern", which licenses her son to give her, his mother, orders, an act that may be interpreted as rude in Malay culture. She views the directness of his words as an example of his serious demeanour, acceptable within a modern perspective. However, Rosliana in the second person is now shifted into a relational role with Saniah, adding contrast to the son's directness through addressing his mother with *you*.

(8) SANIAH: *Hmm. Tak banyak cakap senyaaap je. Kalau dia nak ajak* Aunty *pergi dinner pun.* "Ah, mama, [unclear] hari bulan are you *free or not?" I say, "why?" "We go out for dinner ah. Don't, if* you *already confirm, jangan buat appointment lain tau?" Ah [unclear] tengok very serious je kan? Kalau nak joke dengan dia ah tapi kalau* Aunty *hantar surat, email, joking pulak.*

Hmmm. Not talkative, just quiet. Even if he wants to invite me (Aunty) to dinner, "Ah mama, on this date are you free or not?" I say, "why?" "We go out for dinner okay. If you have confirmed with me, don't make other appointments okay?" Ah see (he is) very serious right? If you want to joke with him... if I (Aunty) write letters, emails, then he jokes.

In (9), Rosliana uses the English pronouns to take a stance against the attitude of her family members. She narrates an incident where her brother-in-law borrowed $20 from her mother. She wants to show this as an example of her sister and her husband's neediness and lack of self-reliance, which are stereotyped as negative characteristics in the conception of the "modern Malay". Elsewhere she presents her family as unaccepting of her independence and very conservative. When she begins, Rosliana uses her own name in self-reference, and the intimate pronouns *aku* and *kau* when referring to herself and her sister/brother-in-law in reported speech, thus presenting the incident in a non-urban area. However, when she scolds her sister, she switches to *I* and *you*, signalling a shift in stance, from that performed by an urban, educated individual to an urban Malay identity unrelated to the person she spoke to in the story.

(9) ROSLIANA: *Ah! Tapi dia takut! Tapi sudah kantoi sebab* **[own name]** *nampak dekat side mirror! Lepas tu* **[own name]** *jumpa Mat Jo, er er er "Mat Jo, asal ah..." masa tu dah macam gangster tapi duduk se-sebelah la kan? Masa tu isteri dia taka da la. "Asal kau pinjam duit mak aku dua puluh ringgit ah?" "**Aku** ni balik setahun sekali tapi kalau **kau** buat perangai macam tu **aku** tak suka ah". Dia diam. Dia terus pergi. Lepas tu my sister datang dia terus marah, "Eh apasal ah **Kak [name]** marah Mat Jo macam tu?"*
Ah! But he is afraid. But he is busted because I (name) saw him in the side mirror. Then I meet Mat Jo... "Mat Jo if", ... that time (he) was like a gangster but he was sitting next to (me). That time his wife was not there. "You borrowed money from my mother $20?" "I come back once a year but if you behave like that I don't like it." He is quiet. He just left. Then my sister came, she was angry. "Eh why were you (older sister Rosliana) angry to Mat Jo like that?"

Marah la apa ni you *minta dua puluh ringgit dari ibu buat apa,* you *kena bagi dua puluh ringgit dekat ibu, bukan* you *minta dua puluh ringgit!* **You** *tak malu ke kahwin dengan*

dia? Eh, you *kena ingat tau. Sekarang* you *nak gadoh dengan I tak pasal kahwin? Lagi sekali* you *tukar topik macam tu, next year I tak balik. 2011 I tak akan balik Raya kalau* you *come up lagi [laughter] that thing.*
"What are you angry about, you asked $20 from mother for what, *you* have to give $20 to her, not you ask for $20! You are not ashamed to be married to him? You have to remember you know. Now you want to fight with me about not being married? Once again, you change the topic like that, next year I won't return. 2011 I will not return for Raya if you come up again." [laughter] that thing.

Pas tu "Ye la, ye la **Kak [name]** *la yang menang, apa la" dia cakap macam tu. Lepas tu merajuk. Sampai sekarang. I tegur dia sebab I terperanjat sebab I thought, "uh".*
After that, (she said) "Yes, yes, you (older sister Rosliana) win, whatever." She said like that. After that, she sulked. Until now. I scolded her but I was shocked because I thought "uh".

The departure from the intimate forms used between family members to the English forms indexes the intensity of Rosliana's anger and reproof. Immediately after this, Rosliana asks Saniah if she was "too rough" or *kasar* in her manner, to which Saniah replies: "Bukan (not) too rough. That is the Western way of handling matters which is transparent lah. ... You want things to be transparent." Her comment suggests Malays are having to navigate two cultural traditions, with *I/you* consistently used to index values associated with modernity, and Malay forms, with family and tradition.

The final example (10) in which negotiations of suitable address forms in an encounter with a stranger highlights the limits of appropriate use. Ariff, a young Malay man (aged 20), begins chatting to Siaw, the 72-year-old Chinese driver of the taxi he has just entered. Ariff begins with the respectful vocative *Uncle* and English *you* in addressee reference. Arguably, his experiences are guiding him to expect his Chinese co-participant to accept the second-person pronoun *you* even though there is a significant age difference between them. As soon as Siaw uses the Hokkien first-person singular pronoun *gua*, Ariff switches to respectful forms *saya* to refer to himself and *Uncle* to refer to his addressee for the rest of the 20-minute exchange, while Siaw continues to use *gua* (I) and *lu* (you).

Although it needs further documentation, anecdotally, Chinese speakers have a propensity to adopt the English forms in interlocutor reference. The Chinese are stereotyped by Malays as a social group most accepting of modern trends (Daniels 2005) and the Chinese in Kuala Lumpur typically use the English pronouns nowadays. The use of Hokkien forms by Chinese in Kuala Lumpur is likely to represent an older Pasar Malay (or Bazaar Malay), a contact variety of Malay which emerged around the 19th century and used in interethnic communication across the Malay archipelago (now spoken in Malaysia and Singapore mainly by older people). Whether Ariff assumed Siauw embodied this stereotype or took Siaw as indexing his Chineseness, he interpreted Siaw's choice of forms as a signal not to use the English forms anymore; instead Ariff selected forms that mark social levels (lower to higher)—in other words, no participation in democratic, neutral *I/you*.

(10) ARIFF: *Uncle, you sini kat mana tinggal?*
Uncle you here loc where live
'Uncle, you live where?'
SIAW: *Gua tinggal di sana.*
1sg live loc there
"I live there."

To summarise, the shifts to and from the English forms indicate that the use of *I* and *you* are interpreted relative to Malay norms with the forms being associated with modernity linked to knowledge of English, education, science and technology, economic prosperity, urban Kuala Lumpur, being a professional, and more generally, Western[6] values, for example, democracy, individuality and directness. Emergent usage patterns noticed, such as the forms as gendered for urban Malays and as preferred in exchanges involving non-Malay interlocutors,[7] suggest they are a recognised strategy used to circumvent hierarchical and distance relations indexed in the traditional Malay forms.

Conclusion

This chapter has demonstrated that using *I* and *you* in Kuala Lumpur Malay talk is a strategy that speakers adopt to circumvent Malay norms that disallow pronominal use by a speaker of a perceived lower status to an addressee of a higher status. In urban Kuala Lumpur, where modernity has influenced the way people treat social hierarchy and led to new social identities and roles, being modern when talking in Malay means bringing in English, including the pronouns *I* and *you*, to index relations traditionally considered unequal. For a higher-status addressee, perhaps the association between these pronouns with modern values provides an adequate reason for using them. However, simultaneous ideological support for Malay cultural values and the continuing practices of using Malay forms (with the implied asymmetry) in Kuala Lumpur and across the country means that the use of the English forms is emerging as part of the overall practices of indexing social relations in Malay.

In everyday urban interaction, using *I/you* instead of Malay forms is not categorically better or worse because both represent a reference practice that is highly potent, useful and productive, reflecting the very real hybridity of ethnic Malay urbanism. Their co-existence allows social actors to select forms to fit particular discursive environments or mediate the addressee's expectations better. The examples shown indicate that far from conveying social neutrality, the English forms are construed relative to the Malay norms for indexing social hierarchy. The shifts to and from the English forms within a single conversation suggest that the Malay "system" of interlocutor reference is dynamic and rich, utilised to express attitudes and stances.

This chapter has proposed that Kuala Lumpur urban talk be considered as a contact register in which resources from Malay and English are drawn upon in the practice of indexing modernity. Using *I* and *you* when speaking Malay is a strategy that speakers can adopt to negotiate social relations that are not readily permitted by Malay conventions. The non-relationality of the English pronouns has been reconceptualised to enable speakers to index egalitarian-type participant relations, thus creating the appearance of democratic and neutral relations.

Notes

[1] The term "Malay" can have different meanings in the Malaysian context. "Malay" by itself refers to the language or people of Malay background. Making a distinction between ethnic Malays and the other (two) main ethnic groups (Chinese and Indian) is necessary because the social value systems of these other groups have different trajectories and are instantiated differently.

[2] First names include given names.

[3] While some Chinese languages, especially their formal registers, may have a "polite" variant, this is not the case with spoken vernaculars such as Malaysian Hokkien and Cantonese, the vernacular Chinese lingua franca in Kuala Lumpur.

[4] Hokkien *gua* (I) and *lu* (you) does not appear to be widely used in contemporary Kuala Lumpur Malay talk.

[5] Manom's daughter's friend is around 11 or 12 years of age and her friendship with Manom's daughter has come about because they attend the same Mandarin-speaking primary school. Her communications with Manom are likely to be mainly in Malay since she is probably not conversant in English, and Manom, not in any Chinese languages.

[6] In the age of superdiversity due to globalisation (Bloomaert 2012), the assumption in Malaysia that only Western practices can be considered modern seems to be receding gradually as alternative or complementary practices from elsewhere, e.g., East Asia (Mandarin) and the Middle East (Arabic), are becoming highly relevant to Malaysian urbanism and is worth exploring in future studies.

[7] The extent to which the English forms can be associated with certain social identities requires further in-depth investigation.

PART 3

Intimacies

CHAPTER 6

"Respect Those Above, Yield to Those Below": Civility and Social Hierarchy in Vietnamese Interlocutor Reference*

Jack Sidnell

In Vietnamese, speakers make reference to themselves and their addressees using a wide range of forms (see Luong 1990; Pham 2002; Sidnell and Shohet 2013; Sidnell 2019). Pronouns, names and titles of various kinds are all quite common, but, in conversation at least, kin terms constitute the default, unmarked means for accomplishing interlocutor reference. Particularly important, especially among same-generation peers, is the use of sibling terms: *anh* (elder brother) (EB), *chị* (elder sister) (ES) and *em* (younger sibling) (YS) (on the extended use of sibling terms, see Haas 1969). As these examples suggest, in Vietnamese, all kin terms indicate a difference of either age or generation—there are no reciprocally usable terms equivalent to English *brother* or *sister*—and thus extended use of these terms, in reference to persons who are not genealogical relatives, inevitably invokes an age and/or generation-graded hierarchical system modelled after the family unit. In this model of social organisation, persons are tied to one another, as they are in a family, by relations of mutual entitlement and obligation. On the one hand, a senior party is entitled to deferential displays of respect from the junior. On the other, the junior can expect a certain degree of care and consideration from the senior. This ethics of intimate interpersonal hierarchy is captured by the oft-cited expression, *kính trên, nhường dưới* (respect those above, yield to those below).[1]

In what follows, I consider a single conversation among four persons—two couples—wherein the use of sibling terms performatively constitutes the social relations between the participants on the analogy of an hierarchically organised family unit with seniors taking precedence over juniors while at the same time "yielding" to them where appropriate.[2] Precedence in this context is realised in an entitlement to speak, to direct the course of the conversation, and to explicitly evaluate the contributions of others as well as in the overt displays of attention and concern that those others direct towards a senior co-participant.[3] Following Goffman, we could say then that the precedence of seniors is displayed both in their own demeanour and in the deference that others pay to them (Goffman 1956). "Yielding" is most apparent in the way seniors accept, with good humour, teasing by those that are junior.

While this organisation into senior and junior, performed through the use of sibling terms, constitutes the default, baseline social arrangement, the participants in this conversation also, at times, report upon or collaboratively imagine quite other possibilities—social relational models that stand in stark contrast with the intimate hierarchy of the family unit. In these other contexts, whether reported or imagined, persons refer to one another using occupational titles, names and pronouns that cast social organization not in terms of mutual ties of entitlement and obligation but rather in terms of top-down relations of power and authority. In comparing these alternatives, my larger point is that social hierarchy is not a brute fact. Rather, any social arrangement, hierarchical or otherwise, is a reflexive semiotic model of conduct composed of both object signs through which it is performed and metasigns through which the significance of such object signs is construed (see Agha 2007, 2015). The more local and ethnographic goal is to situate the practices of interlocutor reference that these persons actually employ in relation to the alternatives that they report upon and collaboratively imagine. Specifically, I aim to show that these semiotic models, implicitly articulated within the warp and weft of interaction, themselves serve as signs by which the participants reassure themselves of their own civility (*văn minh*) and urban sophistication in relation to imagined, barbarous (*dã man*) others.[4]

Sibling Terms in Interlocutor Reference

Among same generation peers, with one or two exceptions to be discussed momentarily, sibling terms constitute the unmarked, default means of accomplishing interlocutor reference. As noted, these terms differ from English "brother" and "sister" in so far as they indicate relative age and thus are not used reciprocally (see figure 1).[5]

Civility and Social Hierarchy in Vietnamese Interlocutor Reference 113

Figure 1. Kin-terms used in reference to persons not genealogically related to speaker

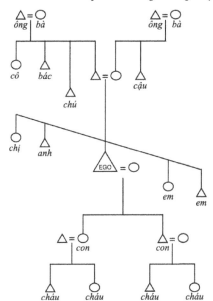

In the conversation I am concerned with here, there were 289 distinct references to the co-participants. This number includes references to the co-participants which cast them as third parties to the exchange, for example, as neither speaker nor addressee. Excluding these and considering for the moment only instances of true interlocutor reference, sibling terms accounted for 75 per cent or all cases, 72 per cent of references to speaker and 80 per cent of references to the addressee.

Figure 2. Participants in VNR 05

When used for interlocutor reference, sibling terms are calibrated to the relative ages of the participants. In the conversation I will be discussing the participants are ordered, from youngest to oldest, as follows: Linh (female), Phuong (female), Hung (male), Thanh (male). So, in speaking with Linh, Phuong is *chị* (elder sister) in both address and in self-reference, but when she addresses Thanh or Hung she becomes *em* (younger sibling). We can see this in the following segment. Here Phuong first self-refers using *chị*, thereby showing that she is addressing Linh. A few seconds later, she self-refers as *em*, thereby showing that she is addressing the group as a whole and, as a matter of decorum, orienting to its oldest member.

(1) VNR 05

57 PHUONG: *Chị ngày cấp ba mơ ước mãi cận*
ES date level three dream forever close
When I was in level three, I dreamed of being nearsighted,

58 *để đeo kính. Tối nằm cứ dí-i-i mắt này đọc truyện này*
to wear glasses. Night lie just stare eye this read story this
so that I could wear glasses. At night, I'd lie there reading a story like this.
((holding a book to demonstrate close reading))

59 THANH: *Nhục*
INTJ
Shame.

60 PHUONG: *Thế mà nó không cận*
yet COMP 3 NEG close
Yet I did not develop near-sightedness.

61 HUNG: *Để đeo* [*kính*
to wear glasses
So that you could wear glasses?

62 PHUONG: [*Đau thật*
pain real
Real pain

Civility and Social Hierarchy in Vietnamese Interlocutor Reference   115

63   PHUONG: *Lớp của em hai mươi lăm đứa thì*
              class of YS twenty-five kids
              My class had twenty-five kids

64   *có khoảng hai mươi hai đứa cận*
              have about twenty-two kids close
              about twenty-two of whom were nearsighted.

65   *Em là một trong ba đứa không cận*
              YS was one in three kids not close
              I was one of three who was not nearsighted.

Figure 3. Video stills for section of transcript (1)

Chị ngày cấp ba   *đọc truyện này*   *Lớp của em*

As can be seen from the video-stills in figure 3, when she begins the talk given as line 57 of the transcript, Phuong turns to gaze directly at Linh and self-refers using *chị* (elder sister). Then, as she begins the re-enactment of reading at night (line 58) she redirects her gaze towards the booklet she is holding. And, after both Thanh (line 59) and Hung (line 61) respond to her story, Phuong shifts her gaze again and, now addressing the group as a whole, self-refers with *em* (younger sibling). The example illustrates an important collateral effect of using kin terms in interlocutor reference. Specifically, it is often the case that the addressee is identified by the term selected for speaker self-reference.

In a case such as this then, sibling terms cast the relation between each co-participant dyad in terms of relative seniority. While stratified and asymmetrical, these relations are defined as much in terms of what senior owes junior as junior owes senior. As noted, this bi-directional, asymmetrical relation, and the interactional ethics it implies, is captioned by the oft-cited expression *kính trên, nhường dưới* (respect those above, yield to those below) which is routinely invoked both to account for one's own conduct and to understand that of others.

Participants in interaction orient to the first dimension, *kính trên* (respect those above) in a range of ways. In the conversation between Linh, Phuong, Hung and Thanh this orientation is most apparent in a certain solicitousness that Phuong and Hung direct towards Thanh. Consider for instance the following case which begins with Thanh complaining that the staff at the café have not turned on any music. Hung, seeking a remedy to the problem identified by Thanh's complaint, first registers the problem before asking Thanh whether he wants to watch the TV.

(2) VNR 05

411 THANH: *Bọn này nó không mở thêm tí nhạc nữa nhỉ*
Group PROX 3 NEG open more music more PRT
These people don't switch on the music

412 HUNG: *Không có nhạc. Anh có xem ti vi không*
NEG have music. EB Q watch TV Q
They don't have music. You want to watch TV?

413 THANH: *Hử*
Q
What

414 HUNG: *Em mở cho anh xem*
YS open give EB watch
You want me to turn it on so you can watch?

415 THANH: *Đấy*
PROX
yeah

Notice that after Thanh initiates repair (in line 413), Hung modifies what he has said (in line 412) in such a way as to make explicit his own proposed action and thus to foreground the deferential display implicit in such an offer (in line 414).

The second dimension, *nhường dưới* (yield to those below), is more difficult to see, at least in this context. In cases of conflict between children, a parent will often insist that the older sibling acquiesce to the demands of the younger.[6] In the conversation between Linh, Phuong, Hung and Thanh, yielding is visible in rather more subtle ways. Most notable is the way Thanh responds to Hung's teasing of him. Near the beginning of the recording, for instance, the participants are calling out their orders to the server and Thanh asks for a mango smoothie. Hung treats this selection as remarkable, repeating the order with a somewhat astonished intonation. Apparently hearing a challenge in Hung's talk, Thanh defends his choice saying *Thích thế đấy* (I like it), but Hung persists making the tease explicit with *Em nhìn anh cũng có tuổi rồi* (I see you are already quite old). Hung thus treats ordering a smoothie as a remarkable thing to do and then develops the tease by accounting for this with the explanation that Thanh is quite old and therefore concerned to order something "healthy". Hung, having so far failed to elicit any significant response from Thanh and the other co-participants, continues, saying *Nhìn anh ấy có tuổi rồi* (See he is already quite old). This time however, Thanh interrupts, exclaiming *Ừ nhể! Bọn này!* (Oh please! These guys!) and then calls to the server with *Em ơi* (Hey you). Hung, though, seizes on the opportunity provided by Thanh's hanging vocative construction, completing his order with *Chọn cho anh cái quả ương ương ấy nhá. Đừng chín quá* (Choose for me fruits that are a bit young. Not too ripe.) The implication is clear and this appropriation of Thanh's voice by Hung elicits collective laughter from the group.[7] The tease then works by exaggerating the difference in age between Thanh and the other co-participants, treating that which, in fact, provides a basis for respect and deference as something undesirable or unfortunate. The key point for present purposes is that Thanh himself eventually appreciates the joke, laughing along with the other co-participants in response to Hung's appropriation of his voice.

When used in interlocutor reference then these sibling terms—*anh, chị, em*—unavoidably index differences of age and concomitant relations of seniority. Modelling the larger social universe after the intimate relations between family members, sibling terms help to constitute a particular kind of hierarchical arrangement in which a generally respectful stance towards seniors combines with a somewhat permissive attitude toward juniors. This hierarchy is completely transparent—everyone knows their place within it—yet it is also mostly gentle and forgiving.

Some Minor Variations

As noted, the vast majority of interlocutor references in this conversation are accomplished using sibling terms. Before exploring this usage further, consider two exceptions to the general rule. Numerically, the most important of these involves the use of *mình* in self-reference. *Mình* is derived from a word meaning "body" and is used also in certain reflexive contexts. A full account of its use as a term of self-reference would take us too far afield but a few remarks are in order. First, note that although it can be used in singular reference to speaker, it can also be used in collective self-reference ("we", "one" and so on) and in reference to the addressee. Indeed, a familiar expression, *mình ơi*, in which the word appears appended by the vocative particle *ơi*, is a term of endearment appropriate in addressing a husband, wife or lover.[8] Secondly, it is associated with personal, subjective experience and a speaker prototypically uses *mình* to talk about their own feelings. In this sense it is similar to Javanese Ngoko which Errington (1998, 38), citing Siegel (1986), suggests, "is the medium of internal thought and feeling, the most immediate or 'natural' means for exteriorizing or ex-pressing subjective, occasional states. All *bậsậ* styles, on the other hand, [...] serve generically to mark and presuppose a speaker's stance of polite awareness, *qua* speaker, to some interactional other as addressee."

In these ways, *mình* differs from *tôi*—a true pronoun which is, unlike *mình*, specified for number and person (see Marr 2000; Tran 2017). In a conversation such as the one considered here, *mình*, while allowing for indepedent self-reference, does not convey distance the way that *tôi* would. At the same time, *mình* offers a solution to the problem of self-reference when talking to a group of people consisting of some who are older and some who are younger than the speaker. The fragment given as (3) provides an illustration. Earlier Hung had shared his sandwich with Thanh and here he jokes that if he had known he would end up sharing it he would have asked the person making the sandwich to spread the meat out evenly across its surface. Instead, all the meat was on the side of the sandwich that ended up going to Thanh. Hung is ostensibly talking to Phuong, but he clearly means for Thanh to overhear. Such complexities of address as well as the fact that he is talking about his own subjective experience make *mình* an ideal term of self-reference (SF) here (lines 478, 479, 480).

(3) VNR 05

471 HUNG: *Anh ăn bánh mì rồi thấy.*
 EB eat bread already PRT.
 You already ate a sandwich!

472 *Đoạn nhiều thịt nhất em phần rồi*
 Section many meat most YS share already
 I gave you the part with the most meat.

473 THANH: *Nhưng mà ít quá*
 But little bit too much
 But that's too small.

474 PHUONG: *Tí chia tiền nhá. Chia tiền nhá.*
 Distribute share money PRT. Distribute money PRT.
 Perhaps you should pay the money. Give the money.

475 *Chỗ của anh mười nghìn.*
 Place of EB ten thousand.
 Your share is ten-thousand.

476		*Hai chỗ bọn em năm nghìn.* Two place group YS five thousand. Our two pieces were five thousand each.
477		*Hai mươi nghìn một cái đấy* Two ten thousand, one CL there. Twenty thousand for the whole thing there.
478	HUNG:	*Cái thằng ôn vật ấy. Mình lại không chú ý* CL guy scamp there. SF again NEG attention That bastard! I wasn't paying attention!
479		*Mình không nghĩ ra trường hợp đến đây phải campuchia*[9] SF NEG think of situation come here must share, I didn't realise that we would share
480		*đâm-ra mình không bảo nó rải đều ra cái* turn SF NEG tell 3 spread even out CL I would have told him to spread it out evenly.
481		*Nó lại rải chỗ thịt chỗ rau riêng* 3 spread place meat place vegetables separately. Instead he put meat on one side and vegetable on the other
482	PHUONG:	*Thế anh không được miếng thịt nào à* So EB NEG get piece meat any PRT So, you didn't get any of the meat?
483	HUNG:	*Nói rồi. Không có thịt thì anh* Say already. NEG have meat that EB Exactly. No meat for me!

The other important exception to the general use of sibling terms is seen in the distinctive way that senior Thanh addresses junior Hung. This he does by adapting a practice of referential perspective shift particularly frequent in interaction between parents and their children (see Luong 1984, 1990; Luong and Sidnell 2020). For example, if a father is talking to his son Khánh about Khánh's younger brother Nghé who is also present, he may address Khánh either as *con* (child) (that is, his own perspective) or as *anh* (older brother) (that is, Khánh's perspective in relation to his younger brother). Such usages involve a deictic recentring in which the utterance *origo* is transposed from the speaker to another, typically, co-present party.

In addressing Hung, Thanh adopts the perspective of his own, nonexistent child, referring to Hung as *chú* which, when used among kin, refers to the father's younger brother (FYB) (see figure 1 above and compare *bác* [father's older brother]).[10] Here, then, *chú* refers to a male addressee who is younger than, and junior to, the speaker (that is, not someone in the parent's generation). Used in this way, *chú*, like *em*, pragmatically presupposes the speaker's status as older than, and senior to, the addressee while at the same time, unlike *em*, conveys that both are of sufficient age to have children of their own. Such a shift in referential perspective thus recasts the *dyadic* relation between speaker and addressee as a triadic, intergenerational relation between two adult men and the speaker's child.[11]

Thanh uses *chú* to refer to Hung throughout this conversation. In (4) for instance, Thanh has been telling a story about how he had posted a picture to Facebook of his wife (Linh) holding a small child in order to trick people into thinking that he had recently become a father. Here, in the aftermath of the telling, Hung suggests that only people who didn't know the couple well would have been taken in (line 167) and then (at line 169) that he himself did not believe it.

(5)   VNR 05

166   HUNG: *Nhưng mà anh nói thế là*
              But EB say that COMP
              But wouldn't you say that

167   *chỉ cái bọn không biết nó mới tin đúng không*
              only CL group NEG know 3 just believe correct NEG
              only those who don't know anything would believe that right?

168   THANH: *Ừ*
              INTJ
              Yes

169   HUNG: *Em thì làm sao em tin được*
              YS do why YS believe get
              As for me, how could I believe that?

170 PHUONG: *Sao không tin*
Why NEG believe
Why wouldn't you believe it?

171 THANH: *Tin quá đi. Gớm. Chú mà không tin*
Believe too much PRT. Incredible. FYB PRT NEG believe
You totally believed it! Incredible! You believed it completely!

172 HUNG: *Tin làm sao được*
Believe do why get
How could I believe it?

173 PHUONG: *Làm sao*
Do why
Why not?

174 THANH: *Chú là ngày xưa chú tin quá đi*
FYB day old FYB believe too much PRT
In the past, you always believed everything

175 *nên chú mới cưới con Phuong sớm thế*
so FYB just marry CL Phuong early PRT
that's why you married Phuong just like that so quickly!

176 *Con này nó nói, nó vừa nói phát là phải cưới ngay*
CL this 3 say, 3 just say emit COMP must marry immediate
This girl just said one thing, just said it and (you) married her immediately!

When Hung claims not to have been taken in by the ruse, both Phuong and Thanh are skeptical, and Thanh challenges Hung in an especially strong way, suggesting, at line 171, that he was completely duped. When Hung continues to deny this, Thanh suggests that Hung is generally gullible. At lines 174–5, Thanh provides evidence for this by proposing that this is why Hung married Phuong "so quickly". She only had to say one thing—that is, that she was pregnant—and Hung married her immediately.

When used to address a younger man, *chú* differs from *em* most importantly in invoking the overriding importance of *intergenerational hierarchy*, a theme which receives extensive elaboration in the reported scenes of interaction to which I now turn.[12]

Alternative Arrangements: Reported and Imagined

The use of sibling terms then casts social relations as asymmetrical but nevertheless bi-directional bonds characterisable by metapragmatic expressions such as *kính* (respect) and *nhường* (yielding). This contrasts markedly with other possibilities which these participants both report upon and imagine, and which are constituted in and through quite different practices of interlocutor reference. Consider, for instance, the following story, told by Thanh, about a time that he went out drinking with some classmates.

(6) VNR 05

222 THANH: *Hôm vừa rồi, cái đám bạn cùng lớp của anh ấy, đi nhậu*
day recent CL group friends class of EB PRT, go drink
The other day some classmates of mine went out drinking

223 *Thế là có ba. Ngồi đấy là bốn thằng với thêm anh nữa là năm*
so is have three. Sit there is four guy with add EB more is five
So there were three guys. Sitting there, a fourth guy, and myself makes five

224 *Anh chưa có vợ thì chả nói gì*
EB yet have wife not at all say what
I wasn't yet married, I didn't say anything.

225 *Mà bốn thằng kia, ba thằng*
but four guys there, three guys
But these four guys, three of them

226 *nâng li nó cạch với nhau cái*
raise glass 3 clink with each other
raised their glass to cheers

227 *Thế xong cái thằng kia đòi nâng li cạch*
so after CL guy there ask lift glass clink
So then this guy asked to toast with them,

228 *Bọn nó bảo rằng không, mày chưa. Mày là ngồi chiếu dưới*
group 3 say that NEG, 2S yet. 2S sit mat below
they said no, you are not yet (one of us). You go sit below.

229   *Chưa đủ- Chưa có đủ tuổi, chưa được cụng*[13]
            yet sufficient- Yet have sufficient age, yet get knock/hit
            You are not yet- you are not old enough to toast with us.

230   *Các anh đây mới được cụng*
            PL EB here just get to toast
            Only we older brothers get to join in the toast

231 PHUONG: *Thế là lúc đấy chưa lấy vợ à*
            so COP time that yet take wife PRT
            Because, at that time, he did yet have a wife?

232 THANH: *Không phải, thằng đấy nó chưa có, chưa có*
            not have, guy this 3 yet have, yet have
            No, this guy didn't yet have, didn't yet have-

233 GIANG: *Chưa có con trai=*
            yet have child boy
            Not yet have a son!

234 THANH: *=chưa có con trai. Thằng đấy là đứa đầu tiên là gái*
            yet have child boy. Guy this COMP child first COP girl
            Didn't yet have a son. This guy, his first child was a girl.

235   *Ba thằng kia đầu là trai hết rồi*
            three guy there first COMP boy finished already
            Three of the guys there, they already had sons

236   *Bắt đầu cạch với nhau còn mày thì chưa đủ tuổi*
            start toasting with each other still 2S yet sufficient age
            Start toasting with one another, saying, you are not old enough

237   *Mẹ. Kích nhau kiểu đấy mới bực*
            EXP. Attack each other way that just angry
            Shit! Just attacking each other that way someone is sure to get upset!

Here Thanh reports on an occasion when he along with four other young men were having drinks. At this time, notes Thanh, he was not yet married and, as a consequence, "said nothing". The key piece for present purposes begins at lines 225–7 in which Thanh says that after three of the men raised their glasses to toast one another, a fourth asked if he could join in. The others responded by denying this request and further by suggesting that he should go sit below at another mat, implying that he would have to sit with the women and children. In Thanh's story, then, the men are engaged in an activity in which each participant's contribution is identical to that of the others. The activity of toasting is, in other words, a diagrammatic icon of egalitarian solidarity. In this context, one of the men is singled out and excluded from the activity and directed to sit at a lower mat. The public humiliation and demotion involve a complex configuration of linguistic and other signs. With respect to the former, Thanh employs direct report, animating the voices of the men, in this way preserving in the report the original forms of interlocutor reference that they purportedly used. Notice that the participants in this represented scene refer to the excluded man not with a kin term but rather with the second-person, non-honorific singular pronoun *mày* in a way which not only denies any bond of kinship between speaker and addressee but also, in this context, conveys a clear lack of respect and/or consideration.[14]

As already noted, in the Vietnamese kinship system seniority by generation overrides seniority by age and here, despite Thanh's initial formulation, the man is excluded not because he is too young but because he does not yet have a son. Fully adult male status is, in this way, equated with having fathered a son and in this case is expressed most explicitly in the suggestion that the excluded man must go sit at a "lower" mat, which is to say, sit with the women and children.[15] The male-focused form of social hierarchy implicated here is strict and decidedly "unyielding", no allowances are made, and the junior person is ridiculed and publicly demoted (see Luong's 1984 discussion of what he describes as the "male-oriented model for kinship relations" in Vietnam).[16]

The story provides some evidence of the various ways in which the participants in this conversation think about social hierarchy. And, in response to Thanh's story, Phuong tells one of her own in which a group of her friends make exactly the same discrimination, excluding one of the men from the communal activity of drinking because he has only a daughter and no son. What is particularly remarkable in Phuong's story is that this status criterion overrides the importance of relative age. The excluded man in this case is actually older than those who exclude him and is addressed as *anh* (older brother).

(7) VNR 05

257 PHUONG: *Họp lớp lớp em chả thế*
meet class class YS not at all that way
It's the same when my classmates get together[17]

258		*Thằng Sơn xoè để con gái ấy* CL Sơn spread birth child girl PRT This guy Sơn had a daughter
259		*Xong thằng Quý cứ thôi anh Sơn ơi, anh Sơn ơi* so CL Quý just only EB Sơn VOC, EB Sơn VOC So Quý goes, "Hey elder brother Sơn, elder brother Sơn,
260		*anh dịch ra kia để bọn em nói chuyện* EB move out there, let group YS talk Elder brother move out of there, let younger siblings talk,
261		*bọn em uống rượu với nhau tí.* group YS drink wine with together a little bit we are drinking together."
262	GIANG:	*D(h)ã ma(hh)n* barbaric Barbaric
263	PHUONG:	*Ừ, mà nó khích kinh lắm,* yes, PRT 3 provoke so much, Yes, just being so provocative
264		*[khích từ đầu đến cuối ấy* provoke from beginning to end PRT Yes, just being provocative the whole time
265	GIANG:	*[khích thế:: em mới bảo là::* provoke that YS just say COP That's why I said, it is
266		*khích cái kiểu ấy thì* provoke CL type PRT PRT it's provocative
267	PHUONG:	*Ừ, thế xong thằng Sơn nó cười xong nó bảo cái gì là thôi* yes, that done CL. Sơn 3 smile done 3 say CL Q COP only That's it! He was smiling, and said something,

268   *anh Sơn ơi*
                    EB Sơn VOC
                    hey older brother Sơn

269   GIANG: *Dã man*
                    barbaric
                    Barbaric

270   PHUONG: *Tí anh cứ ngồi một mình một mâm thoải mái thôi*
                    PRT EB just sit one person a tray comfortable only
                    He just had to sit alone with his tray like that.

In Phuong's story, the status derived from having a son (and by this, belonging to the "parent" generation) overrides the status derived from age-based seniority. In that sense, the model of social relations invoked here stands opposed to that captioned by the expression *kính trên, nhường dưới* and emblematised by the reciprocal use of sibling terms. I want to take special notice of the way Linh responds, in line 262, with the interjection *dã man*. I will return to consider this in more detail in the conclusion. For now, it is enough to note that the expression can be glossed as "barbaric" or "savage" and is used here to negatively evaluate the conduct being reported, that is, insisting that an older, same-generation male peer must, because he does not yet have a son, go and sit at a lower mat, in this way, excluding him from the exclusive community of equals engaged in the ritualised activity of communal drinking.

In some ways, even more striking is the following case in which the participants imagine an alternate possible world in which Hung is Thanh's "driver". This begins with Phuong wishing, somewhat dreamily, that Thanh (and Linh) would buy a car and give her and Hung a ride in it. Clearly, this keys to class aspirations, routinely expressed, in Vietnam as elsewhere, in ideas about mobility, free movement and the luxury of travel (see Tran 2018; Truitt 2008). Hung then develops this bit of fantasy by suggesting that if Thanh were to buy a car he would learn how to drive and would sometimes serve as Thanh's chauffeur (using the verb *chở* which conveys the meaning of "transport" or "carry"). What Hung says here clearly implies an occupational hierarchy—of a boss and his driver—and Phuong elaborates this in the subsequent talk by saying that Thanh should feel free to *quát nạt* (shout at) Hung even in a public place (line 373). Thanh contributes to this jointly imagined scenario, asking Phuong if he should speak to Hung, *Cứ như kiểu lính* (Just like he was a soldier).

(8) VNR 05

368 PHUONG: *Mua ô tô đi. Nhà anh Thanh mua ô tô đi*
buy a car PRT. Family EB Thanh buy car PRT
Buy a car! Your family should buy a car,

369 *thỉnh thoảng cho bọn em ngồi cuốc*
sometimes give group YS sit ride
Sometimes you can give us a ride.

370 HUNG: *Anh mua đi, em đi học lái xe*
EB buy PRT, YS go learn drive car
You buy it, I will learn to drive it.

371 *Thỉnh thoảng anh đi đâu em chở anh đi cũng được*
sometimes EB go where YS transport EB go also get
Sometimes when you go somewhere, I can drive you.

372 *Gọi em lên xong em chở đi*
call YS up ready YS transport PRT
You just call me up and I will drive you.

373 PHUONG: *Mà anh cứ quát nạt*
PRT EB just shout
You just shout at him.

374 *Đến chỗ đông người anh cứ quát nạt thoải mái*
come place crowded people EB just shout comfortable
Come into a public place and feel comfortable to shout at him

375 *Gọi dạ bảo vâng đàng hoàng*
call yes, say yes correctly
Call yes, say yes correctly

376 THANH: *Cứ như kiểu lính đúng không?*
just like way soldier Q?
Just like he was a soldier, right?

378 PHUONG: *Đúng.*
              correct
              Exactly.

Notice the contrast in the way Thanh's conduct is characterised in the descriptions of Hung at line 372 and of Phuong at line 373–4. In Hung's imagined scenario, Thanh "calls up" and Hung, the chauffeur, dutifully responds without hesitation. The relation so characterised is one of command and control but there is no sense of impropriety. Phuong, however, imagines a relation of verbal abuse that involves shouting at Hung in a public place, such that the relation, or its behavioural manifestation, is made a sign of itself.

With this stereotyped social relation established, the participants begin to enact it, imagining the way in which Thanh would speak to Hung. First Thanh, in lines 379–80, imagines ordering Hung to carry his briefcase and clean his shoes. Here, he uses Hung's name to address him (rather than *chú* [father's younger brother], see above) and self-refers using *anh*.

(9) VNR 05

379 THANH: *Hưng ra xách cho anh cái cặp*
               Hung go carry give EB CL suitcase
               Hung, go bring my suitcase!

380   *Hưng chùi chùi anh cái giày*
               Hung wipe wipe EB CL shoes
               Hung, clean my shoes

381 PHUONG: *Thôi, chùi giày thì*
               enough wipe shoe PRT
               Enough! clean shoes!

This elicits laughter from the co-participants and a further development from Phuong (line 381). Hung now introduces a modification to the imagined scenario—suggesting that he will have his own subordinates to whom he can delegate lowly tasks such as cleaning shoes. Phuong helps Hung elaborate this possibility, first by animating Thanh directing Hung to clean his shoes, and then, by animating Hung delegating this task to his henchmen. In the first of two imagined directives, Hung is addressed again by name. In the second, Phuong uses the second singular non-honorific pronoun *mày*. When Hung subsequently animates himself in line 387, there's no explicit reference to the addressee, only a reference to Thanh as *sếp anh* (elder brother's boss). Phuong however corrects this in next turn position, replacing *anh* with the first-person singular pronoun *tao*.

(10) VNR 05

382	HUNG:	*Đâu, chùi giầy thì em bảo đệ em*
		no wipe shoe comp YS tell subordinate YS
		No, I will tell my henchmen to clean the shows.
383		*Em còn có đệ nữa*
		YS will have subordinates also
		I will also have henchmen.
384	PHUONG:	*Bảo Hưng chùi anh cái giầy*
		say, Hung wipe EB CL shoe
		Say, "Hung clean my shoes!"
385		*Hưng lại bảo, ê, mày chùi cho anh cái giầy*
		Hung again say, hey, you wipe for EB CL shoe
		Then Hung will say, "Hey! You clean my shoes!"
386	LINH:	*Bọn đánh giầy thiếu quái gì*
		group rub shoe lack EXP what
		Shoe cleaners are everywhere!
387	HUNG:	*Chùi cho sếp anh chứ*
		Wipe for boss EB PRT
		"Clean the shoes for my boss, eh!"
388	PHUONG:	*Chùi cho sếp tao cái giầy.*
		Wipe for boss 1SG CL shoe
		"Clean the shoes for my boss, eh!"

In this imagined social arrangement then, hierarchical social relations are conveyed not by age-grading sibling terms, not by terms that index a kin-like relationship, but rather by titles such as *sếp* (boss) and by pronouns. In interaction, such pronominal forms are used in a very restricted range of contexts. Although considered appropriate among intimate friends who are close in age, most often they occur in asymmetrical relations such as between parents and children.[18] In asymmetrical relations *mày* can convey derogation and *tao*, arrogance (see table 1).[19]

Table 1. Personal pronoun levels according to Thompson (1988)

	FIRST (Speaker)	SECOND (Hearer)	THIRD (Referent)	GENERAL
RESPECTFUL	tôi			
SUPERIOR	ta			
FAMILIAR				mình
ABRUPT	tao	mày bay (pl)	nó	

Non-reciprocal use of these forms thus represents social relations in terms of a simple, top-down relation of power and authority, implied most obviously by the fact that one member of the dyad is entitled to use them while the other is not. In the imagined scenario, this is, of course, also reflected in and indexed by the very nature of the act itself, namely demanding that one party clean the other's shoes. This is further elaborated in the subsequent talk. Specifically, Thanh imagines holding out his feet and demanding that Hung remove his shoes. While he initially addresses Hung as *chú* (father's younger brother) (in line 399), at line 402 he animates himself saying *Ê, mấy thằng kia, đánh anh đôi giày* (Hey you there, clean my shoes), now referring to Hung with the pejorative term *thằng* which is a classifier for "boys" or "inferiors" but is also used, as it is here, as a derogatory, human-denoting noun (see Luong 1988 for a discussion of its use in colonial period newspapers).[20]

(11) VNR 05

399 THANH: *Mình bảo ờ, chú đi đánh anh cái giày cái*
SF say VOC, FYB go clean EB CL shoe CL
I will say "hey, you go clean my shoes"

400 *Thế là mình giơ-giơ chân ra*
so COMP SF present-present feet out
And then I hold out, hold my feet out

401 *Thế là Hưng cúi xuống gỡ giày*
so Hung bend descend remove shoe
So Hung can bend down and take off my shoes.

402 *Ê, mấy thằng kia, đánh anh đôi giày đúng không*
hey few guy there, clean EB CL shoes correct Q
"Hey, you there, clean my shoes!" Right?

Civility and Social Hierarchy in Vietnamese Interlocutor Reference

403 HUNG: *Sếp- Đến bố của sếp mà bảo sếp là*
boss- To father of boss but tell boss COMP
Boss- Even if your father told you to

404 HUNG: *đánh cho bố cái giầy thì*
clean give father CL shoe PRT
clean his shoes for him,

405 *sếp cũ(hh)ng bắ(hh)t bố phải cởi ra chứ*
boss also insist father must take off PRT
you will also ask him to take off his shoes, right?

406 *Để con cắm xuống mà cởi thì thôi nghỉ bố nhá*
let child plunge descend but take off only rest father PRT
If he lets you kneel down to take it off for him, you'd never do that.

407 *Bố cứ để bẩn thế mà đi*
father just let dirty PRT PRT PRT
Just keep the dirty shoes to yourself

408 G, T, P: ((Laughter))

409 PHUONG: *Tóm lại là nói cũng phải vừa phải*
briefly speaking, also must be fair
Generally, it must be fair.

410 *Nước mắm cũng không thể hâm cả tiếng được*
fish sauce also cannot boil whole hour PRT
Fish sauce cannot be boiled for a whole hour

408 HUNG: *Nó ở mức độ cho phép thôi chứ*
3 LOC level permitted only PRT
It should be an acceptable level

409 PHUONG: *Mức độ cho phép thôi*
level permitted only
Acceptable level only

Interestingly, here the co-participants feel that a line has been crossed in the imagined scenario. A first inkling of this is evident in the way Thanh, after performing the boss's command, reorients towards Hung, adds the tag *đúng không* (right?) and taps him gently and perhaps playfully with his foot (figure 4).

Figure 4. Video stills for line 403 of transcript (10)

Ê, mấy thằng kia,   *đánh anh đôi giày*   *đúng không*

A number of distinct semiotic modalities, distributed across two event frames, are at play here. On the one hand, as can be seen in the first still, as Thanh begins to enact the imagined scene in which he, as the boss, calls to Hung, he looks forward across the table, away from the co-participants, raising his hand as if to beckon the addressee. Here he enacts the summons portion of the represented talk, but he then reorients so as to gaze at Linh and Phuong as he delivers the final portion as mere direct report. And, finally, as he produces the final tag question, he reorients again, now toward Hung, tapping him softly with his bare foot. The body is thus mobilised as a semiotic modality in both the represented speech and in an effort to engage Hung and elicit a response from him. Notice that the foot figures both in the imagined scene, as the potentially defiling object with which the employee is expected to have contact, and in the co-present relations of attention and involvement, serving as a participant deictic that selects Hung from among the co-participants as the addressee of the tag question. There is then a resonance between these two frames such that by using his foot to select Hung as the addressee, Thanh momentarily seems to bring the actual and the imagined worlds momentarily into alignment so that they interanimate one another.

To this jocular teasing, Hung responds with a remarkably complex thought-experiment, suggesting that even if the father of the boss (that is, Thanh's father) were to request that the boss clean his shoes, he would first remove them. One extreme form of hierarchy is that which exists between a father and son, but even here, according to Hung there are limits that must be respected.[21] Phuong aligns with this remarking, *Nước mắm cũng không thể hâm cả tiếng được* (Fish sauce also cannot be boiled for a whole hour). Thus, the co-participants seem to agree that demanding that another remove one's shoes is beyond the pale and that even in the most extreme forms of hierarchy such as exist between a father and a son, or an employee and a boss, such a demand violates basic expectations. What is at stake here is a sense of essential human dignity, one that ultimately challenges and stands in opposition to a Confucian conception of strict and inviolable hierarchy between sovereign and subject (or boss and employee) and between father and son.

These alternative social imaginaries thus provide a striking contrast with the intimate, bi-directional forms of hierarchy indexed by the use of sibling terms and by which these participants performatively constitute their relations to one another in the here and now context of an afternoon chat at a local café. However, even these extreme forms of asymmetry, at least as they are imagined by the co-participants, have their limits. In jointly telling the story of a boss and a driver, Thanh, Hung, Phuong and Linh stumble upon, and so reveal the contours of, a kind of baseline interactional ethics, which prominently includes an expectation that the more powerful member of a dyad will not abuse their power by demanding that the other commit acts that are necessarily self-polluting. Removing another's shoes serves as a synecdoche for acts which are denigrating and deny the dignity of a subordinate.

Conclusion

These alternative social arrangements stand in marked contrast to the familiar and intimate hierarchy constituted in and through the use of sibling terms and the participants implicitly hold them up as a counterpoint to the relations which they themselves enact in the course of their talking together. Moreover, they not only describe these alternate social forms, they also evaluate them. For instance, in the story about toasting (6), Thanh displays throughout his telling that he does not endorse the behaviour he describes and at the conclusion of the story he remarks, *Mẹ. Kích nhau kiểu đấy mới bực* (Shit! Attacking one another that way, someone is sure to get upset).

Even more revealing, I think, is Linh's response with *dã man* to the story that Phuong tells about Sơn being demoted to a lower level because he does not have a son, despite the fact that he is the oldest member of the group. Now, the word *dã* means "wild, savage, rustic" and one finds it in such collocations as *dã quỳ* (wild sunflower) or *chim hoang dã* (wild song bird). The specific expression Linh uses, *dã man*, is often glossed as "savage" or "barbarous" and is routinely paired with the term *văn minh* (civilised, civility) as its semantically opposed antonym. For instance, in the 1904 "A Civilization of New Learning", the Tonkin Free School collective proposed a new approach to education that would allow Vietnamese to compete more effectively in the modern world (see Dutton et al. 2012, 369). The authors concluded their influential discussion with the following:

> Alas, we are asleep while the rest of the world is fully awake, and we are stationary while others have crossed the river. Accordingly, how can we

gain access to the next level of civilization (*văn minh*)? (...) What in the past was a civilized society is now only a half-civilized one. What previously was a partly civilized society is now a barbaric (*dã man*) one.[22]

While *dã man* often occurs, in contemporary Vietnamese conversation, as a generalised and semantically bleached intensifier (similar, perhaps, to English "wicked", for example, *ngon dã man* [incredibly delicious]), Linh's use in this context indexes the still very much current meaning of "barbaric" and "uncivilised" in at least two ways. First, as Linh uses it, *dã man* has a clearly negative valence and expresses her own condemnation of that which Phuong has described. Second, in this context, *dã man* applies to conduct in interaction and to social relations, that is, to matters appropriately evaluated in terms of civility or a lack thereof.

The highly elaborated notion of *văn minh* (civility) has been a focus of much historical and anthropological work on Vietnam. For instance, in his ethnography of a Saigon urban development project, Erik Harms suggests that the idea of civility provides "a way of imagining possibilities for new forms of social interaction" (2016, 60). And that, the concept is deployed "as a means to comment on the actions of others, and to express (...) hopes and aspirations for the way" persons might "act in relationship to each other" (2016, 63). He goes on:

> despite its often unsavory pretensions to elitism, the language of civility sometimes affords a way to speak critically about moral relationships, to make demands about social rights and responsibilities, and to engage in a critical discourse that in other political systems might be understood as a political discourse of citizenship. (2016, 63, see also 2011, 193–220)

This sense of contrast between the modern civility of urban life and the barbarous traditions of a rural or in some other way unsophisticated alternative, is not only implicit in the conduct of these participants but also in the comments of many others with whom I have talked about these scenes. That is to say, there is a widespread sense that sophisticated people living in cities do not attach importance to the fact of having a son, that they would not exclude someone from a communal activity because he had no son, and that they do not aim to publicly humiliate others. Whether true or not, this then is suggestive of the fact that these stories serve as moral exemplars and as a means to define, by way of contrast, the attitudes of the present co-participants. In telling these stories, and in converging in their evaluation of the events recounted in them, the co-participants assure themselves of who they are and how they are related to one another—they justify their own gentle forms of hierarchy over and against the backward, barbaric forms depicted in the stories they tell (see Gal and Irvine 2019; Hastings and Manning 2004, see also Sidnell 2021).

An influential line of thinking, most clearly articulated by Agha (e.g., 2007, 2015), suggests that any social arrangement is a reflexive semiotic model of conduct composed of both object signs through which it is performed and metasigns through which the significance of such object signs is construed. The materials discussed here well-illustrate: the object signs of interlocutor reference are subject to construal by both contextually proximate and more distal metasigns. At the same time, these materials encourage us to unpack what is involved in "construal". Specifically, construal by metasigns is not just the means by which object signs become intelligible. It is also, unavoidably, evaluative. This implies that the norms that govern interaction, including those that govern interlocutor reference, are never completely stable and can never be simply and unproblematically invoked. Rather, in invoking norms participants are necessarily endorsing, condemning or otherwise implicitly commenting on them. And, in so taking up any such stance, participants in interaction are simultaneously positioning themselves. In the case I have considered, participants convey their own "urban" civility by positioning themselves in relation to practices, customs and traditions that they characterise as rural, backward and even barbaric. In other words, the alternative that Linh, Phuong, Hung and Thanh both allude to in their evaluation of other possibilities and performatively constitute through their practices of interlocutor reference, is one in which persons are related to one another through a set of intimate, mutual and yet asymmetrical obligations.

Notes

* This essay owes a great deal to the comments and suggestions of the other workshop participants, especially Novi Djenar, Nick Enfield, Luke Fleming, David Gil and Zane Goebel. A subsequent version was presented to the Linguistic Anthropology Working Group at Berkeley. For comments, suggestions and intensely engaging discussion on that occasion I thank Laurie Graham, Bill Hanks, Randeep Singh Hothi, Kamala Russell, Eve Sweetser and Robyn Holly Taylor-Neu. I would also like to thank Asif Agha, Joseph Errington and Chip Zuckerman all of whom offered suggestions for improvement of an earlier written version. For help with transcription and analysis of the materials discussed here I thank An Thùy Trần, Hương Thị Thanh Vũ and Thanh Hà Nguyễn.

[1] Both *kính* and *nhường* are of Sinitic origin. *Kính* from Chinese 敬 meaning "respect, honour." *Nhường* from the exopassive of 攘 "to remove", meaning "to remove oneself", "to yield; to concede". The general sentiment seems largely compatible with Confucian ethics, though I don't know if there is a direct connection. For discussion see Gammeltoft (1999: 172–3) also Rydström (2003) who cites a passage from Trinh T. Minh-ha's film, *Surname Viet Given Name Nam* the script of which is collected in her (1992) *Framer Framed*. See also the important work of Merav Shohet especially her 2021 book, *Silence and Sacrifice: Family Stories of Care and the Limits of Love in Vietnam*.

[2] The participants in this conversation, close friends for many years, gathered at this cafe at the request of Linh. At the time the recording was made, all four had completed an undergraduate degree and Phuong had also completed a masters. Thanh was working as a journalist, Hung

as an engineer in a hospital while Phuong and Linh were studying as graduate students. Like many others, these people consider Hanoi their home although each of them also has family in the countryside and make periodic visits to their natal village to attend death anniversaries, weddings and other important events.

[3] These relations also manifest in patterns of other-initiated repair, see Sidnell et al. (2020).

[4] On the discourse of civilization in Vietnam see Marr (1981), Bradley (2004), Harms (2011, 2016). For discussion of similar notions across the Southeast Asian ecumene see especially Winichakul (2000) as well as Turton ed. (2000).

[5] One exception to this, discussed in Sidnell and Shohet (2013), involves the reciprocal use of *anh* (elder brother) in address and the pronoun *tôi* in self-reference.

[6] See Sidnell (2019) for an example and some discussion, see Shohet (2021) for a more expansive consideration.

[7] Note the use of *anh* rather than *anh ấy* thereby implying that this is self-reference and thus that Hung is speaking as Thanh. See Goffman (1974) on "sayfors" and Errington (1998) on "speech modelling".

[8] The expression is difficult to gloss but its use in translation may help to clarify its meaning. For instance, one film (*Avengers: Endgame*, 2019) used it to subtitle a situation in which a husband is trying to find his wife, calling out to her, "Babe?".

[9] Campuchia—word play, see *chia* 'split'

[10] It is important to note that, while Thanh refers to Hung as *chú*, Hung does not refer to Thanh as *bác* (father's elder brother) despite the fact that this is precisely what the referential perspective shift effected by Thanh's use of *chú* implies. Instead, Hung refers to Thanh as *anh* (elder brother) and to himself as *em* (younger sibling).

[11] While this conversation does not provide materials to fully ground the argument, there is some evidence that such shifts in referential perspective are a means to avoid positioning a younger male addressee as *em* (younger sibling), which can be heard as both slightly infantilising and, due to the use of the *anh-em* pair among romantic partners, subtly emasculating.

[12] In the Vietnamese kinship system, a male speaker will address the child of his father's elder brother (the speaker's "cousin") as *anh* (elder brother) or *chị* (elder sister) even if that person is younger than he is.

[13] *Cụng*, means collide, knock, hit used here to mean toast, cheers etc.

[14] In one respect this story further illustrates the intimate hierarchy that the use of sibling terms indexes. These men, after all, characterise themselves as brothers. But here we also see the darker side of this social arrangement which involves not only internal differentiation in terms of relative seniority but also the possibility of exclusion.

[15] In the emphasis on having a child and specifically on having a son, there's something distinctly Confucian about the social order being invoked.

[16] Although I do not thematize it here, to the extent Vietnamese interlocutor reference involves the use of kinship terms, gender ubiquitously implicated in such practices. There is also some evidence to suggest that pronouns are used differently by male and female speakers (see Pham 2002 and the introduction to this volume).

[17] *chả thế* 'isn't it'.

[18] See Zuckerman (this volume) for a discussion of the reciprocal use of comparable Lao terms. At one point earlier in the conversation, Hung reports himself talking to a friend at work saying, *tao mà như mày thì tao bỏ rồi* (If I were you, I would have left already) (roughly) using the pronouns in an intimate, symmetrical way.

[19] See Thompson (1988, 249): "The abrupt forms *tao* 'I', *chúng tao* 'we (exclusive)', *mày* (or *mầy*) 'you', *chúng mày* (*chung mầy*) 'you (pl.)', *bay* (or *bây*) or *chúng bay* (*chúng bây*) 'you (pl.)' express either a deep familiarity between the speaker and hearer or signal that the speaker considers the hearer grossly inferior."

[20] It is, perhaps, a little like referring to the addressee as "boy" in English.

[21] See the five cardinal relations of Confucianism: Sovereign and subject, father and son, elder brother and younger brother, husband and wife, friend to friend. Only the last of these is symmetrical.

[22] Translated by Jayne Werner and Luu Doan Huynh and collected in Dutton et al. (2012).

CHAPTER 7

"Friends Who Don't Throw Each Other Away": Friendship, Pronouns and Relations on the Edge in Luang Prabang, Laos*

Charles H.P. Zuckerman

> "As the Thai build their simple bamboo houses so that they can be readily modified and quickly dismantled, so too they build their groups."
> – Lucien M. Hanks (1972, 80)

The messaging program WhatsApp became important during the final months of my research in Luang Prabang, Laos. When I returned to the city after a break, the "group" or *kum1* of male friends (*siaw1*) with whom I was spending time had started a chat "group" (again, *kum1*) using it.[1] WhatsApp allowed us to effortlessly trade photos and messages. The *kum1*'s name in the app, *phùan1 bòo-thiim5 kan3* or "friends who don't throw each other away", referenced a then-popular Thai love song. The song's chorus howls, "we promised not to throw each other away!", a line that the bunch of us would often sing, drunk, late at night, and as loudly as possible.

But soon after I joined the WhatsApp group, one friend Dii sent a frustrated message. "Where did everyone go? If no one is going to chat, I am going to leave the group!" And he left. Another friend, Muu, then pasted an image of a poem—a "gift" he called it: "One good friend with worth is better than many friends who are jealous; one friend with compassion is better than many friends without heart." The group administrator responded with the English word *"destroy"*, and

Friendship, Pronouns and Relations on the Edge in Luang Prabang, Laos 139

then removed almost everyone. With that, the group—a digitally crystallised social structure, a consciously constructed communicative channel—disintegrated. I joked to Dii and Muu later that the "friends who don't throw each other away" had, in the end, thrown each other away, discarded one another into the digital heap. They laughed. It was funny because it was true.

Figure 1. The image Muu sent to the group

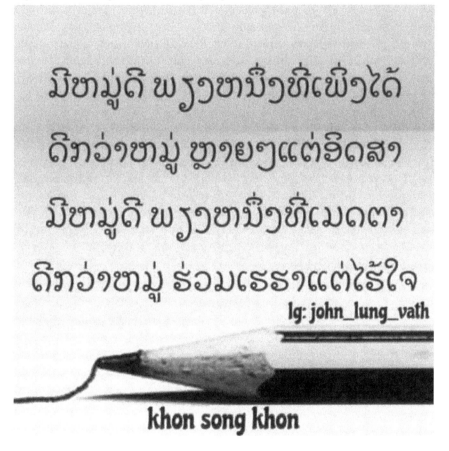

The men in "friends who don't throw each other away" called one another *siaw1* (close friends of the same in age) and understood themselves as equals. In Luang Prabang, *siaw1* friendships are set-off as fundamentally different from other relationships, which like relationships across Southeast Asia tend to have a hierarchical tilt, especially legible in language (Scupin 1988; Simpson 1997;

Howard 2007; Enfield 2007b, 117). In a sea of linguistically encoded hierarchy, *siaw1* stand as self-styled egalitarian islands.

In this chapter, I track the dissolution of "friends who don't throw each other away" to explore the "problem of peers" (Sidnell and Shohet 2013, 623) in otherwise hierarchical Laos. My argument draws a parallel between how *siaw1* relations are imagined and enacted, and ideologies surrounding the "bare" pronominal forms these men use to refer to one another and themselves. Borrowing from a classic anthropology of "loose structures", I show that both ideas about *siaw1* relations, generally, and the bare pronouns *siaw1* employ involve a mixture of aggression and solidarity. *Siaw1* alternately represent and enact their friendships as perduring, stable, and sturdy social knots, bound "to the death", and as delicate ties that might unexpectedly fray or snap. These ambivalent forces contradict one another, but they also work together to prove the resilience of friendships. In acting in ways that might otherwise be taken as offensive, *siaw1* make their friendships more meaningful (see, for comparison, Keane 1997 on "risk"; Stasch 2009, 206–7). The same analysis illuminates the pragmatics of the bare first- and second-person pronouns *kuu3* and *mùng2*. Many have described these (and similarly "low" pronouns cross-linguistically) as having two separate expressive forces—one intimate, the other aggressive. But in *siaw1* friendships, *kuu3* and *mùng2* serve to entangle intimacy with masculine aggression, such that "aggression" is not distinct from "solidarity" but, rather, a means for expressing it.

The Substance of *Siaw1*

"... there is no friend without time... that is, without that which
puts confidence to the test."
– Jacques Derrida (1997, 14 and 17), paraphrasing Aristotle

I joined the "friends who don't throw each other away" group of *siaw1* through Dii. We first met at a money gambling *pétanque* court, where he taught me about the French game similar to bocce. After several weeks of running into each other at the court, where we would compete and drink beer, he started inviting me to join his friends elsewhere. Being a man of roughly my age, Dii called me *siaw1*; his friends followed suit, and I began to tag along with them to drink beer, attend parties, and play games.

While *siaw1* are often talked about as relationships fostered since childhood, ritually cemented in a string-tying ceremony (see Enfield 2014, 138), they frequently develop quickly and casually like this: from fleeting encounters to more enduring, citable bonds. The majority of the eight or so *siaw1* in "friends who don't throw each other away", for example, had begun to spend time together recently; only a few had known each other for longer. While these men spoke generically about *siaw1* relations as if they hovered above the crassness of everyday life and, thus, outside of interaction, they always represented and forged their relations with one another in concrete interaction (Wortham 2006, 29)—during nights of competition, drinking, and acts of economic egalitarianism that mixed intimacy and hostility.

Much of what the group did involved masculine competition and concomitant social risk. Competitive games like soccer, *pétanque*, *katòò4* (a Lao form of rattan ball), draughts, cards, and snooker were the centrepiece of their activities. As they played, the men alternately emphasised both their fundamental equality of opportunity to win (Robbins 1994) and the inevitable inequality that games produced in separating winners from losers (Lévi-Strauss 1966, 32–3). These games made clear that the *siaw1* relation is both dyadic and a property of a friend group, defined by common age and status. Some pairs of friends are closer than others in the group, and some individuals are more central to the group than others.

The groupness of the group was made especially palpable during games of soccer played against other teams of *siaw1*, as the structural opposition gave the group a temporary internal cohesion and boundedness that the men sometimes stressed. But many of these games pitted them against one another, and caused tension and fractures within the group. To limit the ferocity of play and potential for hard feelings, they explicitly prohibited gambling for money (Zuckerman 2020). But they still always gambled for something, usually comestibles such as beer and grilled meats, and they treated the ban on money gambling not as a strict, Kantian rule but as a suggestive limit on competition, a mnemonic touchstone for the hope that things might be contentious yet remain within the boundaries of love and comradery.

In line with this hope, the *siaw1* also frequently poked and prodded one another—teasing each other about missing shots in games, personality quirks, or physical characteristics (see, for comparison, Zuckerman 2016). Mostly, these otherwise inoffensive jabs were taken in stride, and when someone did take issue with a quip or gag that crossed a line, the usual response was for the offender to frame what they had done explicitly with a simple "just joking" (*vaw4 jòòk5*; see, for comparison, Haugh 2016).

Drinking was also fundamental to the substance of "friends who don't throw each other away", and the men often drank as competitively as they played games and teased one another. Rivalry infused their revelry. They competed over who would pay and how much they drank. Toasting was prevalent. Instead of the common polite gestures, the friends often crashed their glasses together in aggressive "diagrammatic icon[s] of solidarity" (Sidnell, this volume). Sometimes the group would drink using a single rotating glass called a *còòk5 lòòp4*. The server would pass—often push—the *còòk5 lòòp4* to a reveller for him to down in a few gulps. In forcing everyone to drink the same quantity of beer, *còòk5 lòòp4* epitomised the competitive, egalitarianism of consumption among *siaw1*. While *siaw1* grumbled about this pressure at times, they were also quick to emphasise that pressuring people to eat, drink, and stay during sessions of partying were signs of "love" (*hak1 phèèng2 kan3*) and fun.

Competitive drinking, constant joking, and games are not limited to *siaw1* in Laos, but these activities are core to what it means, practically and in generic abstraction, to be a part of these groups. The "friends who don't throw each other away" tended to do these activities, furthermore, in ways that marked them as uniquely egalitarian and competitive parts of their lives. For instance, people in Luang Prabang generally talk about the substance of good relations as an accretion of iterated hosting or "feeding" activities (*liang4*; Van Esterik 1996, 33), where one person pays for the others. The "friends who don't throw each other away" sometimes engaged in "feeding" like this, but they stressed that they only ever did so in a reciprocal and generalised way, which balanced out over time (see, for comparison, Brown 2017). Mothers "feed" children (High 2011), older brothers "feed" younger brothers, bosses "feed" employees; the first of each pair is the *phuu5 ñaj1* or "big person" to the second, congealing qualities of greater age, esteem, merit and wealth which explode the egalitarian core of any *siaw1* relation. Thus, when they drank at bars, snooker halls or *pétanque* courts, as they mostly did, they rarely "fed" each other. Nor did they pay in the style associated with "foreigners", where one pays for whatever one ordered. Instead, they underlined their egalitarianism on the spot and split the bill evenly. This could be tricky as it sometimes yielded "leftover money" (*ngen2 lùa3*), which *siaw1* would either save for another day, ideally with the same participants, or insist on spending there and then on more beer, no matter how ready everyone was to head home.

Siaw1 take these economic details seriously for good reason; monetary squabbles are the fault lines along which many relations break. Dii, who tried never to leave the house without money, explained that friends always say don't worry and cover the bill, but as they "feed" you, they grow to resent you. "Paying together" precludes unbalanced feeding (*liang4*) and thus hierarchy. Paying together also has a clear effect, which people are very much attuned to: because friends pay the same amount, and because friendship is imagined in part as the product of mutual consumption, for friendships to last, for a group of *siaw1* to persist as a group that drinks and eats together, *siaw1* must be able to spend at the same level (see, for comparison, Mills 1997, 46). One night, on a motorcycle ride, Muu spelled this out for me. He told me that, before I met him, he had more money and a different group of *siaw1*, but the police confiscated his stock of ill-harvested rare wood and he lost it all. As we rode by one of these friends' houses, giant and adjoined by a car dealership, Muu reminisced about the old group. He did not go with them anymore, he said, because it was not worth it; they spent too much money, and he was trying to save for his family.

That *siaw1* relations are among equals does not mean that, across the city, *siaw1* relations are the same. There are countless groups of *siaw1*: young and old, rich and poor, gay and straight, male and female, lay and monastic.[2] At the end of my fieldwork in 2016, all but one of the men in "friends who don't throw each other away" were in their late twenties or early thirties and married with children. Well-to-do for Laos generally, they were neither rich nor poor in Luang Prabang city. These traits formed their lives as masculine, urban, and aspirationally upwardly mobile young family men. So too did they mould the shape of their friendships. Their particular form of youthful, cosmopolitan masculinity was clear from the style in which they spent time together (see Kitiarsa 2005 on Thai masculinities). They played soccer on new and expensive faux grass fields rather than cheaper fields of cracked earth or mud, and they wore high-quality matching team jerseys. They drank huge volumes of Heineken from small bottles and cans, rather than Beer Lao from large bottles or cheap rice whisky, and thus tested not just their bodies' masculine capacity to metabolise alcohol, but also their wallets' capacity to keep the beer flowing.

They said that drinking with women—especially unmarried, beautiful women (*phuu5 saaw3 ngaam2*)—was more "fun" (*muan1*), and at bars they often recruited nearby women to join them and flirted with beer waitresses. They frequently spoke about extra-marital sex—about going to find "girls" (*phuu5 saaw3*) whether sex workers or not—even as they only occasionally engaged in such activities (see, for comparison, Vanlandingham et al. 1998). This talk quieted when the *siaw1* went out with their wives, who often acted as foils both to their husbands and to the women their husbands otherwise courted. The *siaw1*'s wives mostly drank less and preferred Spy brand wine coolers, a sweet, juicy, and brightly coloured drink, over beer (see, for comparison, Saengtienchai et al. 1999, 81). Kêq, the wife of one *siaw1*, is an illustrative exception: she was said to "drink beer well" (*kin3 hia3 kêng1*), and actively participated in the toasting, drinking challenges, and drunkenness. She also faced criticism for this. Muu, for example, said this was childish. His wife, Tia, in contrast, rarely went out with us and drank little when she did. Muu took this as a sign that Tia was mature and responsible, a family woman.

Often, Tia seemed to take pride in being a homebody as well. During conversations with me, most of the *siaw1*'s wives, in fact, downplayed their own friendships and fun and complained about their husbands' revelry. This does not mean that they never went out with friends or had friends over—they did—but self-fashioning as oriented to the home, they emphasised that now that they had children, they, unlike their husbands or the groups of younger women who packed bars around the city with their own *siaw1*, had little time for the frivolity and partying that friendship required. CamPaa, for instance, said that her only friends were women from her school days. One lived in China now, and they had not spoken in months, "Since I've started a family," she said, laughing, "I haven't ever had any friends."

For their husbands, the expectations were markedly different, and the emphasis was refracted (see, for comparison, Keyes 1984; Cassaniti 2015, 103; Petit 2015, 420; Zuckerman 2018; and, for a different view, Ockey 1999). Going out with friends, drinking, and playing games competitively was core to their evolving identities as cosmopolitan young family men. But this fun was nevertheless only justifiable for them insofar as the rest of their lives were in order. They stressed that they had the means and time to support their families through work *and* to have fun (see, for comparison, DeFillipo 2020). Their friendships were thus set apart. In these egalitarian spaces, in which they competed with and against one another, got drunk together, and, occasionally, sang loudly about not throwing each other away, they were conspicuously engaged in something more electric and socially capricious.[3]

"Loose" Friendships

> "How uncertain is the ground upon which all our alliances
> and friendships rest, how close at hand are icy downpours
> or stormy weather, how isolated each man is!"
> – Nietzsche (1996, 148)

One morning during my fieldwork, a man was found hanged over the riverbank in the UNESCO-protected part of Luang Prabang. A few people showed me the gruesome scene on their cellphones. Rumours swirled about what had happened. He was a young man, probably around twenty. I assumed that it was a suicide, but others suggested that he was murdered and put up there on display. But who would have killed him like that? I asked one woman. Probably, she said, it was his *siaw1*. Others told me similar things: a *siaw1* had killed this man.

At the time, I thought this was a bizarre inference. Even more so because of the matter-of-factness with which people said it. Why would people assume that the young man's *siaw1* would be the one to kill him? Why not a maniacal stranger? A serial killer? A bookie? Some people gave possible backstories: Maybe they were involved in a love triangle? Or maybe his *siaw1* was jealous of his money? But these just dressed up the same premise. Many men might love the same woman, many people might be jealous of another's wealth. Why would it be a *siaw1*?

I believe now that these guesses were just that, guesses. But their intuitiveness was not random, it was informed by a broader sensibility in Luang Prabang—a lurking concern that those who are close to you might do you harm. Signs of this concern are easy to find. Take a 2004 article in the *Vientiane Times* (2004), in which the editorialist dwells on the prevalence of theft through betrayal: "In some cases, thieves go to visit the family, claiming to be relatives.... Another case sees friends betraying each other." These are the ambivalent figures that one should worry about: strangers who claim to be kin, friends who act like strangers. Or take another article (*Vientiane Times* 2009) that documents how obsessions with sports, drinking, and gambling can "cause a lack of warmth" in players' households and lead to disputes within a family and among friends: "many sports involve gambling and there are many people who owe their friends money. Because of this, best friends sometimes become enemies."

The idea that those who are close might turn against you resonates with an older theme in Thai studies, in which scholars argued that Thailand contrasts with the more "tightly woven" cultures of Japan and Vietnam because of its "loose social structure", in which relationships are fleeting (Embree 1950). The idea struck a nerve when it was first introduced (for example, Evers 1969), but it has not aged well since (Silverman 1972). Bilmes (1998, 1–2) averred that "loose structure" was "little more than a hook on which to hang anecdotes and observations about Thai behavior".

I am not interested here in defending "loose structure" as an analytic. But even if it was only a hook on which to hang curious anecdotes about Thai behaviour, many of these anecdotes resonate with what I found some sixty years later in Luang Prabang: people worry about those close to them changing—that their intimacies might be turned inside out, from relations of love to relations of distance, estrangement or, worse yet, conflict and discord. The point is not that such fissions are especially common in Laos versus anywhere else, but that they "occur frequently enough to exist as potentialities" (Phillips 1966, 30) and have become prominent in the local imagination (see High 2011, 217).

In the "loose structure literature", some researchers stressed the fleeting quality of Thai friendship in particular. Foster (1976, 251) wrote that "Thai friendship ... is usually viewed as a sort of prototype of the loose structure which is said to characterize Thai society"; Phillips (1963, 106) observed that, "All villagers have friends of varying degrees of intimacy ... numerous gossip, drinking, and gambling groups, but these associations are notoriously unstable and involve little psychic investment"; and Piker (1968, 200) made the idea the centrepiece of his imaginative essay, "Friendship to the Death in Rural Thai society".

Piker's piece in particular is worth reflecting on here. He begins by introducing a contrast in Thailand, which *siaw1* in Luang Prabang make as well, between "friends to the death" (*phùan1 taaj3*) and less close friends (often called "eating friends" in Luang Prabang). He depicts the former "friends to the death" as oases of warmth in an on-the-whole mutually suspicious society, where "The typical villager approaches his interpersonal world, in virtually all of its aspects, with a pervasive sense of distrust ... and, correspondingly with a degree of caution and hesitancy that makes [durable] interpersonal commitment ... unlikely" (Piker 1968, 200). In the context of this bleak, cynical depiction, "friends to the death" appear to be an anomalous kind of person, someone trustworthy, a mind one can know. And yet, Piker argues that even "friends to the death" reveal that people are ultimately suspicious of others. He argues this point with a simple fact: most pairs of "friends to the death" (61 of 70 surveyed) did not live in the same village. Piker saw this distance not as accidental, but crucial, as it allowed these friendships to sit outside the cynical distrust of others. These friendships were thus fantasies away from the realities of Thai peasant life, outside of time, vehicles for men to have relations unburdened and untested by the daily drudgeries of interacting.

Piker's essay, and the literature on "loose structure" more generally, is marred by the obsessions and pockmarks of its time—an unwavering commitment to framing life in terms of "social structure", a too-broad notion of the peasant, an exoticism—but as an account of a discursive emphasis, it fits well with what I found among the "friends who don't throw each other away". For them, friendships are often haunted by whispered reminders of the potential of failure. The true friend, the friend to the death, thus serves as a desirable but elusive figure of personhood, a horizon toward which they build, judge, and risk these friendships, testing them to see of what they are made.

"Bare" Friendships

While in Lao interaction generally, kinterms are common, these terms automatically encode hierarchy and *siaw1* thus avoid them (see, for comparison, Sidnell and Shohet 2013). Rather, to refer to one another, they use a combination of pronouns, names, prefixes and status address terms (see Enfield 2007b, 2013). Here, I focus especially on the pronouns. In the rapidly urbanizing city of Luang Prabang, the pronominal forms *siaw1* tend to select carry an ambivalence that resonates with how people tend to imagine *siaw1* relations. In the same breath, they can both perform intimacy and signal an uncouthness and aggression that tests social relations as much as it presupposes them. While many have considered these two pragmatic forces of such "bare", non-restraint forms as inherently separate and contextually bound (see, for example, Simpson 1997, 44; see, for comparison, Brown and Gilman 1960, 278), I show that for the *siaw1*, the two forces congeal, paralleling the masculine, affective ambivalence that characterises many *siaw1* interactions.

Cross-linguistically, address terms are often salient for speakers (see Errington 1988, 234; Simpson 1997; Agha 2007). For people in Luang Prabang, pronouns are especially so. When asked, the *siaw1* easily—if not always accurately—describe which forms they use with which people in what contexts. They, similar to most Lao speakers, readily order their pronouns into speech levels of differing degrees of "politeness" (*suphaap4*), "lowness" (*tam1*) or "intimacy" (*sinit1*).

Table 1. Three levels of pronouns[4]

	Bare	Less Bare	Even Less Bare
1st person (SG)	*kuu3*	*haw2*	*khòòj5*
2nd person (SG)	*mùng2*	*too3*	*caw4*

For this chapter's purposes, I focus most on the "bare" forms *kuu3* and *mùng2*.[5] Both locally and in the literature, *kuu3* and *mùng2* are said to be reserved for both the closest of relations and the angriest of moments. Both "fighting words"—"the language one loses one's temper in" (Errington 1985a, 9; cited in Irvine 1992)— and the words you use with intimates. People also wield them metapragmatically, for example, to talk about the quality of relationships—someone might say a close pair are all "*kuu3* and *mùng2* together"—and to frame conversations as coarse or dissident—all "*kuu3 kuu3 mùng2 mùng2*" (see, for comparison, Pressman 1998, 469; Errington 1988, 105).

Kuu3 and *mùng2* are said by locals to be similar in level to several other forms for person reference in Lao, namely the second-person plural *suu3* and the third person singular *man2*, not included in table 1, as well as the following prefixes *bak2* and *qii1*, which are used before names (see Enfield 2007b):

Table 2. Two levels of prefixes[6]

	Bare	Less Bare
Male	*bak2*	*thaan1*
Female	*qii1*	*naang1*

For their capacity to evince both intimacy and coarse, aggression, these barer terms are presumed to be used among *siaw1*. Some string-tying ceremonies that formally bind *siaw1* are reportedly even accompanied by the new *siaw1* switching to *kuu3* and *mùng2* on the spot (Enfield 2014, 138). The *siaw1* in "friends who don't throw each other away" did, in fact, tend to use these barer forms, but they also sometimes switched to the slightly less bare pronouns *haw2/too3*. While I never heard them use *khòòj5/caw4* with each other, on occasion they also used the "sweet sounding" (*siang3 vaan3*) first-person forms *khaanòòj4* (associated with the temple) and *khaaphacaw4* (associated with business and the state) for jokes, which, in terms of non-bareness, are literally off-the-chart of table 1. Muu, for example, once made a bet with another *siaw1* in which the loser had to tell the winner, "I give in" or *khaanòòj4 ñòòm2*. The pronoun underlined the humiliation.

Enfield (2014, 136) writes that *kuu3*, *mùng2*, and the other "bare" forms of person reference, are "the most exposing—or, more accurately, the least covering...." This metaphor, reminiscent of Geertz's (1976, 248–60) classic discussion of Javanese linguistic etiquette as a kind of wall-building around one's emotional life, captures why the bare forms are appropriate in hierarchical kinship relations—for example, in the speech from grandmother to child—as it also illuminates why they are connected to qualities of aggression and impingement.

It is this latter capacity of the bare forms to impinge on their referent that makes them appropriate for the most common insults, which literally curse the referent and addressee (*bak2 haa1 mùng2* and *qii1 haa1 mùng2*). To use these forms with unfamiliars or those deserving of respect is said to offend and enrage; the "friends who don't throw each other away" frequently hurl them at one another (see, for comparison, Haugh and Bousfield 2012). That such bare forms are associated with impingement is also evident insofar as they are at times equated with physical violence, especially blows to the head. Just as *siaw1* use bare forms with each other, so too do they proclaim and sometimes demonstrate that they can hit each other's head without offence (see, for comparison, Siegel 1993, 44). To allow someone to do this to your head—the most sacred part of the Lao body—is to expose oneself completely, to offer your throat to their knife. Accepting or giving a blow to the head are—alongside cursing at one another, making otherwise offensive jokes, and telling one another the truth, even when it is difficult—acts that convert violations and impingement into signs of intimacy. When expected or forgiven, these acts evince an ethic of mutual "nonrestraint" (see Enfield 2014, 143; Cooke 1968). When unexpected or poorly responded to, these acts can lead to argument (see Enfield 2014, 140). The ambiguity as to whether offense or intimacy is intended is yet another way in which *siaw1* relations are formed within the semiotic borderlands of friendship and enmity (Bateson 1972).

The extent to which a bare form can both track social relations and produce them is clearest in moments where people switch from one pronominal form to another, and thus "break[] or reset[] a pattern of established pair-part usage" (Silverstein 2003, 210; Friedrich 1979). I saw many such breakthroughs in Luang Prabang, and they were salient for locals as indices of anger, humour, and drunkenness (see, for comparison, Simpson 1997, 46). Take the neat pronominal arc of one side of an argument I overheard between Muu and his wife, Tia. When it began, Muu spoke calmly and used *khòòj5* and *caw4*. As his voice grew angrier and angrier, moving to a yell, he switched to *kuu3* and *mùng2*. Then, after cooling down, he began to use *khòòj5* and *caw4* again, the pronouns one would expect a respectful married couple to use.

When prompted, people in Luang Prabang tend to talk about *kuu3* and *mùng2* in terms of the addressees with whom they are appropriate. In this respect, they are "addressee focused" (Irvine 1992, 256).[7] But this does not exhaust their (meta)pragmatics. People also recognise and treat them as indexical of the qualities of those who use them (see Silverstein 2003, *inter alia*). They debate, furthermore, how this speaker focus works. Some say that the bare forms are not inherently bad words: that it is not *if* you use them, but *how* you use them that matters. One man told me, "if [*kuu3* and *mùng2*] are used with people you really love, people you really, really love, then you can say them. [But] if ... people of different ages [are speaking to each other], then you should not use them." He then enthusiastically described "one ethnic group" that only used *kuu3* and *mùng2*, even with strangers: "They talk to each other, saying *kuu3 kuu3* and *mùng2 mùng2* just using [the words] on each other, just speaking and using [the words] on each other." "You have to understand where they are coming from," he continued, these words mean they "really, really love" you. "If you don't understand them ... haha ... there is just going to be fighting right then ... haha."

Other people, and some of the same people at different moments, talk about the forms as indefeasibly bad words (Irvine 2011), not to be uttered because they bespeak rudeness, childishness and coarseness. For example, I was drinking with Muu outside his house when his brother-in-law and sister-in-law began to fight viciously, screaming at each other and throwing things. During the argument, their toddler son approached us pushing a bike. I asked him what he was pushing around, and he said, defensively, *khòòng3 kuu3*, (It's mine!). Before I could respond, Muu asked his nephew where he had learned the word *kuu3* and ordered the boy not to use it. I became immediately curious, Where do you think he learned it, I asked Muu, Other kids? His parents, Muu said confidently, referring to the couple intermittently screaming the word to each other a few paces away. They use it all the time. In telling his nephew not to use the word at all, rather than just with me, Muu implied *kuu3* was not just a word one should keep in reserve, but a bad word.

For the *siaw1*, whether bare pronouns were more about the people with whom they were used (addressee focused), or the people who used them (speaker focused), was a live question. Can one be "rude" (*bò-suphaap4*), aggressive, or "low" (*tam1*) to some people without also being a "rude", childish person? The stakes of this question were infused by their concerns with appearing as responsible, cosmopolitan family men, on the one hand, and with fashioning themselves as masculine men with close friends, on the other. Alongside playing competitive games, telling offensive jokes, and drinking beer, *kuu3* and *mùng2* were one of many small battlegrounds where these identities came into tension.

This was clear from my own experiences of stubbornly trying to use *kuu3* and *mùng2*. But, before I recount this, let me briefly reflect on one term of reference that *siaw1* use that rarely carries ambivalence: that is, the term *siaw1* itself. When not using the term to reflect generically on the substance of *siaw1* (see Zuckerman 2021a; 2021b), people use it specifically to characterise relationships ("They are *siaw1* with each other"), prefix names in title-like fashion ("*siaw1 Muu*", for Muu), refer to one another in possessive constructions ("His *siaw1*"), and grab attention (similar to other familiarisers such as *mate* or *dude*, but less ubiquitously applied; see, for comparison, Ewing, this volume). The term tends to be more restricted and warmer than similar—and encompassing—available forms for "friend" such as *muu1* and *phùan1*, which can reference company and intimates, generally (see De Young 1955, 27).[8] The "friends who don't throw each other away" peppered the word *siaw1* throughout their conversations with each other. Take, for instance, how Muu told Dii to wait during a game of cards: waving his hand in Dii's direction, he said "*faaw4 siaw1*" or "[Don't] rush, *siaw1*".

Figure 2. Using "siaw1", Muu tells Dii not to rush during a card game

As I began to spend more time with the group, everyone quickly began calling me *siaw1*. They never hesitated to do so because the term has only positive connotations. While one might find it presumptuous or annoying if a younger

person called him *siaw1* (as I heard people occasionally complain), and while there are popular jokes about men getting drunk and becoming *siaw1* with their fathers-in-law (funny because of the inversion of hierarchy and decorum), the term lacks the dual capacity of *kuu3* and *mùng2*, the power to index both love and aggression. It was sometimes funny to have a foreign *siaw1*, but it was never bad.

But changes to using barer pronominals with me took much longer and happened unevenly. When the *siaw1* met other Lao men of similar age they would use *khòòj5* and *caw4* only briefly (if at all), quickly shift to *haw2* and *too3*, and then, maybe, and especially if alcohol was involved, downshift again to *kuu3* and *mùng2*, like a Dodge Charger picking up speed. With me, some *siaw1* stuck for months to *khòòj5* and *caw4* before using *haw2* and *too3*. They were not concerned about my feelings, but rather how they felt such uses would reflect on them. When they eventually did use *kuu3* and *mùng2* with me, overhearers would sometimes comment and laugh that a Westerner and a Lao person were "using *kuu3* and *mùng2* together" (*kuu3 mùng2 kan3*). Sii complained about this. When I pestered him for using *khòòj5* and *caw4* with me in a bar, he shot back: "What would people think of me if I used *kuu3* and *mùng2* with you?" Months earlier, when I first asked Sii to use *kuu3* and *mùng2*, he was similarly hesitant. He first incredulously claimed that he never used them with other *siaw1*, and then, when I pushed him more, said he would use them with me, but not in front of women or his children. The problem was, it was *bòo-ngam2* (not beautiful), and would make him look immature, like a "child" (*dêk2 nòòj4*) rather than "an adult" (*phuu5 ñaj1*). Another *siaw1*, Khêêng, told me that "real *siaw1*" use *khòòj5* and *caw4*. Months later, he reluctantly agreed to use *kuu3* and *mùng2* with me, but stressed that now that he was a father, he disliked using the words. The hesitance, strongest when we were out and about, came from the stigma. Publicly using the forms—especially with me—exposed the *siaw1* to judgements of being careless, coarse and unrefined with a foreigner, a class of person that the mature, cosmopolitan Luang Prabang man is expected to treat with care, as if he is representing not just himself but the nation.

My shift in pronouns with Muu, the first person in Laos with whom I used reciprocal *kuu3* and *mùng2*, is the most trackable. When we first met on 1 October 2013, he surprised me by using *haw2* and *too3* immediately. On 29 November 2013, at the end of a long night of drinking, he told me that we were really *siaw1* now. I asked him if that meant we could call one another *kuu3* and *mùng2*, and he said that those words weren't important, what mattered was that we could always stay at each other's houses and that we could even "hit each other on the head". We then proceeded to slap each other's heads just above the neck, late at night, standing in his driveway, and hard enough to remember the next morning. In early January 2014, at the end of another long night out, I asked Muu again if we could use *kuu3* and *mùng2*. His response was drastically different: he said he was really happy I had asked because he had not been "brave" enough to ask me. We already had the strongest friendship as possible, it now made sense to use *kuu3* and *mùng2*. We did so on the spot, and I revelled in each token.

Our pronominal conversion was never entire, however. I, unaccustomed to switching pronouns, often clumsily stumbled across different forms. Muu, for his part, alternated between *kuu3* and *mùng2* and the less bare *haw2* and *too3*. While my switching was random, Muu's was relatively systematic. He, like the rest of *siaw1*, was much more likely to use *kuu3* and *mùng2* at night when drinking.[9] For them, as for many young men in Luang Prabang, alcohol and late-night partying were bridges to the development of *kuu3* and *mùng2* relations, just as drinking and partying were said to be a bridge to the development of friendship generally (see, for comparison, Chirasombutti and Diller 1999, 118). "It's all love within the drinking circle", people say, and many drinking sessions begin at one pronominal level and conclude at another. As nights go on, as people get drunker, as the stakes in games go higher, as mock fights, and occasionally real fights happen, people make a full shift from *haw2* and *too3* to *kuu3* and *mùng2*. At a New Year's party at Sii's house, for example, I saw a man that I had long known from the *pétanque* court. We had always used *khòòj5* and *caw4*, but that night, loaded and heavy lidded, he used *kuu3* and *mùng2* immediately. The roughness of his pronouns fit with his affect generally: in apparent jest, he put me in a headlock or two, wrestled and swore at me. I, a bit confused and irked, returned his pronouns and literal jabs in kind.

As anyone passingly familiar with the Lao language knows, *kuu3* and *mùng2* are not exclusively tied to drinking or the rough masculinity of some *siaw1* relations. They are used in families, in schools, and among monks and novices in temples, often reflexively and without comment. But while they are used broadly, for male *siaw1* in Luang Prabang *kuu3* and *mùng2* have come to index drinking and gambling and the sometimes agonistic, unrefined, sociality that goes along with these activities. In some ways this fits with these bare forms' more general association with rural areas rather than urban ones—in cities people are said to *vaw4 dooj3* or speak with more polite affectations (similar ideologies exist throughout mainland Southeast Asia). These indexical ties partly explain why the *siaw1* might feel uncomfortable using the forms publicly, say, to a foreigner like me on the street or in front of their wives and children. But it also explains why *siaw1* are attracted to these forms as semiotic resources generally: they can wield *kuu3* and *mùng2* in moments of rough sociality as tools, to monitor and mould their friendships, to signal closeness, but also enmity or ambivalence. They can also use these forms as metapragmatic objects for self-fashioning, topics for reflecting on themselves and the kinds of language they use, material for enacting and displaying the kind of people they hope to be and the kind of relationships they hope to have.

Thrown Away Friendships

When "friends who don't throw each other away" disbanded, I was invited to another WhatsApp group with most of the same people. Muu was not. Cracks in his relationship with the others had appeared long before, but one night stood out as a turning point. It began with an afternoon game of rattan ball and a trip to a bar. We then decided to play snooker. As we rode over to the snooker hall, I sat on the back of Muu's bike, and he and Khêêng, another *siaw1*, rode close and jawed about who would win. When we arrived, they convinced the group that they should start by playing a game, one-on-one, for six bottles of beer—higher

Figure 3. Muu and Khêêng pose with a crate of beer

stakes than normal. Muu lost, but when it came time to pay, he offered less money than he owed. He argued with Khêêng and Bêê as the rest of us looked on. Back and forth they went. People occasionally told them to 'quiet' (*mit1*) and calm down (*caj3 jênø-jên3*), but they persisted. Muu said they were acting like 'little kids'. Khêêng told him to pay what he owed. To cool the fire, Nòòng had Khêêng and Muu pose for pictures with a crate of beer, ritualizing the giving of the six bottles that Muu had lost.

In the picture (Figure 3), Nòòng stands on the left side of the frame, trying to get the two men to look at the camera and shake hands, to pose around the transfer of goods like the Lao Development Lottery poses around its big cheques to the nation. Khêêng offers his hand, Muu eventually takes it, but the photo-op did little to resolve the tension. After more bickering, Muu admitted that he did not have enough money, but would pay what he could. The group then decided to go to its third competition of the night: *pétanque*.

It was already late, and the *pétanque* courts were closed, but one of the *siaw1*'s family owned a court that we could use. On the way there, Muu and Khêêng again rode near one another, jawing. Muu yelled to Khêêng about the group generally, with the bare second-person plural *suu3*: "You guys (*suu3*) bicker like little kids" and "you guys (*suu3*) don't sympathise with your friends". Khêêng yelled back. "Who are you referring to with *suu3*," he asked, "Do you mean *kuu3*?" Muu, furious, did not answer, and turned off the road to grab money from his house. Now alone with me on the quieter side road, he complained that Khêêng and Bêê were like children. He did not like their "characters" (*nitsaj3*) or the way that "they wanted what others had".

Khêêng and Bêê were waiting at the *pétanque* court with a new case of beer cans. We turned on the weak court lights, and Muu continued to argue and gamble for more beer with them. They all used *kuu3* and *mùng2* throughout. I remember feeling a strange shift happening as they yelled. Rather than a "breakthrough" into a new relationship by way of a change in pronouns (Friedrich 1979), it felt as if the same pronouns shifted in meaning, from indexing the intimacy of being *siaw1* to indexing anger; they "broke through" from signalling mutual exposure and mutual nonrestraint to signalling mutual destruction. The dimly lit *pétanque* court was something like a stage, and the rest of us slipped into the darkness and watched the devolution from the benches.

Eventually, Muu won the games, and someone suggested another picture of him with his winnings. After the photo, he told Khêêng that they could either not be friends anymore or just not like each other, but still go and drink and eat together. Unphased, Khêêng chose the second option and left for home. Muu was so angry he wouldn't be able to sleep, and he asked Dii and me to stay and drink. Dii, looking depleted, said he needed to go home. When we got back to our neighbourhood, Muu told me that he was not actually going to spend any more time with Khêêng. I could, but he was done.

And yet, Muu did spend some more time with Khêêng. They occasionally argued with each other, or became visibly annoyed, but they often also acted as if nothing had happened, as if their relationship was never strained. Perhaps they were, like they had said, going out together without liking one another, or perhaps they had gotten past it, but it always seemed to me like the answer was simpler. They had returned to the intermediary space from which they began the argument, a mixing of unease and "love", of jokes and serious offenses, of tension and friendship.

As Muu's relation with Khêêng stabilised, his tensions with others in the group grew. Slowly, over the next few months, a consensus developed that Muu was selfish—that he 'wanted what others had,' that he was too invested in arguments, too competitive. Muu's style of play in soccer was said to be especially symptomatic of his character. He did not look for his friends as he ran down the field; he never assisted on goals, only tried to make them. People would groan as he dribbled the ball, wave their hands wildly for him to pass. Dii took it upon himself to talk to Muu, to tell him that others had a problem with his style of play. He understood himself to be giving Muu exactly the kind of frank, "straight" talk that both tests and evinces friendship, like a hit to the head (see Zuckerman 2022). But Muu took offence, and many long nights were spent with three or four of us drinking, me sitting quietly, Muu telling Dii how the problem was that his teammates were unskilled, and Dii telling Muu that he, not them, was the problem.

Dii told me he knew that Muu wasn't listening. Eventually, people in the group stopped inviting him to play soccer. Because he and I lived so close, they began picking me up down the road so Muu wouldn't see us in our uniforms. When "friends that don't throw each other away" was disbanded, I was similarly told not to tell Muu about the new group. But he clearly knew. One night when he was feeling especially upset, he asked me to come and drink with him to settle himself down. He told me that he did not have any "friends to the death" (*muu1 taaj3; siaw1 taaj3*) in Luang Prabang, only "eating friends" (*muu1 kin3; siaw1 kin3*). In the province where he was from, he had some friends to the death, he added, his real friends, but not here.

Lasting Friendships

When I left the field a few months later, Muu's relationship with the group had almost evaporated. As a going-away party, I asked everyone to go to a bowling alley with me. Muu arrived late with another man whom we didn't know well. They left quickly. The others explained that Muu was scared we would beat him up: that's why he brought the other man, for protection.

Like that, the *kum1* that seemed so solid when I arrived in Laos had been thrown away, or at least morphed into something else. Years later, when I was first writing these passages, Muu, had moved back to his home province, messaged me telling me that he (*kuu3*) "missed" me (*mùng2*) and sent me photographs of us drinking together with the *siaw1*. I sent him photographs as well, including the last from the night of the argument, in which Muu and Khêêng are shaking hands and holding the beer Muu had just won.

The picture was not out of place. Taken in the heat of an argument, it nevertheless effaced its origins. I now wonder whether that was what motivated those who took it. Even as the camerawork and poses were sloppy with drunkenness, the photo looked like many formal photos of exchanges in Laos. It purported to capture something extant, but it was fundamentally creative and hopeful. The men had organised it to rescue the relationship between Muu and Khêêng. The beer in between them, the cause of the argument, a sign of both the bond and the wedge, manifested friendship in the instant that friendship was at risk.

Conclusion

In Luang Prabang, Laos, a place where hierarchical relations are the norm, *siaw1* relations stand apart in their presumed equality. The men in "friends who don't throw each other away" were committed to this equality and hoped for it to endure in the form of a lasting fraternal love. They worked hard to reify their relations in photographs and team jerseys and frequent messaging and drinking together.

But as they made monuments to their lasting friendship, they also flirted with its destruction. Much of what they did to evince their strong social relations invited low levels of conflict that tested those same relations: they told one another painful truths, they joked with one another, they smacked each other's heads, they constantly competed in games and drinking, and they either split bar bills evenly, no matter how unequally people imbibed, or they gambled for those same bills, creating asymmetries in who was forced to pay.

The *siaw1* constantly invited conflict, but conflict was never their stated goal. It was rather a means to prove the quality of their relations and thus their own qualities as emerging cosmopolitan family men with friends so close they need not worry about being thrown away. By flouting etiquette, by telling one another the undiluted truth, and by inhabiting nonrestraint (Enfield 2014, 143; Cooke 1968), they evinced the power of their relations to endure. Like all good tests, these tests of lasting fraternal love sometimes strained that love too far. Sometimes friends did care and take offense. Sometimes, they stopped being friends. The risk of lost friendship was real.

Figure 4. Muu, Khêêng and Muu's winnings

A parallel logic captures how the men used *kuu3* and *mùng2*. These pronouns of nonrestraint evidence relations because they test them. Both locals in Luang Prabang and scholars studying similar forms elsewhere have tended to describe such bare forms as having two separate meanings, depending on the context: one intimate, one angry. Reflecting on person reference in relatively unstable relations such as those of the "friends who don't throw each other away" makes clear that the apparent interplay of these sharply contrasting uses is more than just an enticing paradox for analysts. In male *siaw1* relations, the anger that the use of these forms can unleash is not separate from their capacity to express intimacy. Bare forms such as *kuu3* and *mùng2* are powerful signs of intimacy because, like a slap to the head, they are construable as something else, because, in the right circumstances, they can shift in pragmatic force as quickly as "friends who don't throw each other away" can turn on one another.

Notes

* This research was conducted with the support of a Wenner Gren Dissertation Fieldwork Grant, a Fulbright-Hays Doctoral Dissertation Research Abroad Fellowship, and the University of Michigan. I wrote this chapter while working under an Australian Research Council Discovery Grant (DP170104607). For comments on versions of it over the years, I thank Kimberly Ang, Nick Enfield, Judith Irvine, Webb Keane, Alaina Lemon, Michael Lempert, John Mathias, Kamala Russell, and Cheryl Yin. Thanks also to an anonymous reviewer and the editors, Novi Djenar and Jack Sidnell, for inviting me to contribute to this volume. Finally, endless love and appreciation to "the friends who don't throw each other away" for letting me join in this slice of their lives: may we all appreciate the friendships we have for however long they last. *kuu3 hak2 suu3 talòòt4 paj3 dee3*!

[1] For transliteration of Lao, I follow Enfield (2007a). All names are pseudonyms.

[2] Of course, while *siaw1* relations centre on similarity, they, and especially dyadic *siaw1* relations, often also span obvious differences of sex, class, etc.

[3] That this is an urban way of being *siaw1* is clear from my subsequent research in the rural Nam Noi watershed (see Enfield, this volume). There, *siaw1* relations among people over 30 are dyadic and between men of different villages or towns, especially locals and outsiders. Only younger villagers, both male and female, use *siaw1* like people in Luang Prabang—a few older people told me that these practices referred to "play *siaw1*" (*siaw1 liin5*), modelled on relations in the towns and cities.

[4] Table 1 is a "metonymic reduction" (Agha 2007, 286), which treats the forms themselves as if they, without the help of context, did all of the pragmatic work (cf. Enfield 2014, 143–4), but it also illuminates insofar as it roughly captures how locals talk about and use the forms.

[5] I use "bare", following Enfield (2007b), because the term parallels local ideas about how these forms work and avoids implying that they are *automatically* rude.

[6] *thaan1* and *naang1* are used most in institutional contexts, alongside full legal names (cf. Enfield 2007b, 103).

[7] The third person forms *man2, khaw2, laaw2*, in contrast, are talked about as primarily referent focused.

[8] *phùan1*, commonly used, feels Thai to many Lao speakers.

Friendship, Pronouns and Relations on the Edge in Luang Prabang, Laos   **159**

⁹ I surveyed twelve recordings of Muu helping me during transcription sessions; these spanned our switch in pronouns. I marked the first time Muu referred to me or himself with a pronoun, expecting to see a clean transition from *haw2* and *too3* into *kuu3* and *mùng2*. To my surprise, in each case Muu used *haw2* or *too3*. In the less sober and serious videos I have of us drinking, in contrast, Muu frequently used *kuu3* and *mùng2*.

CHAPTER 8

Interlocutor Reference and Deferential Relations in Indonesian Political Interviews*

Dwi Noverini Djenar

Speakers of Indonesian use a range of terms to refer to themselves and their addressee in conversation. In addition to pronouns, kin terms, names and titles are widely employed in acts of interlocutor reference. Common kin terms include *adik* (younger sibling), *kakak* (older sibling), *abang* (older brother), *ibu* (mother), and *bapak* (father). Pronouns denoting speaker and addressee roles such as *aku* ("I"; Malay, Javanese), *saya* ("I"; from Sanskrit noun *sahāya* [companion, follower]), Malay *kamu* (you) and a mid-century coinage *anda* (you) are broadly differentiated based on the indexical contrast between "personal" and "public" and implications for "politeness", "intimacy" or "distance" that the use of these pronouns in acts of reference can generate. This chapter examines these resources as they are mobilised by participants in Indonesian political interviews.

The interviews considered here exemplify what Lauerbach calls "panel or debate agenda interviews" (2007, 1394), involving interviewees responding to interviewer's questions by taking opposing positions, and in doing so, putting forth their perspectives on a particular issue to the critical audience (Lauerbach 2007, 1394). The interviews examined are focused on pre-election and post-election issues. Within the institutional framework of these interviews—by which is meant the configuration of persons inhabiting institutional roles, for example, journalist, interviewee and audience (see Agha 2007, 86)—the way the interviewer (henceforth IR) and interviewees (henceforth IEs) refer to each other can tell us something about how political relations are enacted publicly. In the broadcast

160

setting, IEs are expected to engage in political disagreements in a civil manner. As described by Hannah Arendt (1998, 26) in relation to the Ancient Greek experience of the *polis*: "To be political, to live in a *polis*, meant that everything was decided through words and persuasion and not through force and violence." Examining the organisation of talk in these interviews helps us understand how the institutional format may pose constraints on the kinds of relationship that can occur (Clayman 2006, 137). It is moreover an opportunity to understand how the forms employed in interlocutor reference as object signs are not just caught up in discourses circulating at a particular time but also shape those discourses.

The literature on turn-taking in the news interview has shown that examining questioning practices is useful to understand the way journalists and politicians manage their relations, and how journalistic practices change over time. Journalists are known to operate under rules of conduct that are in tension with each other. On the one hand, they are required to maintain objectivity, which they do by taking a "neutralistic" stance toward interviewees' "statements, positions and opinions" (Clayman and Heritage 2002a, 120), and on the other, they are expected to be "appropriately adversarial" in performing their role in the interest of serving the public (Clayman 2002; Heritage and Clayman 2010, 227).

Studies by Clayman and Heritage (2002a, 2002b) on one-to-one news interviews show that journalists in the US and the UK have tended to become less deferential and more adversarial in interviewing, as evidenced by the way they ask questions. Other studies (Rendle-Short 2007, 2011 on Australian interviews; Clayman 2010, 2013a on US interviews) demonstrate that journalists and politicians differ significantly in their address practices, both in terms of the forms they use and where they use them in talk. Politicians tend to address journalists by name and have greater flexibility in terms of where they position address terms, whereas journalists mainly address politicians by their institutional role or by title and last name, and are more limited in terms of where they position address terms (see Rendle-Short 2007). These studies have offered useful insights into the relations between journalists and politicians in anglophone contexts. Outside these contexts, such as those of Southeast Asia, much less is known about how interview participants orient to the institutional format in their interaction with each other. This study contributes to filling this gap.

Several key points can be noted from the linguistic literature on political interviews. One is that interview practices are known to vary across genres. The influential study by Clayman and Heritage (2002a) is based mainly on the news interview, an "elite" genre in which public figures are asked to account for their perspectives and decisions to a sceptical audience (2002a, 341). By virtue of its one-to-one format, the news interview lends itself to adversarial questioning and evasion by the politician (Clayman and Heritage 2002a; Lauerbach 2007, 1394).

Montgomery (2010, 188) points out that the news interview only represents one genre and that privileging this genre in the study of interview discourse has led to the unfortunate consequence that the news interview is treated as representative of political interviews more generally. According to Montgomery, the news interview is characteristic of "single-voiced enunciation" of an interview event (2008, 275). He argues that, while it is no doubt an important genre, the success of news relies on a broad range of sources which are often presented in dialogue with each other. News, Montgomery asserts, "has become a thing of many voices", and the voice of experts, reporters and members of the public is as worthy of attention in the study of interviews as that of the politician (2008, 275).

Another key point noted in the literature is that interview practices vary from country to country (Patrona 2011) and across cultures (for example, between public and commercial channels; see Lauerbach 2004, 1394). Accordingly, one could expect that the way journalists orient to the norms of neutralism and adversariality also varies greatly. Patrona shows, for example, that Greek journalists frequently "breach" the neutralism norm by talking aggressively, dominating the conversation, and making their ideological leanings known to the public, thus, "imposing" preferred interpretations of political events in the service of entertaining programming (2011, 174). Variation in the interview format itself has also been noted. While some interviews follow a traditional format for a certain genre (for example, the news interview), others are presented as a "hybrid" talk show (see Ekström 2011) in which "serious accountability interviewing" is combined with "small talk" (2011, 136) and the adversarial interviewing style characteristic of the news interview is mixed with a style associated with celebrity talk show.

Despite the variety of genres discussed in the literature, most studies on political interviews focus on showing how the standard turn taking procedures which require IR to limit their role to asking questions and IEs to direct all talk to IR are observed or violated. In other words, they focus on how IEs' turns at talk are mediated by IR (Greatbatch 1992). Compared to that standard, unmediated talk is "interruptive" and "violative" (see Greatbatch 1992, 280–7). Panel interviews, unlike news interviews, are characteristically multi-party, and therefore, it is almost inevitable that unmediated talk occurs. How is talk that is structurally interruptive and violative is also, in Lauerbach's (2007, 1394) words, "more deferential" than the news interview? How is deference to be understood in this case?

I would suggest that one way to interpret Lauerbach's claim is by considering how interview participants, including the journalist, orient to the audience. The defining characteristic of broadcast talk is talk designed to be heard by the audience (Heritage 1985; Greatbatch 1992; Clayman and Heritage 2002), and therefore showing deference to co-participants can be understood as a public display of the participants' awareness of the institutional character of their interaction. This study focuses on self- and addressee reference in Indonesian panel interviews to explore the question of how they display that understanding. I argue that interlocutor reference is among the resources interview participants make use of to enact alignment or opposition deferentially. As will be shown, deferential acts are distributed across the participant framework, approximating what Goffman calls "symmetrical deference", that is, deference that "social equals owe one another" (1956, 479). In this study, I consider deference not as a property of the genre itself but as acts performed by all participants within a broadcast setting. To this end, the question of whether the panel interview as a genre is "more deferential" than the (one-to-one) news interview, as Lauerbach (2007) suggests, will not be pursued here.

This chapter is organised as follows. I begin in the next section by delimiting deferential acts to acts that orient to the audience, performed by showing respect to an addressee through self- or addressee-reference and accompanying signs. I discuss alternation between different forms of self- and addressee-reference to show how form alternation mediates deference. From there I proceed to examine acts of deference performed through indirect questions. Two question types are discussed: the *gimana* interrogative and the question cascade. The analysis of *gimana* shows how IR accomplishes questioning by means of a semantically underspecified interrogative construction, while the discussion on the question cascade focuses on the way in which an interviewee taking the initiative to speak can turn journalistic deference into a collaborative construction of deference. The section that follows discusses the use of hand movement in conjunction with language to signal different levels of deference. In the panel interview where interviewees are expected to oppose each other's views, differentiating between the levels of deference one accords to different co-participants can be an effective way of enacting (dis)alignment. In the final section of analysis, I discuss an act of addressee-reference in which a kin term and a pronoun are juxtaposed to achieve a particular goal, namely, to pressure an addressee to respond. This section explores how IR "breaches" the neutralism norm by aligning with the position of certain IEs, and thus, standing at odds with their putative role as "report elicitor" (Greatbatch 1992). This act results in a reworking of the institutional framework and illustrates the way the configuration of persons inhabiting institutional roles in a broadcast event is sensitive to change.

This study is based on interviews broadcast over a period of one year, from the beginning of the 2019 election campaign period through to a month prior to the presidential inauguration (23 September 2018 to 27 September 2019; see the next section for background). Nine interviews from two major programs totalling 200 minutes in duration are included. *Mata Najwa* (Najwa's eyes; henceforth *MN*), hosted by award-winning journalist, Najwa Shihab, was aired for the first time in November 2009 and typically features two to eight, even nine interviewees and a studio audience. *Layar Pemilu Tepercaya* (Reliable election show; henceforth *LPT*), hosted by Budi Adiputro, was a program dedicated to the elections and includes between two to four interviewees, with no studio audience.[1]

Indonesian Panel Interviews and the 2019 General Elections

On 17 April 2019, Indonesian citizens went to the poll to elect the president, vice president, members of the People's Representative Council (*DPR*) and regional councils, all on the same day.[2] With more than 80 per cent of the 190 million eligible voters turning up to vote at over 800,000 polling stations across the country—many at logistically challenging locations—it was a mammoth undertaking. Unsurprisingly, of all the elections, the presidential election attracted the most attention. The two candidates, the incumbent Joko Widodo (better known as Jokowi), and his challenger, former army general Prabowo Subianto, had met head-to-head five years earlier in the 2014 election. This time, Jokowi campaigned to win a second term, and Prabowo, his first.

The battle over who should win or lose at the elections was fought on all grounds, involving participation from various sections of society, across all forms of media. Media coverage during the seven-month campaign period leading to the elections was wide and intense, with daily coverage on television, newspapers and social media all playing an important part in forming opinions on who should be elected. Amidst all this, there were concerns that inexperienced voters would be easily swayed by fake news and align themselves too readily with identity politics. *Pemilih milenial* (youth voters) constituted nearly 45 per cent (or around 85.5 million) of the total number of eligible voters, among which were five million first-time voters. Increased social polarisation, a perceived threat of Islamism and, more generally, patterns of democratic erosion in the lead up to the elections intensified the competition to win youth votes, thus turning the elections into a high-stakes battle.

Media practitioners concerned about the election process saw it as their responsibility to encourage young voters to exercise democratic rights by casting their votes instead of abstaining. Well-known journalists who are hosts of panel interviews devoted their programs to the topic of the elections, inviting speakers from both Jokowi's and Prabowo's coalitions and Indonesians of various ages, but particularly young voters, as their audiences. In the aftermath of the elections, concerns about disunity and democracy being under threat turned the wider media discourse towards the need to reunite the nation and *merawat demokrasi* (safeguard democracy). As the institutional setting of the interviews and the journalists' frequent references to *publik* (public) make clear, the conversations between them and the politicians are designed to be heard by the whole nation, that abstract and "unmarked subjectivity" (Cody 2011, 41) for whom democracy is a collective ideal.

Panel interviews are of great interest to the Indonesian public because of their relatively new presence in the Indonesian broadcast world, with major programs aired for the first time well after the Reform era (1998–2002), and also because of the varied topics and the wide range of interviewees they attract.[3] Clayman remarks that panel interviews generally attract "a less distinguished cadre of participants" compared to individual interviews and as such they are "a somewhat less prestigious variant of the news interview genre" (2002, 1387; also see Clayman and Heritage 2002a, 299). It is certainly true that people in the highest office, such as presidents and prime ministers, tend to be interviewed individually rather than in a panel; however, Clayman's remark seems to focus too narrowly on the rank of the interviewees as a source of prestige when perceptions of quality and credibility are not dependent on the presence of high-ranking politicians alone. The skills of the journalist, the overall standing of the television station and the resources it provides the interview program surely contribute to prestige in addition to the calibre of the politicians.[4] That the skills of the journalist matter would also explain why, for example, high-ranking politicians are more likely to grant an interview to journalists with a respectable reputation than to those perceived to be professionally weaker.

Self- and Addressee-Reference in Indonesian and Deferential Acts

Indonesian has been described as a language with an "open" pronoun system. In a narrow sense, this simply means that it allows pronoun borrowing, which results in multiple pronouns being available for use in interlocutor reference. This contrasts with languages with the so-called "closed" system (such as English and French) which have historically allowed borrowing to a more limited extent (Court 1998, cited in Thomason and Everett 2005). In a broader sense, an "open" system allows both pronoun borrowing and the inclusion of lexical nouns in the range of forms that can be used in interlocutor reference. Fleming and Sidnell (2020) refer to this system as "Open Class Interlocutor Reference" or OCIR, and they point out that this system is found in many languages of East Asia and Southeast Asia. As lexical nouns can serve a similar grammatical function as pronouns, they are sometimes called "pronoun substitutes" (see Sneddon et al. 2010, 166). The term "imposter", coined by Collins and Postal (2012) to refer to expressions whose denotational structures are incongruent with their grammatical representations, has also been applied to the analysis of interlocutor reference in Indonesian (see Conners, Brugman and Adams 2016).

In the panel interviews studied here, kin terms of various provenance are employed in vocative and referential functions. As vocative, the kin term is positioned outside the clause, while as reference, it points to an argument in the clause. It is not unusual for an utterance to include a kin term used as a vocative and another as reference, as shown in (1). In this example, the two functions are indicated by position and form; the short form *tèh* serves as a vocative, while the long form *tètèh*, an addressee reference. This study discusses referential use of kin terms only (for vocatives, see Ewing, this volume).

(1) *Tèh   Diyah,   Tètèh   apa?*
    older.sister Diyah   older.sister what
    "*Tèh* Diyah, what are you (*Tètèh*) having (for lunch)?"
    (Diyah's younger friend is asking what Diyah is having for lunch.)
    (example adapted from Ewing and Djenar 2019)

In the interviews under study, the most common addressee-reference forms include kin terms and names. The kin terms employed are mainly sibling terms, and more specifically, terms for older siblings. In acts of reference involving these kin terms, the addressee is treated as more senior and the "target" of deference (Fleming, this volume). For the purposes of this study, deferential acts are understood as acts of showing respect within a broadcast setting, performed by means of self- and addressee-reference and accompanying signs, for the benefit of the audience. One of the ways in which orientation to the audience can be discerned is in instances of alternation. Which form is selected in any given moment of interaction depends on various factors, including whether the target of deference is treated as an addressee or a third party. In addressee-reference, a kin term plus name tends to be used, while in third-party reference, the kin term is often dropped. An example of this kind of alternation is shown in (2).

In this example, Adian Napitupulu and Arief Poyuono, spokespersons from Jokowi's and Prabowo's coalitions respectively, are guests on *MN*. In the preceding talk, Arief claims that most politicians in the *DPR* are corrupt. Adian knows that Arief had previously run for a national parliamentary seat but did not win and consequently was not appointed to the *DPR*. Based on this knowledge, Adian treats Arief's criticism of the *DPR* as sour grapes and teases him by suggesting that, instead of criticising, Arief should run again and try his best to win so he could join the *DPR* and gain firsthand knowledge of how decisions are made there. In lines

3 and 11, Adian refers to Arief with the kin term *mas* (older brother [Javanese]) followed by name. Arief similarly uses *mas* but as a vocative (see lines 9 and 13).

(2) [Narasi TV, Catatan Najwa, 13 April 2019: Nobar Debat Pilpres: Bawa Asyik Politik – Final Battle Adian vs Poyuono]

1	ADIAN:	*Nah itu seharusnya bisa dilakukan.*
		So that should have been done.
2		*Bagus-nya=*
		A better (thing to do) is,
3	->	... (.7) ***Mas Arief ini,***
		(for) <u>you</u>,
4		... *ikut PILEG lagi dan menang.*
		to run again in a legislative election and win.
5		... (.7) *Sehingga tahu bagaimana di DPR itu.*
		So (you'll/he'll) know what the DPR is like.
6		... *Gitu lho.*
		Like that.
7		[((AUDIENCE LAUGHING))]
8	NAJWA:	[@@@@]
9	ARIEF: ->	*Saya nggak terta=rik **Mas**.*
		I'm not interested *Mas*.
10	ADIAN:	*Buk-... bukan tidak tertarik.*
		It's not (you who's) not interested.
11	->	*Rakyat tidak tertarik milih **Mas Arief**.* ((LOOKS AT ARIEF))
		The people aren't interested in voting for <u>you</u>.
12		((AUDIENCE LAUGHING))
13	ARIEF: ->	... *Nggak [ter]tarik sungguh **Mas**.*
		(I'm) honestly not interested *Mas*.

In extract (3) Adian treats Arief as a third party and refers to him using name only.

(3) [Narasi TV, Catatan Najwa, 13 April 2019: Nobar Debat Pilpres: Bawa Asyik Politik – Final Battle Adian vs Poyuono (Part 1)]

1	ADIAN (talking to Najwa):	...(.9) *Kalau=... **Arief**,*
		In Arief's case,
2		...(.7) *mau jadi calon rakyat*
		(he) wanted to be a representative of the people,

3   *gagal.*
            (but) failed.

During the entire (one-hour) interview, Adian refers to Arief only four times: twice with a kin term plus name (*Mas Arief*) in addressee-reference, once using the name *Arief* in third-party reference, and once using the "alternative recognitional" (Stivers 2007) *teman kita ini* (this friend of ours). Similarly, Arief uses the kin terms *bang* (from Malay *abang* [older brother]) and *mas* followed by name in addressee-reference and name only when referring to Adian as a third-party.

The interview participants may use different forms in addressee-reference depending on the relations they highlight at any particular moment in the interview. For example, journalist Najwa Shihab sometimes introduces a regular interviewee, Yuniarto Wijaya, with the alternative recognitional *teman saya* (my friend) followed by full name and a description of his position within the organisation he represents, *Direktur Charta Politika* (Director of Charta Politika). During an interview, Najwa sometimes alternates between referring to Yuniarto with a kin term followed by his familiar name (*Mas Totok*), thus orienting to the institutional format, and name only (*Totok*), treating him as someone with whom she is on familiar terms. Yuniarto similarly refers to Najwa with a kin term followed by her familiar name (*Mbak Nana*), or name only (*Nana*).

These examples suggest that both the journalist and interviewees mobilise similar resources, namely, kin terms and name, to orient to the audience, and they vary the form depending on the relation they index at any particular moment during the interview and whether they treat a co-participant as an addressee or a third party.

Indexing Deference through Self-Reference

Indonesian has multiple forms for self-reference. These include kin terms, names and first-person pronouns. It has been observed that in informal, multiethnic conversation, the pronoun *saya* tends to be used "to construct a public social and personal identity, to show deference, and to index social distance" while the use of the pronoun *aku* indexes "personal identities as informal, relaxing the prescribed norms of public language use, and building social intimacy" with co-participants (Englebretson 2007, 84). In the interviews examined, both journalists and politicians use *saya* and *aku* in self-reference, with some tending to maintain the same pronoun throughout a speech event while others alternate between the pronouns. I suggest that pronoun alternation is one of the resources used by the participants to index deference in political interviews. The following examples illustrate this point.

At the beginning of the same interview as (2), Najwa Shihab (IR) describes Arief Puyuono and Adian Napitupulu as *calon wakil rakyat dua-duanya* (both candidates for people's representatives). Arief rejects this attribute, saying he is neither a representative of the people nor member of the *DPR*, referring to himself with *aku* as he does so (lines 3 and 6).

(4) [Narasi TV, Catatan Najwa, 13 April 2019: Nobar Debat Pilpres: Bawa Asyik Politik – Final Battle Adian vs. Poyuono]

1	NAJWA:	*Kan calon wakil rakyat dua-duanya=.*
		But both of you are candidates for people's representatives
2	ARIEF:	*... Enggak.*
		No.
3	->	***Aku** ngga=k wakil rakyat lo=h.*
		I'm not a representative of the people, you know.
4	NAJWA:	*... Loh*
		How come.
5		*Masa merasa enggak mewakili walaupun nggak .. dari rakya=t?*
		Don't you feel that you represent (them) though (you're) not ... of the people?
6	ARIEF: ->	*.. **Aku** kan nggak DPR RI*
		But you see I'm not in the *DPR*.
7		*[Enggak ya enggak].*
		(If I say) no (I) mean no.

Later in the interview, Arief uses *saya* when he claims firsthand knowledge of the significant financial loss suffered by the American company that manages the Freeport mining project in West Papua. (In a preceding sequence of talk, Arief criticises the Indonesian government's decision to take over 40 per cent of the project ownership, saying that, given the financial loss, the decision was unwise.) This is the first instance of self-reference since Arief's use of *aku* in (4).

(5) [Narasi TV, Catatan Najwa, 13 April 2019: Nobar Debat Pilpres: Bawa Asyik Politik – Final Battle Adian vs Poyuono]

8	NAJWA:	*[<itu>] itu asumsi atau --*
		that's that's an assumption or
		it- itu asumsi= atau itu yang anda ketahui= atau seperti apa?_

		that's an assumption or it's something you know or what is it actually?
9	ARIEF: ->	... *Saya* yang ketahui *Mbak.*
		(It's what) I know *Mbak.*
10	->	... *Saya* kan tahu hitung-hitungannya
		I know the numbers.
11	NAJWA:	... *Wes=*
		Gosh.
12	ARIEF: ->	... *Saya* kan nguasain hitung-hitungannya begitu.
		I know how the numbers are worked out.
13	NAJWA:	... *Wes.*
		Gosh.

Arief alternates between *aku* in (4) and *saya* in (5) despite there being no change of addressee. In both instances, the act of self-reference occurs within the context of him making a claim about his role as a public figure, so there does not seem to be a significant shift in the kind of identity he is indexing. However, considering the temporal structure of the debate can help explain why the alternation occurs.

The two excerpts are taken from the final in a series of three events in which Arief and Adian met as guests *MN*. The events were playfully named *Hot Debate*, *Rematch* and *Final Battle*, respectively, reflecting the entertainment value the program derived from having the two interviewees. The *Final Battle*, from which the excerpts are taken, was held in a movie theatre with young Indonesians as audience and the interview panel projected onto the movie screen. Recognition that the venue adds theatricality to the interview is indicated, for example, by Najwa's question to the interviewees if being able to see themselves on the screen made them feel like movie stars. Through her question Najwa also reminded her addressees that the setting was different from the studio space in which her program is usually held. The sequence of talk in (4) occurred at the beginning of interview, after the two politicians had just entered the theatre and were walking to their seats while "Miserlou", a soundtrack by Dick Dale and His Del-Tones from the film *Pulp Fiction*, was playing in the background and Najwa was standing nearby, waiting for the two interviewees to settle. This contrasts with the sequence in (5), which occurred during the interview proper.[5] (Note that it is also within the interview proper that Arief used *saya* in self-reference when speaking to Adian, as seen earlier in example (2), line 9.) The shift to *saya* thus marks an indexical shift in participant relations, from a relaxed and playful relation between three public figures (Najwa, Arief and Adian) to a deferential relation between participants inhabiting institutional roles.

The journalist too makes a similar shift, as shown in (6), which follows directly from (4). Najwa, who has just heard Arief say he is member of a political party but that being so does not make him a representative of the people, is turning to Adian to ask him if he thinks political parties should represent the people. She refers to herself with *aku*.

(6) [Narasi TV, Catatan Najwa, 13 April 2019: Nobar Debat Pilpres: Bawa Asyik Politik—Final Battle Adian vs Poyuono]

1   NAJWA: ->   ... *kalau **aku** nanya Bang Adian,*
              how about I ask Bang Adian,
2   ... *Partai itu juga harus bisa mewakili rakyat enggak?*
              Do political parties have to represent the people or not?

Later, during the interview proper, Najwa shifts to *saya*, as shown in (7).

(7) [Narasi TV, Catatan Najwa, 13 April 2019: Nobar Debat Pilpres: Bawa Asyik Politik—Final Battle Adian vs Poyuono]

1   NAJWA: *Oke.*
              Okay.
2   *Kalau gitu*
              If that's the case,
3   *Kita komentar aja --*
              Let's talk about --
4   *e=*
              er
5   *kampanye aja deh.*
              the campaign, shall we.
6   ->   *[Tadi di] awal **saya** sudah bilang.*
              At the beginning I already mentioned.

The fact that both IE (Arief) and IR (Najwa) shift from *aku* to *saya* suggests that alternating between these pronouns constitutes a shared practice of signalling deference within an institutional context and provides an example of how the interview format both constrains referential practice and is constituted by it.

These alternations are clearly not motivated by a change of addressee. Englebretson (2007, 84) argues that speakers use *aku* to index a personal identity as informal and amenable to social intimacy, and they use *saya* to construct a public identity, show respect and index social distance. That the direction of the alternations we have seen is from *aku* to *saya* can be explained with reference to this conventionalised association between pronominal forms and sociopragmatic meanings, and by taking the interview structure into account.

Indexing Deference through Question Design

In performing their role, IRs make use of the question-and-answer format to elicit information. Asking questions, according to Heritage and Clayman (2010, 227), is "antithetical" to overtly agreeing or disagreeing with IEs, therefore using this format can help IRs to remain accountable and operate in accordance with their role as report elicitor. Clayman and Heritage developed a system for analysing journalistic adversarialness and deference based on question design, one dimension of which is "directness". Direct questions are questions formulated with "blunt" and "straightforward" expressions, while indirect questions "entail some divergence between what is said and what is meant, such that meaning is circuitously implied rather than literally stated" (2002b, 759). Indirect questions, according to Clayman and Heritage, are more deferential than direct questions.

The Indonesian *gimana* (how) (or *bagaimana* in the standard variant) interrogative constructions can come across as deferential, particularly when used for "juxtaposing perspectives", that is, to "engage two IEs [interviewers] in a mediated exchange of alternative (and perhaps contesting) perspectives" (Roth and Olsher 1997, 12). In English-language interviews, juxtaposing perspectives is often accomplished through *what about that* interrogative, which has the following sequential structure (1997, 12):

1	Interviewer:	Question, addressed to Interviewee-1
2	Interviewee-1:	Response
3	Interviewer: -->	*What about that*—addressed to Interviewee-2
4	Interviewee-2:	Response

The nominal *that* in the interrogative specifies the referent the addressee is expected to respond to (that is, the position taken by Interviewee-1). *What about that* is typically followed by an address term specifying the recipient.

The Indonesian *gimana* (and its variant, *bagaimana*) interrogative, when used to accomplish a similar action in the interviews, is typically preceded or followed by a kin term or another lexical noun (for example, *Bung* [comrade], *Bos* [boss]). Like *what about that*, *gimana* can be followed by a nominal or used without it. I call the latter the "bare" *gimana* construction. This construction is commonly used by IRs to ask an IE to respond to a co-IE's position without specifying which position, thus allowing IE greater liberty in designing their response than the *gimana* construction involving a nominal. In the following, I discuss instances involving both types of construction to support this contention.

The "Bare" Gimana Construction

The use of *gimana* interrogative without a nominal is shown in the following two extracts from *LPT*. Puspa, the journalist replacing Budi Adiputro as the host of *LPT*, is interviewing two young politicians: Rian Ernest, a spokesperson from the Indonesian Solidarity Party and supporter of Jokowi, and Faldo Maldini, a spokesperson for the National Mandate Party and supporter of Prabowo. In extract (8), Faldo responds to Puspa's *gimana* interrogative by referring to Rian's position articulated within the immediate sequential context (line 2 in Roth and Olsher's schema). However, because the bare *gimana* does not specify which position to respond to, an IE can treat the interrogative as soliciting a contrasting position but not necessarily the position articulated within the immediate sequence. This is shown in extract (9) in which Faldo responds by referring to Rian's position from a much earlier sequence. The following elaborates on the difference.

In extract (8), Puspa (IR) is asking Rian to respond to her statement in a preceding turn that a report by Indonesia's Bureau of Statistics has highlighted a problem with the government's record on rice production and distribution. Rian responds by conceding that the cost of rice production in Indonesia is much higher than Vietnam and explains that this is partly caused by the uneven amount of rain across Indonesia's rice-producing regions. He then claims the government has been addressing the issue building reservoirs to ensure a more consistent water supply and new roads to improve distribution. At the end of Rian's turn in line 11, IR asks Faldo to comment on Rian's position, using the bare *gimana* interrogative preceded by the addressee-reference *Mas Faldo* (line 12). Faldo responds by attending to Rian's immediate position, dismissing Rian's claim that climate is to blame for the high cost of rice production. Faldo thus treats IR's *gimana* interrogative as soliciting a contrasting viewpoint (see line 14 where Faldo indicates contrast with *Kalau saya* ... "for me ...").

(8) [CNN Indonesia, Layar Pemilu Tepercaya, 6 November 2018: PSI: "Janji stop impor, Prabowo omong kosong"]

1	RIAN:	*Jadi memang harga di Vietnam lebih kompetitif.*
		It's true that the cost (of rice production) in Vietnam is more competitive.
2		*Pe-ernya kita,*
		Our homework,
3		*Pe-ernya pak Jokowi makanya apa.*
		Therefore *Pak* Jokowi's homework is what.
4		*Dibuat logistik lebih baik.*
		To improve logistics.

5		*Dana desa membangun embung-embung di desa*
		Use the rural fund to build reservoirs in rural areas.
6		*supa- pe-ernya setiap tahun.*
		so- (this is) a yearly homework.
7	PUSPA:	*Oke.*
		Okay.
8	RIAN:	*Atau jalannya diperbaiki.*
		Or improve roads.
9	PUSPA:	*Oke.*
		Okay.
10		*Supaya apa,*
		So that what-is-it,
		kita lebih kompetitif,
		we (can be) more competitive,
	PUSPA:	*Nah,*
		So,
11	RIAN:	*dalam sisi ... produktifitas.*
		in terms of productivity.
12	PUSPA: ->	**Mas Faldo** *gimana?*
		How about you (*Mas* Faldo)?
13	FALDO:	*Iya.*
		Yes.
14	->	*... Kalau saya ... cuaca jadi permasalahan,*
		For me ... (if) climate is the problem
15		*Ya itu seharusnya diitungla=h*
		That should be taken into account (in the calculation).
16		*... gitu.*
		like that.
17		*Masak nggak bisa ngitung faktor-faktor kayak gitu.*
		Why can't (you) factor that in in the calculation?

In extract (9) Faldo responds to Puspa's bare *gimana* by opposing Rian's position from a much earlier sequence, thus interpreting the interrogative as asking for a response but not specifying which position the addressee is to respond to. Earlier in the interview, Faldo criticises the Jokowi government for allowing large scale importing, saying it is damaging to the economy. Rian responds to that criticism by arguing there is nothing wrong with importing so long as trade balance is maintained. In lines 9–15, Faldo does not respond to Rian's immediate position (see lines 4–6) but instead changes the topic (lines 9–10) and resumes an earlier discussion about infrastructure, in order to oppose Rian's position that was articulated then.

(9)
1	PUSPA:	*Nggak dosa ya*
		(So) it's not a sin is it
2		*impor dengan banyak --*
		to import on a large
3		*[dengan] jumlah banyak itu.*
		on a large scale like that.
4	RIAN:	*[eh=]*
		er=
5		*Kalo impor itu dosa berarti*
		If importing is a sin that means
6		*... bera- berdagang juga dosa dong.*
		doing business is also a sin, right.
7	PUSPA:	*Oke.*
		Okay.
		((TURNS TO FALDO))
8	->	**Mas Faldo gimana?**
		How about you (*Mas* Faldo)?
9	FALDO:	*Well,*
		Well,
10		*kalo ngomongin infrastruktur,*
		if (you) talk about infrastructure,
11		*data yang dari BPS lagi ni=h.*
		the data from the Indonesian Bureau of Statistics once again.
12		*dua ribu tujuh belas itu datanya empat koma tujuh,*
		in 2017 it was four point seven,
13		*dua ribu delapan belas itu empat koma satu .. persen.*
		in 2018 it was four point one per cent.
14		*Tu=run kok.*
		(It) went down.
15		*Ya.*
		Yeah.

Now compare the previous two extracts with the following, showing *gimana* being prefaced by a referent and the IE treating it as a request to comment on that referent. Sandiaga Uno is Prabowo's running mate and a former deputy governor of Jakarta whose initiative to provide support for small businesses through a scheme he named *Oke Oce* has not been successful. Puspa (IR) asks Faldo to comment on Sandiaga's record of achievements as a former deputy governor of Jakarta, specifying the referent of the interrogative as *rekam jejaknya sebagai wakil gubernur* (his record as deputy governor). This *gimana* interrogative invites the IE to respond to a specific position, and in this respect, it is akin to the English *what about that* discussed by Roth and Olsher (1997).

(10)
1	PUSPA:	*Tapi kalau misalnya Pak Sandi,*
		But in the case of *Pak* Sandi,
2	->	*rekam jejaknya sebagai wakil gubernur **gimana**?*
		<u>how</u> is his record as deputy governor?
3		*Belum sampai a=h -- akhir*
		(He) hasn't reached the end
4	FALDO:	*Pasti ... pasti saya diserang nih,*
		(I) guarantee (they'll) criticise me,
5		*Oke Oce tuh gagal ... gitu kan.*
		"*Oke Oce* has failed" ... like that, right.
6		*... dah kebayang nih.*
		(I can) imagine it.

The bare *gimana* in extracts in (8) and (9) can be considered deferential in the sense that by using this interrogative, the IR asks merely that the IE respond to a co-IE's position, without specifying which position to respond to, thus leaving the scope of the interrogative broad, allowing the IE the liberty to decide which position they would provide a contrast to. Deployed in conjunction with a kin term plus name to designate addressee, the construction is a common resource used by IRs to juxtapose perspectives deferentially.

Cascading Question and the Collaborative Accomplishment of Deference

In panel interviews, it is common for IEs to take the initiative to comment on a question directed to another IE, effectively self-selecting as next speaker by offering their own comment before the target addressee provides a response. This exercise of agency can transform a question-answer pair into a "question cascade" (Clayman and Heritage 2002b, 756), a deferential type of question presented as a series. In a question cascade, IR asks a question, and at its completion, goes on to produce a second version of the question. In the following example, an IE's self-insertion in a question cascade turns questioning into a collaborative act of deference.

In an episode of *LPT* shown in (11), Budi Adiputro (IR) has just had a jocular exchange with IE Philips Vermonte, bringing laughter to all participants. Now turning to Adi Prayitno, political commentator and academic from the State Islamic University Syarif Hidayatullah in Jakarta, Budi taps Adi lightly on the lower arm to signal he is being addressed. With everyone still laughing, Budi asks Adi to comment on the reliability of quick count as a method for predicting election results. He refers to Adi metonymically as *Ciputat*, the name of the suburb where Adi's institution is located, implying he is part of an esteemed establishment, then offers Adi the floor. That Budi's action is understood as deferential can be shown in the response it receives from Toni, another interviewee on the panel.

Toni recognises *Ciputat* as a metonym for the institution Adi represents. In a self-selecting turn, he provides recognition of its standing by calling it Ciputat school (line 4). By metonymically linking Adi to a school, Toni thus elevates Adi's views to the status of a respectable scholarly voice. Budi shows alignment with Toni's action by treating the latter's formulation as a corrective, as shown in line 5, where Budi immediately repeats Toni's formulation. In an overlapping turn, Toni displays further deference by addressing Adi using the kin term *Bang* (from Malay *abang* [older brother]) followed by first name, *Adi*, and shortening Adi's surname, Prayitno, into *Pray*, thereby imbuing it with a sense of youthful coolness.

At the completion of Toni's turn, Budi follows up on his request for Adi to speak, using the *gimana* interrogative followed by the reference formulation *Bang Adi* (older brother [Malay] Adi). Compared to his initial *silakan* (please) request, Budi's *gimana* construction is more specific in that it not only invites Adi to speak but also to give his opinion on a referent (namely, the validity of the quick count method). Budi's questions thus "cascade" from being an offer to take the floor to a request to comment on a specific referent.

(11) [CNN Indonesia Layar Pemilu Tepercaya, 21 April 2019: Caci dan Puji Hitung Cepat Usai Kompetisi]

1 BUDI: -> *Dari Ciputat dulu.*
            (Let's hear) from Ciputat first.
2   ->   *... Silakan.*
            Please.
3   @@@
4 TONI: -> *... **Ciputat school.***
5 BUDI: -> *... **Ciputat** [school]*.
6 TONI: -> [*Bang Adi*] *Pray.*
            Bang Adi Pray.
7 BUDI: -> *Gimana **Bang Adi**,*
            How do you (Bang Adi)
8   *... melihatnya.*
            see it. (-> 'What do you think about it?')

In terms of Toni's contributions to the question cascade, a couple of observations can be made. First, the insertion of his turns in between Budi's question cascade shows how structural positions can be exploited in the exercise of agency through self-selection as next speaker. Second, it illustrates how structural positions can serve as a resource for indexing deference collaboratively. These in turn suggest that the notion of "journalistic deference" could be broadened to include both acts performed by IR and those constructed collaboratively with IEs.

Differentiating Degrees of Deference

In this section I discuss how a participant uses language and hand movements in concert to signal different levels of deference and enact alignment and opposition. Eight speakers were invited as guests on *MN*, four from Jokowi's coalition and four from Prabowo's. The IEs are debating various issues and there is much overlapping talk. Dahnil Anzar Simanjuntak, a spokesperson from Prabowo's coalition is raising his hand to chest height while facing the speakers on the opposite side, in a bid for a turn to speak. Najwa (IR), noticing Dahnil's hand movement, signals he is to speak next, addressing him with *Mas Dahnil* while extending her left hand above shoulder height with palm up (line 2). Dahnil takes up his turn, referring to Najwa with *Mbak* (older sister [Javanese]) followed by the affectionate form of her name, *Nana* (line 4), and extending his right arm up to head height while pointing his forefinger upwards as he aligns with a statement made by Najwa in a previous sequence (line 4).[6]

(12) [Mata Najwa, 10 Oct 2018: Satu atau dua, debat harga tempe vs telur]

```
1    NAJWA:     [Mas] —
2    ->         [Mas Dahnil].
                ((FACING DAHNIL, EXTENDING LEFT HAND
                ABOVE SHOULDER HEIGHT WITH PALM UP
                TOWARD DAHNIL))
3    DAHNIL:    Pertama=.
                First of all.
4    ->         ... Tadi yang Mbak Nana juga sampaika=n,
                ((FACING NAJWA, RAISING RIGHT HAND TO
                HEAD LEVEL WITH PALM HALF OPEN AND
                FOREFINGER POINTING UP))
                What you (Mbak Nana) also said before,
```

5		*itu kan hasil survei.*
		that's survey results.
6	RAHAYU:	... [Iya].
		Yes.
7	DAHNIL:	*[Dan] itu adalah pendapat pu[[blik]],*
		And that's public opinion.
8	ROMLI:	*[[Suara]] [X].*
		The voice.
9	DAHNIL:	*[dan] rasa publik,*
		and sentiments of the public,
10		*dan suara **rakyat**.*
	->	((EXTENDING LEFT ARM OUT <u>ABOVE SHOULDER HEIGHT</u> WITH PALM UP TOWARD AUDIENCE))
		and the voice of <u>the people</u>.
11		...(.7) ***Rakyat** mengatakan,*
		<u>The people</u> are saying
12		*harga-harga mahal.*
		prices have skyrocketed.
13		*... Itu suara **rakyat**.*
	->	((EXTENDING LEFT ARM OUT <u>ABOVE SHOULDER HEIGHT</u> WITH PALM UP TOWARD AUDIENCE))
		That's the voice of <u>the people</u>.
14		*Dan **mereka** bantah.*
	->	((EXTENDING RIGHT ARM OUT <u>AT SHOULDER HEIGHT</u> WITH PALM UP TOWARD SPEAKERS ON OPPOSITE SIDE))
		And <u>they</u> rejected (it).
15		*Kedua=.*
		Secondly.
16		*Ka- --*
		If
17		***Rakyat** mengatakan,*
		<u>The people</u> are saying,
18		*... pekerjaan sulit.*
		jobs are scarce.
19		*... Itu suara **rakyat**.*
	->	((EXTENDS LEFT ARM OUT <u>ABOVE SHOULDER HEIGHT</u> WITH PALM UP TOWARD AUDIENCE))
		That's the voice of <u>the people</u>.

20   *Mereka bantah.*
->   ((EXTENDS LEFT ARM OUT <u>AT SHOULDER</u>
          <u>HEIGHT</u> WITH PALM UP TOWARD SPEAKERS ON
          OPPOSITE SIDE))
          <u>They</u> rejected (it).

Dahnil makes three distinct hand movements in reference to three different groups of participants in this speech event. In reference to Najwa shown previously in line 4, he extends his arm up to *head height* with palm half open and forefinger pointing upwards. This is the highest position at which he places his hand along the vertical axis. The second is when he refers to *suara rakyat* (the people's voice)—lines 10, 13, 19—and extends his arm out *above shoulder height* with his palm open to the audience. The third is in reference to the participants on the opposing side, referred to with the pronoun *mereka* (they), which he performs by extending his arm out *at shoulder height* with palm up while facing Najwa (lines 14, 20). The differing heights at which the arm is extended are in this way iconic of the differing degrees of deference he gives to the different (groups of) participants, with the highest accorded to IR and the lowest, the co-IEs from the opposing side. That they are all deferential, that is, respect giving performed for the benefit of the audience, is indicated by the way referring is accompanied by an open palm—a gesture generally regarded as more deferential than pointing to an addressee—and signs of demeanour that include a gentle tone, smiles and a slow speed of talk.

Neutralism "Breach" and Reworking of Institutional Framework

In this final section of analysis, I consider the way in which object signs can be juxtaposed to enact an adversarial stance deferentially. In the example to be shown, kin terms and a pronoun are used by IR in a move designed to pressure a senior politician to respond to student activists in the panel. The juxtaposition between kin terms and a pronoun produces a semantic "clash" whereby a term denoting kin hierarchy is contrasted with individuation and relations of distance, even anonymity (Errington 1998; see also, Errington, this volume) that is associated with the pronoun. By using the kin term *abang* (older brother) the IR positions the politician as a senior who has a duty to care for their *adik* (younger sibling). These kin terms are contrasted with *anda*, a word coined in 1957 to fill a perceived lack in Indonesian language of a pronoun that could be used to convey egalitarian relations—relations considered characteristic of a democratic, modern society Indonesians aspired theirs to be. The etymology of this term is unclear, though some speculate it was originally a term reserved for a high-status addressee (see

Sabirin 1957). Nowadays, *anda* is commonly used in public announcements, advertisements and institutional settings.

The example is taken from an episode of *MN*. Najwa Shihab (IR) sat with nine interviewees, including two student activists, Atiyatul Muqtadir and Royyan Dzakiy, and Fahri Hamzah, deputy speaker of the *DPR*, the legislative body that drafted the law. (Fahri was himself a student activist who protested against President Suharto in 1998.) Less than a month before Jokowi was sworn in as president for the second term, thousands of students had taken to the streets to oppose a new law ushered in to monitor the work of the state's corruption watchdog, the *Komisi Pemberantasan Korupsi* (Commission for the eradication of corruption). Activists were worried that the law would erode the agency's independence. Among the audience were supporters of the protests.

Atiyatul and Royyan are the first to be invited to speak. Royyan mentions that in the past few days students' requests to meet with the *DPR* have been ignored. Atiyatul adds that they are still waiting for a government response as they speak. Hearing this, Najwa reminds the students that Fahri Hamzah is in the panel, implying this is an opportunity to communicate their concerns directly to a key member of the *DPR*. In an unexpected move, Najwa then turns to Fahri and startles him by asking him to respond to the student activists without specifying which position he is to respond to. Najwa first addresses Fahri with *bang* (older brother) followed by full name, *Bang Fahri Hamzah*, thus relating to Fahri deferentially, before mentioning that his *adik-adik* (younger siblings) (lines 13–14) are awaiting response. She uses the pronoun *anda* to frame her reference to Fahri in the possessive construction *adik-adik anda* (your younger siblings). By being addressed and referred to as an older brother, Fahri is treated as a senior with an obligation to care for his junior counterpart. At the same time, the pronoun *anda* explicitly and singularly identifies Fahri as the bearer of this obligation. That this act is unexpected, particularly in a public broadcast, is indicated by Fahri's change in demeanour and reluctance to respond, as indicated by the silences (lines 15 and 21) and delay in answering (lines 16 and 18).

(13) [Trans7 & Narasi TV, Mata Najwa, 27 September 2019: Ujian Reformasi]

1   ROYYAN: *Dan konferensi pers sudah dilakukan tapi sayangnya tidak ada*
                       And the press conference was held but unfortunately there was no
2   *... kelanju[tannya itu].*
                   follow up.

3	ATIYATUL:	*[Termasuk] ... malam ini,*
		Including this evening,
4		*tidak terjadi juga Mbak.*
		it didn't happen *Mbak.*
5	NAJWA:	*Termasuk malam ini tidak ada respon?*
		Including this evening there is no response?
6		*... Tapi yang hadir,*
		But those who are present (here),
7	((AUDIENCE CLAPPING))	
8		*... tapi ada ketua wakil DPR,*
		but we have here the deputy speaker of the *DPR,*
9		*... yang juga e mantan*
		who is also er a former
10		*... mantan aktivis mahasiswa*
		former student activist
11		*tahun sembilan puluh delapan.*
		(from nineteen) ninety-eight.
12		*Ada Bang Fahri Hamzah.*
		We have here *Bang* Fahri Hamzah.
13	->	**Bang Fahri Hamzah,**
		Bang Fahri Hamzah,
14	->	**... adik-adik anda Bang.**
		(here are) your younger siblings *Bang.*
15		(0.2)
16	FAHRI: ->	*... Soal ap --*
		In relation to
17	NAJWA: -->	*Silakan ditanggapi.*
		Please respond to them.
18	FAHRI: ->	*Soal apa?*
		In relation to what?
19	NAJWA:	*Apakah memang DPR tidak ... ada*
		Is it true that the *DPR* doesn't have
20		*... keinginan untuk membuka ruang dialog itu?*
		the desire to open a space for dialogue?
21		(0.3)
22	FAHRI:	*Ya=m,*
		Well,
23		*... (0.1) saya nggak tahu ya.*
		I'm not sure.

24	*Tapi kan DPR itu memang tempat dialog ya,*
	But you know the DPR is a place where dialogue takes place, right.
25	*... hari-hari ya.*
	on a daily basis, right.
26	*... E=h,*
	Er,
27	*Partainya banyak .. ya.*
	There are many parties, right.
28	*... Agamanya banyak,*
	Many (different) religions,
29	*situ sukunya banyak.*
	many (different) ethnic groups.
30	*... Dan orang tuh beda pendapat semua.*
	And everyone has different opinions.
31	*Ada ekstrem kiri ada ekstrem kanan .. di situ.*
	There are those from the extreme left and those from extreme right there.
32	*... Mantan aktivis ada*
	There are former activists.
33	*... lawyer ada.*
	there are lawyers.
34	*... Dan memang,*
	And actually,
35	*hari-hari ya berdebatlah ... ya.*
	(they) engage in debates on a daily basis ... right.
36	*... Karena itu mustahil anggota DPR menghindari dialog dan perdebatan,*
	That's why it's impossible that members of the DPR would avoid having dialogues and debates.
37	*Karena itu dah makanan hari-harinya.*
	Because that's their daily meals.

The show ended with Najwa offering the space to Royyan, Atiyatul and two other students to read a communiqué. As the students rose from their seats to stand on the stage, Najwa joined in and invited everyone in the audience to stand up and join in the communiqué, with she herself reading every line in the loudest voice. Behind her and the students, a large screen displayed scenes from the protests and lines from the communiqué written in white letters set against a bright red background, calling to mind the red and white of the Indonesian flag. The communiqué ended with everyone shouting a chant, expressing loyalty to student movements and the Indonesian people, and calling on everyone to bring down corrupt politicians.

A panel interview being transformed by the panel host into a venue for a student protest is certainly not a common occurrence. By inviting the students to perform the communiqué and the audience to join in, and by immersing herself in the action, Najwa effectively stepped out of her role as IR to inhabit the role of a "partisan advocate" (Clayman 2013b, 631). What transpired on this *MN* episode illustrates how the institutional framework can be reworked to serve contingent purposes, and that an act of addressee-reference can mark a crucial point that signals a forthcoming change in participant roles. It also suggests that journalistic neutralism can be overridden in the service of other, more pressing goals.

Conclusion

Panel interviews are venues where both IRs and IEs are expected to express and interrogate arguments, and display alignment or opposition. These venues demand that the participants conduct themselves institutionally by talking to each other in a civil manner. The interviews studied here were held at a time when the need for modelling political conduct was high, and therefore the way journalists and politicians refer to themselves and their addressee(s) could influence the way members of the public perceive political relations and judge the degree of success with which Indonesia has traversed the road to democracy. This study has examined acts of interlocutor reference to show how journalists and politicians use sibling terms, names and pronouns to enact deference in these interviews.

I have discussed deference as respect shown toward co-participants in an institutional setting and pointed out that acts of deference are distributed across the participant framework; that is, both IR and IEs perform and are given deference. I have mentioned that the common form employed in deferential acts consists of a kin term followed by name, and that orientation to the audience is sometimes explicit (as in a politician referring to the audience as *rakyat* 'the people') and other times subtle (enacted, for example, through alternation of self-referring forms). I hope to have demonstrated that a study of interlocutor reference can provide a useful avenue for showing how the panel interview is constituted as a broadcast event.

Recent studies in journalism (Statham 2007; Hanitzsh et al. 2019; Van Dalen et al. 2019) of role perception show that, while journalists around the world identify as information providers, reporters and watchdogs, they vary in the way they define these roles. The studies by Hanitzsh et al. (2019) in particular, mention that Indonesian journalists, like other journalists in "new democracies" (for example, in Eastern and Central Europe, Latin America and the Philippines) have a low level of trust in political institutions. They value what Statham (2007, 465) calls the "informative-educative" role, a role involving raising public awareness and knowledge about a perceived problem in society. Although these findings do not directly correlate with practices of showing deference in the Indonesian interviews, they nevertheless suggest that journalists' perceptions of their professional role would to some degree influence the way they perform their role as IR. The journalists hosting *MN* and *LPT* are concerned to ensure that they do what they can to encourage young people to participate in the elections. They perform this informative-educative role by inviting young people as audience members and show alignment with them through various means, including choosing an interview setting that is youth-friendly (for example, a movie theatre on *MN*, a café style studio set-up on *LPT*). Najwa Shihab's participation in the student communiqué on *MN* takes this alignment further in a radical way.

Indonesia is a modern nation, which, like other similarly modern nations, exemplifies what Hannah Arendt (1998, 28) describes as "the body of peoples and political communities" and "a family whose everyday affairs have to be taken care of by a gigantic, nation-wide administration of housekeeping" (Arendt 1998, 28; see Bouchier 2015; Brenner 1999; Platt et al. 2018 for references to the Indonesian nation as a family). The incumbent president, Jokowi, often frames his call for people to resolve political differences in terms of a need for siblings/relatives to make peace with each other. *Kita ini kan bersaudara* (We are all related after all) is a sentence he has uttered on multiple occasions when conflicts arise. The repeated act of metaphoric kinship by a head of state may be interpreted relative to the broader patterns of governance under that person's leadership as reflecting increased patrimonialism (see Bouchier 2015 for patrimonialism under the New Order). The study of interlocutor reference presented here could provide a basis for examining the extent to which reference practices can be said to reflect such power relations. Jokowi's family metaphor is hardly unusual as it forms part of the broader practice of conceiving of social relations as relations between kin.[7] In this conceptualisation, misgivings people have about each other co-exist, perhaps paradoxically, with feelings of familial affection and duty.

Notes

[*] I owe special thanks to Jack Sidnell, Luke Fleming, Sarah Lee, Michael Ewing and Tom Power for valuable comments and suggestions. Thanks also to participants at the Forum on the Dynamics of Discourse, Society and Power in Asia: Language Dynamics in the Asia Pacific, The University of Melbourne, for their generous feedback, and to Refdinal Hadiningrat and Asdit Leonitara for helping me transcribe the data.

[1] The transcription followed here is from Du Bois, Schuetze-Coburn, Paolino and Cumming (1993). Due to space, interlinear gloss is provided only for example (1).

[2] *DPR* is the acronym for *Dewan Perwakilan Rakyat* (People's representative council).
[3] The first episode of *MN*, for example, was aired on 25 November 2009.
[4] Clayman and Heritage (2002a, 30) define "elite" or "successful" journalists as those who "impart their own 'take' on events, and whose interpretations of the background and motivations of political actors are conveyed to the viewing public."
[5] The following are indicators of when the interview proper begins. Before the participants were seated, Arief said he was not a representative of the people, to which Najwa responded: *Yah, belum mulai udah gini* (We haven't even started yet and you're already like this). After all participants were seated, Najwa signalled a shift to the interview proper by prefacing her next turn with *Oke* (okay), thereby indicating to the IEs that they are about to be interviewed.
[6] Note the use of Javanese kin term *mbak* (older sister) by a speaker of Batak ethnic background (Dahnil Simanjuntak) to address Najwa Shihab who is of Arab-Makassarese descent. We don't know whether Najwa identifies herself as Makassarese or Indonesian Arab or both. Similarly, she uses the Javanese kin term *mas* (older brother) in reference to Dahnil, who is clearly not a Javanese (Dahnil comes from a Batak family who grew up in Banten, West Java). This is not unusual among Indonesians but nonetheless shows there is no default indexical relation between kin terms and ethnic identity that earlier studies on address terms in Indonesian suggest (see Kridalaksana 1974; Purwo 1984; Mahdi 2001).
[7] Indeed, Jokowi is not unique in appealing to kinship in his political communication. This practice is attested worldwide (see e.g. Haugevik and Neumann 2019).

PART 4

Theories

CHAPTER 9

Interlocutor Reference and the Complexity of East and Southeast Asian Honorific Registers

Luke Fleming

Honorific registers are uniquely elaborated in the languages of East Asia (Japanese, Korean) and island Southeast Asia (Javanese, Madurese, Sundanese, Balinese, Sasak). Grammaticalised honorifics in these languages index the deference-entitlements not only of the discourse referent (common for honorific vocabularies found elsewhere) but also of the addressee. Additionally, (self-) humbling or "humiliative" vocabularies often form distinct honorific repertoires (for example, Javanese *krama andhap*, Japanese *kenjigoo*). Scholars tend to assume that language-external factors—elaborate social hierarchies with ascriptive status-asymmetries—are the most relevant causal infrastructures motivating the emergence of honorific language:

> Sets of personal pronouns ... are perhaps most diversified and complex in societies characterized by pronounced forms of hierarchical social organisation and status. In such societies, distinctions in personal reference and address are likely to thrive, paradigm cases being found in Southeast and East Asia. (Heine and Song 2011, 588)

However, as Irvine (1992) has shown, any simple correlation between social hierarchy and honorific language lacks predictive power—many hierarchical societies lack elaborated honorific repertoires. And honorific repertoires are found in more egalitarian, kinship coordinated societies, for example, Yele (Armstrong 1928), Mangarayi (Merlan 1982) and Sengseng (Chowning 1985). Although social hierarchy is clearly a necessary condition for the elaboration of the honorific types we will be discussing (Müller and Weymuth 2017), social stratification cannot sufficiently explain the deep typological differences in the pragmatic structure of honorification attested in different linguistic areas. Furthermore, there is a complex causal interplay between pragmatic patterns instantiated in discursive interaction and ideologies of social hierarchy. From the perspective of a Whorfian social pragmatics, sociocultural ideologies of hierarchy (like Confucianism) may be just as sustained by social pragmatic patterns (like the fictive use of kin terms as an idiom for signalling relative statuses) as they are generative of such patterns in the first place (see Fleming and Sidnell 2020).

In this chapter, I argue that a full causal account of the character and distribution of honorific systems must complement attention to factors of sociocultural "complexity" with a focus on language internal factors. I argue that the unique properties of East and Southeast Asian honorific "pronominal address", and the unique properties of East and Southeast Asian "speech levels", suggest that the two should be understood both diachronically and synchronically as a unified phenomenon. I build upon important empirical and theoretical work by Joseph Errington (1985b) concerning the "pragmatic salience" of interlocutor referring expressions in the ethno-metapragmatic modelling of honorific speech in Javanese (see also Suharno 1982) in order to formulate a diachronic argument that explains why uniquely complex honorific registers are only found in East and Southeast Asia. Focusing in particular on Southeast Asia, I argue that patterns of social pragmatic variation in interlocutor reference (in particular, the robust paradigmatic alternation between pronouns and nouns in both speaker- and addressee-reference) served as an affordance assemblage that scaffolded the development of the full range of honorific types (more technically, "indexical focus" types) that give honorific registers in this part of the world their unparalleled richness.

This chapter grows out of ongoing comparative work on social indexicality in person deixis. But it is also deeply informed by work carried out in collaboration with Jack Sidnell on what we call the "social pragmatics of interlocutor reference". The study of so-called "address systems" has emerged from work on European languages. In those contexts, it is typically only in alternations in addressee-referring expressions (that is, second-person pronouns) that the deference entitlements of the addressee vis-à-vis the speaker are non-referentially indexed. In East and Southeast Asian languages, however, both addressee- and speaker-reference are invested with social pragmatic significances. In these languages, "pronominal address" is only a subspace of a larger domain of the social pragmatics of interlocutor reference. This point is central to the larger argument.

The chapter proceeds as follows. In the next two sections, I discuss the problem of Asian honorific registers by offering a functional typology of honorification and a portrait of the cross-linguistic distribution of those types, limiting myself to the class of lexical honorific repertoires. This allows a more precise characterisation of the unique richness of honorific registers in East and Southeast Asia. In the sections following that, I focus on honorification as achieved specifically in interlocutor reference. I show that honorific registers of person deixis (or "T/V systems") have a parallel typological distribution to lexical or morphological honorific repertoires and that—just as in the case of the honorific vocabularies—honorific pronouns (and "pronoun-substitutes") in the languages of this region have highly divergent and marked properties. I conclude with a discussion of the "pragmatic salience" of person referring expressions in honorific registers and show how the particularities of honorific person reference in Southeast and East Asia can be plausibly understood as paving the way for the development of these functionally heterogeneous honorific systems.

I apologise in advance to regional experts; I have never conducted field research in East or Southeast Asia and this chapter is based exclusively upon published primary and secondary source materials. This has the inevitable effect of conflating stipulated norms with actual discursive practices, and of reifying as closed paradigms of interlocutor reference what are surely socially and linguistically much more heterogeneous phenomena. But though the argument is schematic and theoretical, proceeding often only by exemplification, I hope that it opens up pathways for thinking in greater depth about how social pragmatic structure hangs together and how it is scaffolded.

Indexical Focus and Honorification

Honorific words and expressions can have varied significations depending upon their contexts of use and the cultures of language within which they are embedded. Nevertheless, and setting aside for the moment these different social valuations, the default understanding of honorifics is a relational one. As opposed to, say, dialectal markers of speaker identity, the default reading of an (anti)honorific expression is one which concerns the social relationship between individuals. Importantly, the individuals who are related by this social signalling are typically identified with the interactional roles defined by the utterance context (Silverstein 1976; Comrie 1976; Levinson 1983 [1979]). Formalising this insight, Agha (1993a) proposed the analytic framework of indexical focus to capture how social indexicals are mapped onto interactional roles. Here is his account of indexical focus specifically innovated for honorifics:

The signalling of deference entitlement (or simply 'deference') appears to have the structure 'deference to somebody from somebody,' or more precisely 'deference to [role₁] from [role₂].' I will say that the interactional role category to which deference is directed is the *focus of deference*, and the interactional role category from which the deference emanates is the *origo of deference*, so that deference in this sense is always 'deference to [role_focus] from [role_origo]'. (Agha 1993a, 134)

Though I do not substantively revise Agha's account, I will conserve the use of "origo" for the source of deference but replace the term "focus" with "target", for the goal of deference-indexing. By "indexical focus" we will mean the full set of interactional roles which are socially indexed by the use of a token of the pragmatic type.

The indexical focus of honorifics typically treats the (occupant of the) speaker role [S] as the origo of deference (but see Fleming [2018, 580] *infra* on Goffmanian Animator as origo). Intuitively, we think of honorific discourse as speech where the speaker shows respect towards someone else. The target of honorific discourse is typically either the discourse addressee [A] or the discourse referent [R], or their union (see note 6).[1]

Indexical focus can be thought of as part of the metapragmatic content of honorific word *types*. Indexical focus is a metapragmatic framework in the sense that it provides a roadmap for language users to interpret pragmatic acts of honorification—for knowing who defers to whom. But it should be underscored that at the level of actual discourse *tokens* any number of contextual variables may interact with the indexical focus of honorific word types. Use of referent-raising forms—for instance, use of Title + Last Name as opposed to First Name in American English—may signal solidarity with relatively lower-status audience members (Murphy 1988). This happens when one refers to a colleague as "Professor Last-Name" when speaking to a student but as "First-Name" when speaking to another colleague. Inversely, suppression of referent-targeting honorifics may itself count as a trope of deference towards a high-status audience member. Indeed, this was one of the defining of characteristic of *basa kedhaton* or "palace language" employed at the royal court of Solo. In the co-presence of the king, there was a "conspicuous nonuse of *krama inggil* for reference" to anyone other than the co-present potentate (Errington 1982, 91). The point is, honorific word *types* often have indexical focus properties specified in their type-level pragmatics, but honorific *tokens* complexly interact with other aspects of context to create richer pragmatic meanings.

The Markedness of Speaker-Addressee Lexical Honorifics

Lexical alternations which belie a difference in honorificity are found in all languages. So, for instance, in almost all languages, the alternation between proper names and seniority-encoding kin terms constitutes an honorific distinction (Fleming and Slotta 2018). By lexical honorific registers, however, I mean something both more specific and more elaborate. Here we are concerned with a lexical repertoire, typically covering a number of distinct classes of grammatical words (that is, not just limited to human nouns), which is an active and naturally occurring object of metalinguistic reflection for some socially defined domain of individuals, and which, furthermore, is a named speech variety (for example, Tibetan *zhesa* [respect language]) stereotypically understood to be a means for one individual to express deference towards another individual, whatever other effects may actually be accomplished by its use in actual events of speaking (Agha 1998). So while lexical alternations like *gut/stomach*, *clunker/car*, or *slop/food* exhibit parallel pragmatic asymmetries to one another (Allan and Burridge 1991), with the first term in each pair having something like a "speaker-debases-the-referent" function, these and other similar terms do not form—in American English, at any rate—a discrete anti-honorific lexical repertoire whose pragmatic effects are associated with discrete stereotyped effects. (Compare here to the dense ideological scaffolding of the Korowai anti-honorific lexical register *xoxulop* [Stasch 2008]).

In a comparative study of honorific registers—crucially, as defined in terms of this dual metapragmatic-pragmatic structure—Agha (2007, see in particular table 7.6) decisively shows that Speaker$_{origo}$-Referent$_{target}$ is the default or "unmarked" indexical focus type for honorification cross-linguistically (see also Brown and Levinson 1987, 276). This finding is consistent with the biasing of metapragmatic awareness towards referential functions in language (Silverstein 1981) and the related "pragmatic salience" of person referring expressions as sites of social pragmatic alternation (Errington 1985b), a connection which I discuss in greater detail below. Artificially restricting our discussion to *lexical* honorific repertoires, the markedness of Addressee$_{target}$ honorifics with respect to Referent$_{target}$ honorifics is revealed (*i*) in asymmetries in their global distribution cross-linguistically and (*ii*) in implicational relationships governing their co-occurrence language internally.

Lexical Honorifics which only Signal Deference to Addressee are Largely Restricted to Southeast Asia

In many languages, honorification is exclusively accomplished by means of Speaker$_{origo}$-Referent$_{target}$ lexical repertoires. Again, this is a description of the indexical focus of honorific word *types*. For particular discourse *tokens*, the honoured referent may also additionally be the discourse addressee, and, indeed, referent-targeting forms may be used in more exaggerated fashion when the exalted referent is an audience member. With the possible exception of Taba (Austronesian), no language of South East Asia, to my knowledge, exclusively employs, Speaker$_{origo}$-Addressee$_{target}$ lexical repertoires.[2] Outside of Southeast Asia, the only other possible candidates are some of the so-called "mother-in-law languages" of Aboriginal Australia (see, for example, Dyirbal, Bininj Gun-wok, Yanyuwa; for further discussion and citations, see Fleming 2022).

Lexical honorifics in many Austronesian languages are exclusively Speaker$_{origo}$-Referent$_{target}$ focused. The so-called "chiefly languages" of western Polynesia are examples of honorific registers employed in an exclusively referent-targeting manner (Fleming 2016). But such exclusively referent-targeting lexical honorific registers are found in languages scattered all over the world, for example, Nahuatl (Pittman 1948), Tibetan (Agha 1993a, b), Sinhala (Chandralal 2010), Tongan (Philips 2010). Honorific repertoires may be quite large and yet honorific alternants are still only employed where the honorific target is the discourse referent (whether or not that referent is additionally the discourse addressee). In Ladakhi (Sino-Tibetan), a very large number of verbs and nouns have distinct honorific and non-honorific forms (for example, non-honorific/honorific body part term doublets like *mik/rtsan* [eye], *sna/shang* [nose], *lakpa/chak* [hand], *lce/ljaks* [tongue]), and a range of semantically vacuous affixes function honorifically on "neutral" nouns that lack honorific stem-alternations (Koshal 1987). But tokens of these forms always express deference to the individual associated with the reference of the term itself (whether the referent of the subject of the verb, the possessor of a nominal, or the experiencer of an affective state).

> In the case of persons to whom honor is to be given, one uses honorific forms for his worldly possessions (house, dog, horse, etc.), things he uses (water, food, cup, plate, spoon, bedding, etc.), and to all other behavioral actions and states of being (such as sickness, pain, thought, happiness, unhappiness, smile, laugh, etc.). (Koshal 1987, 162)

Intriguingly, formally distinct addressee-targeting lexical honorifics have a distribution which is largely circumscribed to Southeast Asia. (Japanese and Korean possess purely Speaker$_{origo}$-Addressee$_{target}$ [S-A] honorifics, but these are not lexical honorifics, so we leave them aside for the moment.) In particular, Javanese, and nearby languages historically influenced by Javanese, like Madurese, Sundanese, Balinese, and Sasak, have quite large vocabulary sets whose use expresses speaker's deference to addressee independent of the identity of the discourse referent.

The Existence of Addressee$_{target}$ Honorific Vocabularies Implies the Existence of Referent$_{target}$ Vocabularies

Where Addressee$_{target}$ lexical repertoires are employed, (a) formally distinct or overlapping repertoires will exist which can be used to defer to non-addressed Referents, or (b) Addressee-targeting forms can also be used to target Referent.

(a) *Formally distinct Speaker$_{origo}$-Addressee$_{target}$ and Speaker$_{origo}$-Referent$_{target}$ repertoires.* The existence of distinctive referent-targeting and addressee-targeting honorific repertoires is really particular to the languages of East Asia (Japanese and Korean) and island Southeast Asia. In all of the languages of Indonesia just mentioned (again, with the exception of Taba), honorific vocabularies which signal deference to the addressee are complemented by repertoires which signal deference to the discourse referent (e.g., Javanese *krama inggil*; Balinese *alus singgih*). ("The oppositions between krama inggil/non-krama inggil on one hand, and krama/ngoko on the other, are skewed pragmatically: the former keys to connections created by referring to someone, the latter to existential links presupposed in addressing someone" [Errington 1985b, 293].) To be sure, some forms can be used either to honour the addressee (independent of the identity of the referent) or the referent (independent of the identity of addressee)—that is, some items double as both *krama* and *krama inggil* forms. This reflects important historical overlap between the repertoires, with *krama inggil* forms diachronically being recruited into Speaker$_{origo}$-Addressee$_{target}$ [S-A] function (Silverstein 1979). But there are also numerous forms differentially enregistered in one or the other repertoire, e.g., *tindak* versus *késah* as referent-targeting versus addressee-targeting honorific terms for "to go out", respectively (Errington 1988, 101).

(b) *Honorifics can be employed with either Speaker$_{origo}$-Addressee$_{target}$ or Speaker$_{origo}$-Referent$_{target}$ focus.* In some languages outside of Southeast Asia lexical honorifics can be employed with an S-A focus. But in these cases, the same formal repertoires can also be employed with a Speaker$_{origo}$-Referent$_{target}$ [S-R] focus. I have called this "fluid focus" elsewhere (Fleming 2016). Most of the "mother-in-law languages" of Aboriginal Australia pattern in this way. In languages like Warlpiri (Laughren 2001), Mangarayi (Merlan 1982) and Wik (Sutton 1978), large sociopragmatically suppletive vocabularies are employed in addressing particular "avoidance relations" (typically affinal kin, adult cross-sex siblings, or partners in particular ritual organisations, like those centred around rites of male circumcision, see Fleming 2014, 137–41), regardless who is being referred to. Though their kinship-keyed implementation within the social field is quite distinct from the rank-stratified uses of speech levels, register variation is every bit as constitutive of a relational honorific distinction. Interestingly, in most of these languages the same vocabularies should additionally be employed in speaking about (that is, referring to) avoidance relations. Outside of Australia, the "royal" registers of northeastern Africa, for example, Yemsa, Shilluk, Dirayta (Storch 2011), likely historically functioned in this manner.

To summarise, addressee-targeting lexical honorifics are much more scarcely attested than referent-targeting ones, and where they are attested, they typically co-occur with, or double-as, referent-targeting honorifics.

Southeast Asian Honorifics by Indexical Focus Type

Essentially, up until this point we have simply developed Agha's finding that referent-honorifics are the unmarked type of honorific cross-linguistically. With this backdrop in place, we hope that we have successfully motivated the question of the emergence of "marked" honorific indexical focus types: that is, how does honorification not limited to the indexical targeting of the discourse referent emerge? Here I will answer this question only for the special case of lexical honorifics. Distinct lexical repertoires of addressee-targeting honorifics are essentially only attested in Southeast Asia. In Korean and Japanese, sentence-final particle and mood markers function as pure Speaker$_{origo}$-Addressee$_{target}$ honorifics. Though it seems likely that parallel diachronic pathways can account for the convergent properties of honorific registers in East and Southeast Asian languages, for reasons of textual and intellectual economy we largely limit ourselves to a discussion of patterns of lexical honorifics found in the languages of island Southeast Asia.

Javanese, and a number of languages historically influenced by it, including Balinese, Sasak, Sundanese, and Madurese, have developed elaborate lexical honorific repertoires.[3] Javanese is assumed to be the source for Sundanese speech levels. This is dated to the 16th century when the Mataram empire controlled west Java (Müller-Gotama 2001, 3, citing Purwo 1993, 252; see Fox 2005 for an overview). Nineteenth century connections between Sundanese nobility and the Javanese nobility at the courts of Solo and Yogyakarta would have been a further source of honorific borrowing (Harsojo 1983, 301, cited in Anderson 1993, 108). Clynes (1994) convincingly shows that Balinese speech levels are contact derived from Old Javanese during the 15th century or earlier. This supports a relatively early development of Javanese speech levels.[4] Nothofer summarises Clynes' historical synopsis:

> Bali was culturally dominated by Java between the eighth and fifteenth century and the flow of influence was from Java to Bali only. [....] These contacts came to a halt when Islam arrived on Java and caused the destruction of Hindu kingdoms. Relations between Java and Bali after

the Islamisation of Java consisted mainly of hostile encounters. (Nothofer 2003, 60)

Historical evidence of contact between Lombok, where Sasak is spoken, and Java is less well-established. Parts of Lombok were, however, occupied by Balinese from the end of the 17th to the end of the 19th centuries. And many honorific forms in Sasak have cognate forms in Balinese (Nothofer 2003, 80). But Javanese also likely influenced Sasak speech levels, and that during two distinct periods of contact: "The first one was established when Majapahit dominated Lombok in the 14th century and the second one took place when New Javanese speakers participated in the Islamisation of Lombok in the 16th century" (2003, 62).

What makes Indonesian languages possessing lexical honorifics so remarkable from a typological perspective is the way in which honorific repertoires are differentiated by indexical focus type. Though folk ethno-metapragmatic labels for distinct vocabularies do not map in a one-to-one fashion onto distinct indexical focus properties of the honorifics they classify, they do roughly correlate with them. (Neither does native metapragmatic vocabulary discretely differentiate between utterance-level and lexeme-level judgments—both a word and an utterance may be characterised by Javanese speakers as *krama*, see Errington 1988). The correspondence between our indexical focus characterisation and native metapragmatic categorisation of honorific repertoires is tightest for S-A and S-R types. The S-A axis is of course the speech level axis (that is, *krama*, *madya*, *ngoko* in Javanese). Many lexical alternations are effective only over this axis (e.g., the temporal adverbs $wis_{ngoko}/mpun_{madya}/sampun_{krama}$ [already]). The S-R axis is instantiated by the cross-cutting *krama inggil* vocabulary (e.g., $késah_{krama}/tindak_{krama\ inggil}$ [to go out]).

Particular attention, however, must be paid to forms which are metapragmatically characterised as humbling (often called "humiliatives" or "humilifics" in the literature on East Asian honorifics). Considered in terms of their indexical focus properties, these do not form a unified class either cross-linguistically or language-internally. Rather, they are united by a principle of semantic derogation and associated pragmatic implicature. Javanese *krama andhap* (or "low" *krama*), for instance, does not form a unitary class from the indexical focus perspective. This sub-repertoire includes some verbs, like *caos* (to give), which indicate that the referent of the subject of the verb is evaluated as owing deference entitlements to the referent of the (indirect) object of the verb. In the indexical focus notation, multi-place predicates like *caos* could be characterised as $Referent1_{origo}$-$Referent2_{target}$ [R1-R2] honorifics.[5] But forms (like *dalem* "I") which semantically derogate the referent (prototypically the speaker), and by implication honour the addressee, are also classified as *krama andhap*. These would be given the notation $[Speaker=Referent]_{origo}$-$Addressee_{target}$.

It is the prototypical identity of the debased referent and the occupant of the speaker role which accounts for local understandings which group these diverse forms into a coherent class of humbling honorifics. Multi-place *krama andhap* predicates like *caos* are prototypically employed in constructions involving first-person subjects and second-person objects or indirect objects—that is, they are conceptualised as verbs of petition or supplication. In Japanese, the speaker-anchored privileges of Referent1$_{origo}$-Referent2$_{target}$ forms are reflected in the folk ethno-metapragmatic framing of such forms as *kenjigoo* or "self-humbling" (Uehara 2011, 201). But again, addressee-honouring speaker-referring terms are also often classified in native metapragmatic terminology as humbling forms—for example, Javanese *dalem* (Errington 1988, 157), Sasak *kaji* (Nothofer 2003, 66). Indeed, in Sasak the majority of forms given an emic metapragmatic characterisation as "humbling" are in fact one-place predicates prototypically employed in self-reference. (The honorific register in Tetun, an Austronesian language spoken in West Timor, may be entirely composed of such humiliative terms; see discussion in Fleming 2016, 307.) Though the mapping of social indexical functions onto interactional roles operates in diverse ways, what is common to all of these cases is that denotational debasement counts as honorification and the prototypical—and sometimes categorical—person who is debased is the speaker him- or herself.

Returning to the broader point, this cluster of languages in Indonesia routinely distinguishes between honorifics of at least three distinct honorific types. So, for instance, in Sasak the verb of motion "to go" can be rendered with an addressee-honorific form (*lumbar*) [S-A], a referent-raising form (*margi*) [S-R] or a speaker-humbling form (*lampaq*) [S=R-A]. There are three ways to honour others, and these different ways of honouring are all grammaticalised in distinct honorific lexical repertoires.

Why are Addressee-Honorifics and Self-Humbling Repertoires only Robustly Attested in East and Southeast Asia?

As we have seen, languages of East Asia and Southeast Asia possess remarkably elaborated honorific registers: Japanese and Korean, on the one hand, and Javanese, Balinese, Sasak, Madurese and Sundanese, on the other, possess distinct addressee-targeting and referent-targeting honorific repertoires. And, as if this were not enough, these languages additionally contain a third, albeit more functionally diverse, repertoire of humiliatives forms prototypically employed in speaker-reference (so-called "object honorifics" in the literature on Korean and Japanese). Viewed through this comparative prism, it becomes clear that East and Southeast Asian sociolinguistics offer unique patterns not attested anywhere else. So how should we explain the existence of elaborate S-A lexical honorifics, or "speech levels", as well as of humiliatives, in these two areas? Clearly the existence of elaborate honorifics in this region is importantly contoured by the forms of social hierarchy and political organisation proper to East Asian dynastic kingdoms, on the one hand, and Indonesian sultanates, on the other, and to the norms of honorific language that emerged around institutional centres of royal courts (see Errington 1982). Focusing again on Southeast Asia, there is good evidence for a close fit between distinct honorific repertoires and particular social distinctions in a number of societies in this region. Arka's (2005) discussion of Balinese honorific repertoires, for instance, illustrates the tight linkage between speech level use and social caste. Nevertheless, as important as social hierarchy may be to the ultimate functional instantiation of honorific language within the social field, it is not a sufficient explanatory principle to explain the typological anomalies that we have documented. As Irvine (1992) observes, honorific vocabularies do not pop-up anywhere that social hierarchies are found. Furthermore, even where elaborate honorific registers are clearly linked to social stratification (for example, Nahuatl, Persian, Samoan, Romanian), we typically only find S-R focused repertoires. To understand the *pragmatic structure* of honorific registers we cannot reductively focus on social stratification.

But neither can the answer to the problem of deriving "marked" honorific types be to simply set up a direct diachronic scenario leading from referent-targeting honorifics to addressee-targeting ones, as advocated by Brown and Levinson (1987, 276). Observing the markedness of addressee$_{\text{target}}$ honorifics with respect to referent$_{\text{target}}$ honorifics, they argue that

> referent honorifics are basic and—at least as encoded in address forms— universal, and that addressee honorifics are derived from these [....] We suggest, then, that via the recurrent use of referent honorifics in situations where the addressee-referent relation is a close one (i.e., the respected persons or things belong to H[earer]'s social orbit) they may evolve into direct addressee honorifics. (Brown and Levinson 1987, 277)

They give the addressee$_{\text{target}}$ use of *-nka* in Tamil, derived from the honorific plural ending (for example, honorific second-person plural *ninga*, feminine honorific / third person plural *avanga*). They suggest that "the habitual use of this referent honorific *-nka* led to its acquiring an independent life of its own as a *direct* addressee honorific" (1988, 277). As plausible as this may be for explaining the unique addressee-targeting particle in Tamil, such an account seems insufficient for explaining the diachronic development of the much more morphologically and lexically diverse addressee-targeting repertoires of Southeast and East Asian languages. Nor does it offer a principled account for why such forms are geographically circumscribed to Asia. Finally, it cannot account for the co-occurrence of self-humbling, or humiliative, honorifics alongside addressee-targeting ones.

Complementing sociohistorical factors, I will argue that the development of addressee-targeting and self-humbling honorific repertoires in East and Southeast Asian languages can be understood as an "internal development" (in the sense of the term as employed by historical linguists) which analogically extends a social pragmatic pattern that originally emerged in systems of interlocutor reference highly particular to East and Southeast Asia. In order to properly understand the contours of this argument, we must consider the indexical focus properties of honorific registers of person deixis in a manner comparable to what we have done for lexical honorifics, above.

Indexical Focus in Honorific Registers of Person Deixis

The most common formal locus for the elaboration of honorifics is in human nouns—that is, in forms prototypically employed in person reference (Errington 1985b; Enfield and Stivers 2007). Within this semantic domain, it is the closed-class of person deictics—or pronouns—that often bear the highest functional load in sociopragmatic signalling. In the Europeanist tradition, honorific registers of person deixis (Agha 2007, 278 *infra*) are called T/V systems, where "T" stands for the non-honorific pronoun and "V" the honorific pronoun (Brown and Gilman 1960). Importantly, the indexical focus properties of T/V systems manifest the same markedness asymmetries as lexical honorific registers (Fleming 2017).

Honorific pronouns have typically been treated as having a Speaker$_{origo}$-Referent$_{target}$ indexical focus. In the passage quoted earlier, we saw that Brown and Levinson (1987, 277; *italics* added) contend that "referent honorifics are basic and—*at least as encoded in address forms*—universal". In agreement with Comrie (1976), they argue that:

> [T]he familiar T/V pronoun alternation in European languages is in fact a case of referent honorifics, and not addressee honorifics as might be supposed. For in these European T/V systems, as in all systems based on the speaker-referent axis, it is not possible to express respect to H [=hearer] without *reference* to him or her. (Brown and Levinson 1987, 180)

This is not a totally convincing argument. The indexical target of European honorific pronouns like German *Sei* or French *vous* is simultaneously the discourse addressee and the discourse referent; it is not clear why one interactional role should be analytically privileged over the other.[6] However, when honorification is not limited to addressee-reference and is extended beyond the second person we can sometimes garner evidence which points to either a global S-R or S-A indexical

Interlocutor Reference and the Complexity

focus for the T/V system. And where evidence exists, European languages *do* seem to pattern as Comrie, Brown and Levinson suggest. Self-raising speaker-reference in the attenuated use of the Royal "we" in Latin, but also later in languages like Danish and Icelandic, for instance, suggests that the plural feature value as employed in notionally singular reference honours the referent of the pronoun expressing that value. So too does the extension of honorific pluralisation beyond addressee-reference to nonparticipant-reference (that is, the third person) in a number of Slavic languages (Houtzagers 2018). These are both lines of evidence that support an S-R honorific alignment interpretation for European T/V systems. Most languages of South Asia (for example, Tamil, Telegu, Darai, Nepali, Marathi, etc.) have honorific second and third person pronouns, but lack grammaticalised addressee-honouring first-person pronouns. Honorification is activated in pronominal *reference to* the target of honorification. Cross-linguistically, such S-R alignment is much more common than S-A alignment in T/V systems.

Table 1. Paradigmatic patterning can be diagnostic of the indexical focus of a T/V system. (Shading denotes pronominal forms which have an honorific interpretation when employed in reference to a unique individual.)

SG	DU EXCL	DU INCL	PL EXCL	PL INCL	Person	SG	DU EXCL	DU INCL	PL EXCL	PL INCL
-ŋa	-lijara	-li	-ŋalu	-liwa	1st	iɲ	əliɲ	alaŋ	alɛ	abo
-n(i)	-nbula		-nda		2nd	am	aben		apɛ	
-Ø	-wula		-lu		3rd	uni	unkin		onko	

Djaru nominative verbal suffixes   Santali independent pronouns

Nevertheless, in cases where honorification is achieved by "skewing" of semantic number feature values (for example, plural number is honorific in notionally singular address), two distinct paradigmatic profiles are attested, with skewing in second person complemented by skewing of the same feature value in either the third or first person. In Djaru (Pama-Nyungan), plural number functions as an honorific in both second- and third-person pronominals, but not in the first person (Tsunoda 1981, 215). This common pattern indicates a Speaker$_{origo}$-Referent$_{target}$ alignment of the honorific system: plural forms are employed where speaker indexes deference towards the referent of the pronominal. In the Santali (Austroasiatic) dialect studied by Ghosh (2008), dual number functions as an honorific in both second and first persons, but not in the third person. That is, dual number was traditionally employed in the second person, but also in first-person reference, in respectful address to in-laws. This rarer pattern is diagnostic of a Speaker$_{origo}$-Addressee$_{target}$ alignment of the honorific system; dual forms are employed in all acts of interlocutor reference addressed to a particular individual, not just in acts of reference to the target-of-honorification.

As the Santali paradigm illustrates, just as with lexical honorific registers, Speaker$_{origo}$-Addressee$_{target}$ T/V systems are attested. In these systems addressee-honorification occurs in both speaker-reference (first person) and addressee-reference (second person). The essential point to see here is that in these systems, honorification is activated in pronominal *address to* the target of honorification whether or not the pronoun refers to the target of honorification. Systems of this sort are quite rare (but see discussion of Southeast Asian patterns below); examples include Diuxi Mixtec (Mixtecan), Santali (Austroasiatic), Ainu (the variety described in S. Hattori 1964), Dhimal (Sino-Tibetan), Mijikenda (Bantu) and Guarijío (Uto-Aztecan) (see Fleming 2017 for the full discussion and for any citations not included here). As we will see, particular subsystems of the interlocutor reference systems of East and Southeast Asian languages tend to function in this way. The Aslian language Semelai, for instance, has this same alignment with an honorific distinction in first- and second-person pronouns but not in third person pronouns (Kruspe 2004, 171). We will see more examples below.

Just as with lexical honorifics, S-A honorific pronouns are a rare phenomenon. And just as with lexical honorifics, S-R is the unmarked indexical focus type for T/V systems. Observe that what is really diagnostic of these marked S-A honorific pronouns is the existence of an addressee-targeting honorific first-person pronoun (e.g., Santali first dual exclusive, *əliɲ*). It is important to recognise that these first non-singular honorifics are not cases of the so-called Royal "we" of the kind historically attested in Latin and other European languages. Here, the honorific target is not the speaker, but the addressee. (Remember, the existence of a Royal "we" is evidence for Speaker$_{origo}$-Referent$_{target}$ honorification since it is the occupant of the interactional role of 'Referent' who is elevated across multiple person categories.)

East Asian languages, like contemporary Japanese and Korean, possess these typologically rare honorific alternations in first-person pronouns. In Korean, *ce* is the "V" form first-person pronoun while *na* is the "T" form (Kim 2011). (As in Vietnamese [see discussion below], use of a deictically selective forms [*ne* or *caney*] in addressee-reference counts as a "T" form, while polite address demands the use of a deictically non-selective form [for example, a human noun like "Professor"].) Historical varieties of Chinese also employed addressee-honorific first-person pronouns—often derived from self-humbling nouns (for example, *chén* [servant, vassal])—though these usages are less well attested in contemporary Chinese varieties (Kádár 2005).

The interlocutor reference systems of the languages of East and Southeast Asia prove intractable to the kind of neat indexical focus treatment which we have just applied to honorific pronominal paradigms. Nevertheless, languages in this region often possess honorific first-person pronouns of the Santali type. As an example, consider the pronominal paradigm from Sumbawa (an Austronesian language of Indonesia) in table 2.

Table 2. Pronouns in the Austronesian language, Sumbawa, spoken in Indonesia (after Shiohara 2014, 19). (Shading denotes honorific forms.)

	1st		2nd		3rd	
	SG	PL	SG	PL	SG	PL
		INCL	EXCL				
HONORIFIC	*aku*	*kita*	*kami*	*sia*	*nènè*	*diri*
NON-HONORIFIC	*kaji*			*kau*		*nya*

Note that honorific distinctions are found in all three grammatical persons.[7] We cannot offer a unified treatment in terms of either S-A or S-R indexical focus. The third person *diri* functions as an S-R honorific (that is, the target of honorification is the referent but not the addressee). But the first-person *aku* functions as an S-A honorific (that is, the target of honorification is the addressee but not the referent).

To summarise, honorific registers of interlocutor reference in East and Southeast Asian languages cannot be neatly reduced to a unitary indexical focus treatment. Nevertheless, they activate speaker-reference as a salient domain for addressee-honorification. This is a point which is of considerable importance in understanding the unique properties of honorific registers in this region.

Honorific Interlocutor Reference in Southeast Asia

The treatment of T/V systems in terms of one unified indexical focus type (what Fleming 2017 calls its "honorific alignment") is well-suited to languages where a semantic feature value is "skewed" in honorific reference across multiple persons. It does not, at first blush, appear well suited to understanding honorific interlocutor reference in the languages of East and Southeast Asia. The reasons for this involve the particular formal and functional attributes of interlocutor reference in these regions.

In many East and Southeast Asian languages reference to speaker and addressee is routinely accomplished by forms which do not categorise their referent by participant role (see Luong 1990 on Vietnamese; Agha 2007 for further discussion; Luong and Sidnell 2020; Fleming and Sidnell 2020). As an example, we draw on data from Minangkabau (Austronesian; Sumatra). As in many other Southeast Asian languages, in Minangkabau, reference to speaker and addressee is routinely achieved not with person deictics but by means of status terms, kin terms, and personal names (Moussay 1981). Both of the core arguments in the expression *uni indak dapek pai jo adiak* (big sister cannot go with little sibling) can be interpreted as occupying either core speech participant role or as being a nonparticipant. That is, the same text sentence can be interpreted as an utterance meaning either "I can't go with you", "You can't go with me" or "She can't go with him" etc. Analysing this example, Moussay (1981, 156) offers this summary: "*L'opposition entre les personnes n'est pas marquée linguistiquement. La seule marque qui puisse permettre d'identifier les personnes est une marque extralinguistique, constitué par la situation de l'énonciation.*" (The distinction between grammatical persons is not linguistically marked. The only "mark" that allows one to identify grammatical person [that is, speech participant role] is an extralinguistic "mark" expressed in the utterance context.) In numerous speech communities in Southeast Asia and East Asia, open class nouns like kin terms, titles, and proper names are routinely employed, as in Minangkabau, to refer to speaker and addressee. Fleming and Sidnell (2020) call this "Open Class Interlocutor Reference" or OCIR.

OCIR, and the use of non-deictic nouns in speaker-reference in particular, is marked cross-linguistically. In European languages, deictically selective pronouns are almost always employed in speaker-reference. Illeism—self-reference with personal name—is a circumscribed (and often disparaged) practice. There are some European languages—like Brazilian Portuguese—where open-class nouns are employed in addressee-reference (for example, *O senhor/A senhora quer alguma coisa?* [Do you want something?]). And this pattern is more widespread in South Asian languages, for example, Malayalam (Chandrasekhar 1970). In Sinhala, for instance, use of nouns for addressee-reference is ubiquitous. But although the use of nouns for addressee-reference is attested in Europe and South Asia, the widespread use of nouns for self-reference is largely restricted to the languages of East and Southeast Asia.[8]

OCIR in these languages has numerous interactional knock-on effects which field researchers on these languages have long appreciated (Cooke 1968; Luong 1990; Ewing 2005a; Ewing and Djenar 2019; Luong and Sidnell 2020). In these languages, speakers are expected to attend to social positioning relative to speech recipients not only in acts of reference to those speech recipients but also in acts of self-reference. These acts of interlocutor reference do not employ the deictic ground of discourse—with speaker as the deictic origo—as the relational, coordinate system for reference. Rather, they draw upon more sociocentrically stable coordinate systems, like kinship or institutionally sanctioned role relations as these are mapped onto various individuals present, absent or merely potential (see, for comparison, Lee and Harvey 1973, 38 on Korean teknonyms). The mapping of linguistic forms onto participant roles is not categorical—as is the case with the indexical focus mapping of honorification onto interactional role for non-referential indexicality, or as is the case with the mapping of person deictics onto interactional roles for referential indexicality—but rather inferential. If a token of "elder brother" is employed in a parent's speech addressed to their son, speech recipients infer (the figure of) a younger sibling in the "context". Put differently, the mapping of the two places of the two-place noun, "elder brother" (that is, elder brother: younger sibling), onto interactional roles is contingent on sociocultural factors that are orthogonal to the local, contextual factors determining interactional role inhabitancy. And because the mapping of person-referring expressions onto interactional roles is not categorical, but rather contingent upon inferentially linking participants—actual or virtual—to the role relationships semantically projected through linguistic form, the social indexical functions of kin terms are not limited to signifying either the Speaker-Addressee or the Speaker-Referent relationship but routinely index (often polyadic) relationships involving not only core speech participants, but also bystanders or even absent alters.

Deictic Selectivity and Indexical Focus in OCIR

As we can see then, in OCIR systems, sociopragmatic alternations in interlocutor reference cannot be reduced to, or modelled exclusively in terms of a unitary indexical focus type (in contrast to T/V systems of the kind that we looked at earlier). In Southeast Asian interlocutor reference, choice of referring expression, *where achieved by kin terms, names or other open-class nouns*, is often decoupled from interactional role-inhabitancy. And just as open-class noun reference to speaker or addressee is achieved inferentially, so too are the semantically scaffolded (anti-)honorific functions of such open-class nominal reference inferentially mapped onto interactional roles. The following example of a Malay conversation between a daughter (D), named Ira, and her father (F), taken from McGinn's (1991, 205) study of a fictional corpus illustrates the point:

D to F: *Ira tidak mau pergi ke   sekolah.*
        Ira   not   want go   to   school
        "Ira [= Speaker] doesn't want to go to school."
F to D: *Ayah   mengerti.*
        father   understand
        Ira   pasti   malu   memakai jas   hujan ini.
        Ira   certain ashamed   wear   coat   rain   this

"Father [=Speaker] understands.
Ira [=Addressee] is ashamed to wear this raincoat."

In the Malay conversation between parent and child, *Ayah* is used to refer to the "Father" both in the utterance where he is the addressee and in the one in which he is the speaker. Of course, the age-stratified social pragmatic distinction between name (= "T") and kin term (= "V") is widely attested in languages of the world (Fleming and Slotta 2018). When activated in interlocutor reference, this social pragmatic function is mapped onto speech participant roles in a non-principled manner. That is, the mapping of the sociopragmatic function of the noun-phrase type (to vulgarise, "name" as referent-lowering/"ascending kin term" as referent-raising) onto its referent remains constant independent of the interactional role—speaker or addressee—which the referent of that noun occupies.

Structurally, these open-class honorific variants enter into paradigmatic alternation not only with one another (for example, kin term versus personal name) but also with "true" pronouns. These true pronouns do not have rich semantic properties to entail their sociopragmatic significations. Even when grammaticalised from open-class nouns they typically undergo desemanticisation and phonological erosion (Heine and Song 2011). This means that their honorific functions cannot rely upon the scaffolding of their semantic sense properties (for example, the original use of *saha:ya* [servant] as an addressee-honouring term employed in speaker-reference in Classical Malay [Heine and Song 2011, 611]) but are more purely conventional (for example, the contemporary use of the phonologically eroded and desemanticised *saya* as a polite first-person pronoun in contemporary Indonesian).

In some languages, a higher-order contrast between honorific open-class terms and anti-honorific pronominals can be observed. We exemplify this with an example of status-stratified interactional dyads in Vietnamese. In Vietnamese, "[m]asters and their offspring ... usually utilized the pair *tao ... mày* 'I ... thou' when speaking to their housekeepers" (Pham 2002, 298). Housekeepers, however, would respond with *con* (offspring), for self-reference, and terms like *ông* (grandfather) or *bà* (grandmother) for addressee-reference. Here "mode of reference" (Errington 1985b)—use of denotational indexicals (pronouns) versus pure symbols (kin terms)—becomes intertwined with non-referential or social indexical function. That is, pronouns count as "T" forms *in both Speaker- and Addressee-reference* while kin terms count as "V" forms *in both Speaker- and Addressee-reference*. Limiting ourselves to the case of semantically rich noun phrases, sociopragmatic function cannot be decoupled from semantico-referential function—kin terms which characterise referent as senior (here, the ascending G+2 terms denoting grandparents, *ông/bà*) are referent-raising while kin terms which characterise referent as junior (that is, the term for lineal descending generation kin, *con*) are referent-lowering, and thus by implication other-raising. However, at the higher order level of the opposition between kin terms and pronouns, both noun phrase types function as addressee-targeting (anti-)honorifics. Regardless which interlocutor is referred to by means of the form, the use of a pronoun presupposes the greater deference entitlements of the speaker vis-à-vis the addressee (that is, pronoun = "T") and the use of a kin term presupposes the greater deference entitlements of the addressee vis-à-vis the speaker (that is, kin term = "V"). That is, the opposition between pronouns and kin terms operates—within the microcosm of interlocutor reference—in the same way as speech level vocabularies; that is, the alternation between these phrase types functions along the Speaker$_{origo}$-Addressee$_{target}$ axis.[9]

Table 3. Vietnamese example of asymmetric address between housekeeper and house owners

Sp > Ad	Speaker-referring term	Addressee-referring term	
Housekeeper > House owners	*con* (offspring) [Speaker=Referent]$_{origo}$-Addressee$_{target}$	*ông/bà* (grandparent) Speaker$_{origo}$-[Addressee=Ref.]$_{target}$	V
House owners > Housekeeper	*tao* 1st pro Speaker$_{origo}$-Addressee$_{target}$	*mày* 2nd pro Speaker$_{origo}$-Addressee$_{target}$	T

(Anti)honorification in maximally status-differentiated interactions in Vietnamese can be understood as accomplished in three distinct ways: (1) honouring the addressee by semantic abasement of the speaker-referent (*con* [offspring]), (2) honouring the addressee by semantically characterising the addressee qua referent with esteemed semantic predicates (*ông/bà* [grandparent]), (3) by use of person deictics, which are conventionally understood as anti-honorific toward addressee whether or not they refer to that addressee (*tao* and *mày*). Crucially, because person deictics function as anti-honorifics which target the addressee, at a higher level of abstraction, kin terms and pronouns become paradigmatically opposed as Speaker$_{origo}$-Addressee$_{target}$ honorifics ("*V*") and anti-honorifics ("*T*"), respectively.

Moving beyond kinship terms, it appears that honorific nominals used in participant reference in SEA languages often form pairings of this kind. In Thai, terms related to "hair" (*phom*) and "feet" (for example, *tâajthâaw* [underneath foot]) are paired together as addressee honorifics used in speaker- and addressee-reference, respectively (Cooke 1968; Ishiyama 2010, 23; Heine and Song 2011, table 2). (Here corporeal metaphors of caste and spatial indexing of status are both important, figuring speaker's head as "lower than" [even] addressee's foot.) In many SEA languages, the two-place relational role designators "slave" or "servant" and "master" are employed as honorifics. In all of these cases, status-polarised two-place nouns afford honorific functions. The one employed in addressee-reference semantically characterises the referent with socially valued predicates of, for example, seniority, high rank status, totalising agency, etc., while the term employed in speaker-reference semantically derogates or abases the referent, and by implication signifies deference to addressee. In all of these cases, terms used to refer to the speaker, on the one hand, and to the addressee, on the other, are paired as a function of the degree of honorification which the speaker estimates is due the addressee. As we saw in our discussion above, this paradigmatic organisation is elsewhere indicative of a Speaker$_{origo}$-Addressee$_{target}$ honorific alignment for the T/V system.

The Pragmatic Salience of Interlocutor Reference and the Pragmatic Structure of Honorification

In an important essay, "On the nature of the sociolinguistic sign: Describing the Javanese speech levels", Joseph Errington (1985b) argues that something like an analytic of "pragmatic salience" is necessary for a rich understanding of the native conceptualisation of speech level systems and, through the mediation of that conceptualisation, of their pragmatic structure.

> Pragmatic saliences of morphemes contrast by virtue of their differing objects of reference (if they have any) and their modes of reference (if they refer). More pragmatically salient (classes of) morphemes are tacitly recognised by native speakers to be more crucial as linguistic mediators of social relations, and this awareness is evinced both in their metalinguistic statements, and in linguistic change and variation. [....] First and second person pronouns are doubly integrated into the context of speech exchange, make up the most complex, delicately differentiated paradigmatic sets, and are (as will be shown) most subject to strategic manipulation and metalinguistic use. (Errington 1985b, 295)

Errington goes on to illustrate that the pragmatic salience of interlocutor referring expressions is revealed in the naturally occurring metapragmatic discourses of the *priyayi* elites—ancestral residents of the royal polity of Surakarta—with whom he worked. If asked how so-and-so speaks to so-and-so, speakers tend not to use the metapragmatic vocabulary of levels (such as *krama*, *madya* and *ngoko*) but rather to cite the interlocutor referring forms which would be appropriately employed between the pair (1985b, 296). Addressee-referring expressions, in particular, seem to have maximal salience because they both metonymically exemplify the appropriate speech level and denote the interactional role which is—on the plane of non-referential indexicality—the target of deference (1985b, 297). Correspondingly, alternations of interlocutor referring expressions are the most elaborate and most susceptible to diachronic change and revaluation. Suharno (1982) also argues that Javanese speakers use interlocutor-referring term as a proxy for determining which speech level vocabulary to employ. Pointing towards the tight conceptual connection between the two, he observes that *ngoko*—the term for unrefined speech—is a reduplication of the addressee-lowering term *kowe* (you). That is, *ngoko* vocabulary is the vocabulary one would employ in addressing someone one would address as *kowe*.

The notion of pragmatic salience helps to explain the particular relationship between referential and non-referential indexicality which comes to the fore in the typology of social pragmatics—that is, it helps explain why referent-targeting honorification is the unmarked indexical focus type (see the discussion on this above). The argument here dovetails with Silverstein's (1981) observation that language users have greater awareness of the referential as opposed to the non-referential functions of linguistic form. This biasing of metapragmatic awareness contours the development of honorifics, as well as other social indexical functions (for example, speech act verbs), in language. In essence, the non-referential speech act of deference to another is conflated with, or assimilated to, the speech act of referring to that individual. Though only some languages possess elaborate honorific repertoires, in all languages human nouns enter into sociopragmatic alternation (compare the name/kin term alternation mentioned above).

The pragmatic salience of interlocutor reference also helps to explain why the more marked kinds of honorifics—addressee-targeting honorifics and humiliatives, in particular—are only robustly attested in East and Southeast Asia. If Errington and Suharno are right, interlocutor-referring expressions are privileged exemplars which speakers draw upon in modelling honorific registers more broadly. In most languages, honorific registers of person deixis pattern exclusively in terms of a Speaker$_{origo}$-Referent$_{target}$ indexical focus. But as we have seen, languages which employ open-class nouns in speaker-reference cannot be reduced in this manner. These languages have interlocutor referring expressions that can be interpreted: (a) as deferring to referent (for example, honorific titles, kin terms, etc. employed in addressee-reference); (b) as deferring to addressee by means of the semantic lowering of speaker (for example, use of a term like "younger sibling" for speaker-reference); and (c) "true" pronouns which are conventionally understood as being (im)polite towards addressee (for example, *aku* versus *saya* in Indonesian). It appears that these three kinds of interlocutor referring expressions have served as conceptual anchors or attractors guiding the diachronic development of honorific repertoires in Southeast Asia. That is, these three interlocutor-referring types have paved the way for honorific forms which do not refer to speech participants to be analysed as (a) Referent$_{target}$ honorifics (b) humiliatives, and (c) Addressee$_{target}$ honorifics, respectively.

Given the pragmatic salience of interlocutor reference to native speaker rationalisation of honorific function, the null hypothesis ought to be that Speaker$_{origo}$-Addressee$_{target}$ and humiliative honorific repertoires—so rare elsewhere in the world—emerged in East and Southeast Asia from the ideological reanalysis of the indexical focus properties of (anti-)honorific interlocutor referring expressions. Considering the dynamics of this process in greater detail would require much more in-depth study. (As discussed in note 5, crucial lines of evidence for generating a richer understanding of this process may come from a more fine-grained treatment of the differences and similarities in how humiliatives function cross-linguistically.) Nevertheless, there are indications that this is a plausible diachronic sequence for Indonesian honorific registers. In the final section, I turn to data from Indonesian languages specifically.

From Person Deixis to Speech Levels: Addressee-Targeting First-Person Pronouns in Indonesian Languages

In an earlier section, we saw that first-person, addressee-targeting honorific pronouns are diagnostic of the rare Speaker$_{origo}$-Addressee$_{target}$ indexical focus for T/V systems. The unique dynamics of the social pragmatics of speaker-reference in East and Southeast Asian languages are also seen as crucial to the development of the marked honorific types—addressee-targeting "speech levels", on the one hand, and humilitiaves, on the other—attested in these regions. The prototypical use of humiliatives is in speaker-reference. The use of semantically rich, referent-lowering nominal expressions (for example, "younger sibling", "slave", "hair") in speaker-reference, would have been important models for the development of this honorific strategy. But the activation of speaker-reference as a site for addressee-honorification has also motivated the development of addressee-targeting honorific distinctions in truly deictic first-person pronominals. OCIR seeded honorific first-person pronominals both through grammaticalisation and analogy.

Diachronically, as nouns employed in polite speaker-reference were grammaticalised as first-person pronouns, an addressee-targeting honorific/non-honorific distinction in first-person pronominals emerged. This is what occurred, for instance, in the Chamic languages where the honorific first-person pronouns are clearly derived from a nominal meaning "slave" *ulôn* (see examples from Acehnese, Rade, Jarai, Chru, Haroi, and Cham in Thurgood 1999, 248). Many languages in East and Southeast Asia have dedicated honorific/non-honorific first-person pronominal pairs (e.g., Minangkabau *den* and *ambo*, Korean *na* versus *ce*, etc.; cf. Djenar 2008 on the distinction between *aku* and *saya* in contemporary Indonesian).

But first-person pronouns likely also developed honorific distinctions on analogy to the (anti)honorific use of open-class nouns in speaker-reference. This pattern is robustly attested in languages of Indonesia, many of which employ the kind of feature value "skewing" common in European T/V systems (e.g., honorific skewing of plural in notionally singular reference). Notably, in many languages of Indonesia, first-person plurals are skewed in singular speaker-reference to achieve addressee-honorification. As an example, take honorific skewing of clusivity in Gayo, spoken in northern Sumatra: "[K]in terms are used more often than pronouns when referring to first, second and third persons. Personal pronouns are typically used only in the presence of people of lower age or status, or when referring to people of lower age or status, for politeness" (Eades 2005, 203–4). In some dialects of Gayo, the use of the first-person inclusive and the first-person exclusive can be used as addressee-targeting honorific pronouns in addressee- and speaker-reference, respectively (just as in Old Javanese; see table 4 below). Many other examples could be cited (for example, first-person exclusive, *kami*, not only in Gayo, but also Minangkabau and Totoli; first-person inclusive, *kita*, in Bugis). (For other examples consult Cysouw's (2005) survey of honorific clusives, a survey which unfortunately fails to appreciate the relationship between the overrepresentation of honorific clusives in the languages of Indonesia and the sociopragmatic activation of speaker-reference as a functional domain for addressee-targeting honorification.) In Indonesian languages, the use of non-singular first-person pronouns are readily interpreted as addressee-honorifics (and not as self-aggrandising, as is the case with the Royal "we" in European languages), because speaker-reference is already activated as a site of addressee-honorification in OCIR.

Synchronically, the pronominal systems of the core speech level languages of Javanese, Balinese, Sasak, Madurese, and Sundanese, lack defined paradigmatic structure (that is, lack clusives, lack dedicated plurals, and the same elements can sometimes be used for both first- and second-person reference, cf. *anak*); interlocutor referring expressions are fully incorporated into broader honorific repertoires and rationalised in these terms. Nevertheless, neighbouring languages, like Sumbawa (see table 2), have relatively well-defined pronominal paradigms but still with the typologically marked presence of honorific first- and second-person pronouns. On the model proposed here of the analogic transfer of indexical focus properties from the system of interlocutor reference to the broader honorific system, languages of the Sumbawa-type are good candidates for a starting point for the development of speech level systems. Indeed, Suharno (1982, 112) following Gonda (1948) has argued that Javanese speech levels developed around the 16th century from "a complex pronoun system and word-ending variation." Importantly, the most widely accepted description of the Old Javanese or Kawi pronominal system closely parallels the contemporary Sumbawa pattern, exhibiting the crucial Speaker$_{origo}$-Addressee$_{target}$ pattern for interlocutor reference.

Table 4. Old Javanese/Kawi pronouns. (Shading denotes pronominal forms which have an honorific interpretation when employed in reference to a unique individual.)

	1st person	2nd person	3rd person
honorific	*kami*	*kita*	*sira*
non-honorific	*aku*	*ka(N)u*	*ia*

Source: Becker and Oka (1974).

In MSEA languages, the use of desemanticised "true" pronominals typically has an anti-honorific function, and these languages lack speech levels (but see Diller 2006 on addressee targeting uses of *ra:cha:sàp* [royal Thai]). As we have seen, where open-class nouns are the principal honorific alternants employed in interlocutor reference, honorific function is inferentially mapped onto interactional role. Some deictic selectivity may be necessary, therefore, in order to motivate categorical interpretations of indexical focus—that is, for the ethno-rationalisation of interlocutor reference as a Speaker$_{origo}$-Addressee$_{target}$ system. For this reason, perhaps, the languages of Indonesia were best positioned to develop the uniquely complex honorific systems which have so fascinated sociolinguists and linguistic anthropologists.[10]

Notes

[1] In-law avoidance vocabularies employed in Aboriginal Australian speech communities are often described as "bystander honorifics" (e.g. Levinson 1983 [1979]). Such Recipient$_{target}$ honorifics and, what I have elsewhere called, Nonparticipant$_{target}$ honorifics (Fleming 2018, 586) are characteristic of honorific registers organised around the avoidance of tabooed words. Elsewhere I have argued that these two types are extensions of Addressee$_{target}$ and Referent$_{target}$ honorifics, respectively (Fleming 2014; cf. Rijkhoff 1998).
[2] Bowden's (2001, 2002) description of honorifics in Taba, spoken in North Maluku province, suggests that there is only a distinction of Speaker$_{origo}$-Addressee$_{target}$ speech levels—that is, there is no mention of either referent-targeting honorifics or humiliatives. The metapragmatic labels for the levels (*alus, biasa, kasar*) suggest Malay influence; Bowden also notes that numerous *alus* vocabulary items are borrowed from Ternate, the language of a historically important sultanate in eastern Indonesia. It may be that Referent$_{target}$ honorifics were historically present but that as the speech level system waned, those forms have been lost. "While speech levels were probably an important feature of older varieties of Taba, it appears that the distinctions between levels are being lost under the impact of Malay, and perhaps as a result of decreasing differences in status since the political influence of the sultanates has waned" (Bowden 2001, 21–2). See also: "It

seems fairly clear that while a number of people (mostly older) still have an extensive knowledge of the *alus* forms in Taba, the younger Makianese are not learning them any more and that they are falling out of use" (Bowden 2002, 131).

[3] Though we speak of languages as if they were unitary, honorific vocabularies employed in the "same" language were historically associated with competing royal courts that served as institutional centres in which these honorific repertoires were enregistered and from which they diffused (Fox 2005, 102).

[4] Errington (1982, 90) cites Javanese textual sources that suggest a date around the year 1000 for the development of *basa kedhaton* 'palace language', an honorific register employed in the presence of the king and which presupposes—because of its suppression—the use of referent-honorifics (i.e. *krama inggil* forms).

[5] Referent1$_{origo}$-Referent2$_{target}$ [R1-R2] honorifics are anomalous, with respect to canonical lexical honorifics, in their susceptibility to transpose the origo of deference away from the speaker position. Is an honorific an honorific if it isn't "I" that does the deferring? What, we might ask, is the involvement of the speaker in the evaluation of the status relationship between the two referents? In Tibetan, for instance, there are two verbs with R1-R2 focus: *phüü* (give) and *su* (say/tell). These two verbs are both productively employed in a wide range of compound and phrasal verb constructions (Agha 1993b, 97). Agha (97) writes of these R1-R2 honorifics that they represent "agent's deference to recipient as estimated by speaker." In Korean, the pragmatic implicature may be stronger. R1-R2 honorifics in Korean are felicitous only where the referent associated with the grammatical "object [is] socially superior *both* to the subject/topic referent as well as the speaker" (Brown 2011, 37 citing Yun 1993, 18). If this is accurate then R1-R2 honorifics in Korean might be treated as having a triadic focus, with two indexical origos (i.e. Speaker and Referent1), much as with trirelational kin terms in the Australianist tradition (Garde 2013; cf. Agha 2007, 329 on "conjoined categorial [indexical] focus"). More study is required to tease out how R1-R2 honorifics are employed in voicing constructions and the pragmatic implicatures concerning the speaker's deference entitlements relative to the referents. As I argue below, speaker-referring addressee-honouring nouns, like "slave" or "younger sibling", are the likely historical source for these kinds of humbling honorific repertoires, explaining why they are almost only found in East and Southeast Asia. A typological study of humiliative registers—which would include within its purview impolite repertoires (e.g., impolite pronouns)—would make an important contribution to the typology of social pragmatics.

[6] Pingelapese (Austronesian) lexical honorifics illustrate that some honorifics do have both discourse referent and addressee as indexical target (a special case of what Agha [2007, 329] calls "conjoined categorial [indexical] focus"). The lexical repertoire consists of terms which in other Austronesian languages (including neighbouring Pohnpeian) are employed in Referent$_{target}$ honorification (for example, "face", "head", "to sleep", "to think", "to eat", "to say"). However, these forms appear only to be used in referring to addressees—"'older language consultants reported that the polite vocabulary, *loakaeiah wahu* (language of respect), is used to address high title holders and elders. Women should use it with their brothers, the elders say...'" (2007, 329). Non-honorific expressions can be rendered honorific "by adding the polite second person singular possessive suffix *-mwi* (e.g. *aeawe* [mouth] > *aewae-mwi* [your mouth (polite)])" (R. Hattori 2012, 42). Pingelapese lexical honorifics cannot be given a definitive classification as either S-A or S-R. European T/V systems limited to the second person are similarly indeterminate.

[7] For the sake of full disclosure, I should note that honorification in all three grammatical persons (where speaker-reference is notionally singular) is not only attested in Southeast Asia and East Asia. Examples elsewhere include Kharia (Petersen 2014) and Tuvaluan (Besnier 2000).
[8] See Fleming and Sidnell (2020) for a survey of languages in this region which ubiquitously employ non-deictic nouns in speaker-reference and for a discussion of the historical emergence of this pattern. The crucial thing to observe is that OCIR is attested in Japanese, historically in Chinese and Korean, and then throughout Southeast Asia. That is, it is attested in the two areas—East and Southeast Asia—where complex honorific registers are found.
[9] Note how the formal difference (kin term versus pronoun) diagrammatically figurates the power imbalance between housekeeper and house-owner functionally instantiated on the plane of deference indexicality. The housekeeper employs terms which semantically characterise the relationship between speaker and addressee in terms of enduring frameworks of, albeit age-stratified, kinship. The house-owner declines to ratify this relationality, referring to self and other with terms that presuppose only the evanescent framework of discursive participation.
[10] My thanks to Novi Djenar for pushing me to consider this line of thinking.

List of Contributors

Dwi Noverini Djenar is Associate Professor in Indonesian Studies at the University of Sydney. Her research interests are in topics related to youth language practices, literary stylistics, self- and other reference, and the relations between language and place.

N.J. Enfield is Professor and Chair of Linguistics at the University of Sydney and co-director of the Sydney Centre for Language Research. He is the author of *The Utility of Meaning*, *How We Talk* and *Language vs. Reality*.

Joseph Errington is Professor of Anthropology and former Chair of the Council of Southeast Asian Studies at Yale University. His research and writing, drawing on semiotics and politics of language have focused on linguistic dimensions of modernisation and identity in Indonesia.

Michael C. Ewing is Associate Professor in Indonesian Studies at the University of Melbourne. His current research involves the language of Indonesian youth, and the nexus between standard and colloquial modes of grammatical organisation in everyday conversation.

Luke Fleming is Associate Professor in Anthropology at the University of Montreal. His research and scholarship seek to develop comparative and typological approaches to the study of social indexicality and speech registers. His monograph, *On Speaking Terms: Avoidance Registers and the Sociolinguistics of Kinship*, will be published in 2023 by the University of Toronto Press.

Sarah Lee gained her PhD in linguistics from Rice University and has worked as a researcher at the University of Queensland. Currently an independent scholar, her work focuses on language contact and multilingual practices in Malaysian and Singaporean digital spaces.

Jack Sidnell is Professor of Anthropology at the University of Toronto. He has conducted ethnographic, linguistic and anthropological research in the Caribbean,

Vietnam, India and North America. His interests centre on the intersection of language structure, social interaction and reflexive reanalysis.

Charles H.P. Zuckerman is a linguistic anthropologist who works in Laos. He is currently a 2022–23 Fellow for the American Council of Learned Societies and a visiting scholar at the University of Vermont. His work has appeared in *American Anthropologist, American Ethnologist, Cultural Anthropology,* the *Journal of the Royal Anthropological Institute* and *Language in Society*.

Bibliography

Adelaar, Alexander and John Hajek. Forthcoming. "Pronouns." In *The Oxford Guide to Malayo-Polynesian Languages of South East Asia*, ed. Alexander Adelaar and Antoinette Schapper. Oxford, UK: Oxford University Press.

Adelaar, Alexander and Nikolaus P. Himmelmann, eds. 2005. *The Austronesian Languages of Asia and Madagascar*. New York: Routledge.

Adib, Holy. 2018. Sejarah "Anda". *Berita tagar* (24 November 2018).

Adler, Max. 1978. *Naming and Addressing: A Sociolinguistic Study*. Hamburg: Buske.

Agha, Asif. 1993a. "Grammatical and Indexical Convention in Honorific Discourse." *Journal of Linguistic Anthropology* 3, no. 2: 131–63.

―――. 1993b. *Structural Form and Utterance Context in Lhasa Tibetan: Grammar and Indexicality in a Non-Configurational Language*. New York: Peter Lang.

―――. 1998. "Stereotypes and Registers of Honorific Language." *Language in Society* 27: 151–93.

―――. 2007. *Language and Social Relations*. Cambridge, UK: Cambridge University Press.

―――. 2015. "Chronotopic Formulations and Kinship Behaviors in Social History." *Anthropological Quarterly* 88, no. 2: 401–15.

Alba-Juez, Laura. 2009. "'Little Words' in Small Talk: Some Considerations on the Use of the Pragmatic Markers *man* in English and *macho/tío* in Peninsular Spanish." In *Little Words*, ed. Ronald P. Leow, Hector Campos, and Donna Lardiere, 171–81. Washington DC: Georgetown University Press.

Allan, Keith and Kate Burridge. 1991. *Euphemism and Dysphemism: Language Used as Shield and Weapon*. Oxford: Oxford University Press.

Alves, Mark J. 2021. "Linguistic Influence of Chinese in Southeast Asia." In *The Languages and Linguistics of Mainland Southeast Asia*, ed. Paul Sidwell and Mathias Jenny, 649–72. Berlin/Boston: De Gruyter Mouton.

Anderson, Edmund A. 1993. "Speech Levels: The Case of Sundanese." *Pragmatics* 3, no. 2: 107–36.

Arendt, Hannah. 1998. *The Human Condition*, 2nd ed. Chicago: University of Chicago Press. https://doi.org/10.7208/chicago/9780226924571.001.0001

Arka, I Wayan. 2005. "Speech Levels, Social Predicates and Pragmatic Structure in Balinese: A Lexical Approach." *Pragmatics* 15, nos. 2–3: 169–203.

Armstrong, W.E. 1928. *Rossel Island: An Ethnological Study*. Cambridge: Cambridge University Press.

Arps, Ben, Els Bogaerts, Willem van der Molen, Ignatius Supriyanto and Jan van den Veerdonk. 2000. *Hedendaags Javaans: En Leerboek*, Semaian 20. Leiden: Opleiding Talen en Culturen van Zuidoost-Azië en Oceanië, Universiteit Leiden.

Asmah Hajah Omar. 1983. *The Malay Peoples of Malaysia and Their Languages*. Kuala Lumpur: Dewan Bahasa dan Pustaka.

⎯⎯⎯⎯⎯⎯⎯⎯. 1986. *Nahu Melayu Mutakhir*. Kuala Lumpur: Dewan Bahasa dan Pustaka.

⎯⎯⎯⎯⎯⎯⎯⎯. 1998. "Language Planning and Image Building: The Case of Malay in Malaysia." *International Journal of the Sociology of Language* 130: 49–66.

⎯⎯⎯⎯⎯⎯⎯⎯. 2012. "Pragmatics of Maintaining English in Malaysia's Education System." In *English in Southeast Asia: Features, Policy and Language in Use*, ed. Ee-Ling Low and Azirah Hashim, 155–74. Amsterdam: John Benjamins.

Auer, Peter. 1998. *Code-switching in Conversation: Language, Interaction and Identity*. London and New York: Routledge.

⎯⎯⎯⎯⎯⎯⎯⎯. 1999. "From Codeswitching via Language Mixing to Fused Lects: Towards a Dynamic Typology of Bilingual Speech." *International Journal of Bilingualism* 3, no. 4: 309–32.

Axelson, Elizabeth. 2007. "Vocatives: A Double-Edged Strategy in Intercultural Discourse Among Graduate Students." *Pragmatics* 17, no. 1: 95–122.

Badenoch, Nathan. 2016. "Bit Personal Pronouns in a Northern Mon-Khmer Context". *Annals of Foreign Studies* 92, *Researches in Asian Languages* 10: 5–23.

Baetens Beardsmore, Hugo. 1982. *Bilingualism: Basic Principles*. Clevedon: Tieto Ltd.

Bakar, H.A. 2009. "Code-switching in Kuala Lumpur Malay: The 'Rojak' Phenomenon." *Core* 9: 99–107. Manoa: ScholarSpace at University of Hawai'i at Manoa.

Banks, David J. 1974. "Malay Kinship Terms and Morgan's Malayan Terminology: The Complexity of Simplicity." *Bijdragen tot de Taal-, Land- en Volkenkunde* 130, no. 1: 44–68.

Bateson, Gregory. 1972. "A Theory of Play and Fantasy." In *Steps to an Ecology of Mind*, 177–93. Chicago: The University of Chicago Press.

Becker, A.L. and I Gusti Ngurah Oka. 1974. "Person in Kawi: Exploration of an Elementary Semantic Dimension." *Oceanic Linguistics* 13, nos. 1–2: 229–55.

Benjamin, Geoffrey. 1983 [1978]. "The Anthropology of Grammar: Self and Other in Temiar." Paper presented at the Second Austroasiatic Conference, Mysore, India.

⎯⎯⎯⎯⎯⎯⎯⎯. 1999. "Temiar Kinship Terminology: A Linguistic and Formal Analysis." Penang: Academy of Social Sciences (AKASS), Universiti Sains Malaysia.

Bibliography

———. 2013. "Aesthetic Elements in Temiar Grammar." In *Sound and Meaning in the Languages of Mainland Southeast Asia*, ed. Jeffrey P. Williams, 36–60. New York: Cambridge University Press.
Benveniste, Emile. 1966 [1958]. "Subjectivity in language." In *Problems in General Linguistics*, translated by Mary Elizabeth Meek, 223–30. Coral Gables, Florida: University of Miami.
Berman, Laine A. 1992. "First Person Identities in Indonesian Conversational Narratives." *Journal of Asian Pacific Communication* 3: 3–14.
Besnier, Niko. 2000. *Tuvaluan: A Polynesian Language of the Central Pacific*. Oxford/New York: Routledge.
Biber, Douglas, Stig Johansson, Geoffrey Leech, Susan Conrad, and Edward Finegan. 1999. *Longman Grammar of Spoken and Written English*. London: Longman.
Bilmes, Jack. 1998. "Two Models of Villager-Official Relationships in Northern Thailand." *Tai Culture* 3: 108–18.
Bloomaert, Jan. 2012. *The Sociolinguistics of Globalization*. Cambridge, UK: Cambridge University Press.
Bouchier, David. 2015. *Illiberal Democracy in Indonesia: The Ideology of the Family State*. Abingdon, Oxon: Routledge.
Bourdieu, Pierre. 1984. *Distinction—A Social Critique of the Judgement of Taste*, translated by Richard Nice. Cambridge, Mass: Harvard University Press.
Bowden, John. 2001. *Taba: Description of a South Halmahera Language*. Canberra: Pacific Linguistics.
———. 2002. "The Impact of Malay on Taba: A Type of Incipient Language Death or Incipient Death of a Language Type?" In *Language Endangerment and Language Maintenance*, ed. David Bradley and Maya Bradley, 114–43. New York: Routledge.
Bradley, Mark. 2004. "Becoming *van minh*: Civilizational Discourse and Visions of the Self in Twentieth-Century Vietnam." *Journal of World History* 15, no. 1: 65–83.
Brandom, Robert. 2000. "Facts, Norms, and Normative Facts: A Reply to Habermas." *European Journal of Philosophy* 8, no. 3: 356–74.
Braun, Friederike. 1988. *Terms of Address*. Berlin: De Gruyter. https://doi.org/10.1515/9783110848113
Brenner, Suzanne. 1999. "On the Public Intimacy of the New Order: Images of Women In the Popular Indonesian Print." *Indonesia* 67: 13–37.
Brown, Lea. 2005. "Nias." In *The Austronesian Languages of Asia and Madagascar*, ed. Alexander Adelaar and Nikolaus P. Himmelmann, 562–89. Abingdon, Oxon: Routledge.
Brown, Lucien. 2011. *Korean Honorifics and Politeness in Second Language Learning*. Philadelphia: John Benjamins. https://doi.org/10.1075/pbns.206

Brown, Panitee Suksomboon. 2017. "Shades of Friendship among Thai Women in the Netherlands." In *Conceptualizing Friendship in Time and Place*, ed. Carla Risseeu and Marlein van Raalte, 250–67. Leiden: Brill Rodopi.

Brown, Penelope and Stephen C. Levinson. 1987 [1978]. *Politeness: Some Universals in Language Use*. Cambridge, UK: Cambridge University Press. https://doi.org/10.1017/CBO9780511813085

Brown, Roger and Marguerite Ford. 1961. "Address in American English." *The Journal of Abnormal and Social Psychology* 62, no. 2: 375–85.

Brown, Roger and Albert Gilman. 1960. "The Pronouns of Power and Solidarity." In *Style in Language*, ed. Thomas A. Sebeok, 253–76. Cambridge, MA: MIT Press.

Bucholtz, Mary. 2009. "From Stance to Style: Gender, Interaction, and Indexicality in Mexican Immigrant Youth Slang." In *Stance: Sociolinguistic Perspectives*, ed. Alexandra Jaffe, 146–70. Oxford: Oxford University Press.

Bunnag, Jane. 1973. *Buddhist Monk, Buddhist Layman: A Study of Urban Monastic Organization in Central Thailand*. Cambridge, UK: Cambridge University Press. https://doi.org/10.1017/CBO9780511557576

Bunnell, Tim. 2002. "Kampung Rules: Landscape and the Contested Government of Urban(e) Malayness." *Urban Studies* 39, no. 9, 1685–1701.

Cassaniti, Julia. 2015. *Living Buddhism: Mind, Self, and Emotion in a Thai Community*. Ithaca, NY: Cornell University Press.

Chandralal, Dipesh. 2010. *Sinhala*. Philadelphia: John Benjamins. https://doi.org/10.1075/loall.15

Chandrasekhar, A. 1970. "Personal Pronouns and Pronominal Forms in Malayalam." *Anthropological Linguistics* 12, no. 7: 246–55.

Chin, Yee Mun, Lee Yok Fee, Jayum Jawan and Sarjit Singh Darshan. 2015. "From Individual Choice to Collective Actions: Ethnic Consciousness in Malaysia Reconsidered." *Ethnic and Racial Studies* 38: 259–74.

Chirasombutti, Voravudhi and Anthony Diller. 1999. "'Who Am "I"' in Thai?' The Thai First Person: Self-Reference or Gendered Self." In *Genders & Sexualities in Modern Thailand*, ed. Peter A. Jackson and Nerida M. Cook, 114–33. Chiang Mai, Thailand: Silkworm Books.

Choksi, Nishaant. 2010. "The Dual as Honorific in Santali." *Proceedings of the 32nd All India Conference of Linguists*, 125–30.

Chowning, Ann. 1985. "Rapid Lexical Change and Aberrant Melanesian Languages: Sengseng and Its Neighbours." In *Austronesian Linguistics at the Fifteenth Pacific Science Congress*, ed. Andrew Pawley and Lois Carrington, 169–98. Canberra: Pacific Linguistics.

Clayman, Steven E. 1992. "Footing in the Achievement of Neutrality: The Case of News Interview Discourse." In *Talk At Work: Interaction in Institutional Settings*, ed. Paul Drew and John Heritage, 163–211. Cambridge, UK: Cambridge University Press.
_____. 2002. "Disagreements and Third Parties: Dilemmas of Neutralism in Panel News Interviews." *Journal of Pragmatics* 34: 1385–1401.
_____. 2006. "Understanding News Media: The Relevance of Interaction." In *Talk and Interaction in Social Research Methods*, ed. Paul Drew, Geoffrey Raymond and Darin Weinberg, 135–54. London: Sage.
_____. 2010. "Address Terms in the Service of Other Actions: The Case of News Interview Talk." *Discourse & Communication* 4, no. 2: 161–83.
_____. 2013a. "Agency in Response: The Role of Prefatory Address Terms." *Journal of Pragmatics* 57: 290–302.
_____. 2013b. "Conversation Analysis in the News Interview." In *The Handbook of Conversation Analysis*, ed. Jack Sidnell and Tanya Stivers, 630–56. Chichester: Wiley Blackwell.
Clayman, Steven E. and John Heritage. 2002a. *The News Interview: Journalists and Public Figures on the Air.* Cambridge, UK: Cambridge University Press. https://doi.org/10.1017/CBO9780511613623
_____. 2002b. "Questioning Presidents: Journalistic Deference and Adversarialness in the Press Conferences of U.S. Presidents Eisenhower and Reagan." *Journal of Communication* 52, no. 4: 749–75.
Clynes, Adrian. 1994. "Old Javanese Influence in Balinese: Balinese Speech Styles." In *Language Contact and Change in the Austronesian World*, ed. Tom Dutton and Darrell T. Tryon, 141–79. Berlin: Mouton de Gruyter.
Cody, Francis. 2011. "Publics and Politics." *Annual Review of Anthropology* 40: 37–52.
Collins, Chris, ed. 2014. *Cross-Linguistic Studies of Imposters and Pronominal Agreement.* New York: Oxford University Press. https://doi.org/10.1093/acprof:oso/9780199336852.001.0001
Collins, Chris and Paul Postal. 2012. *Imposters: A Study of Pronominal Agreement.* Cambridge: MIT Press. https://doi.org/10.7551/mitpress/9780262016889.001.0001
Collins, James T. 1989. "Malay Dialect Research in Malaysia: The Issue of Perspective." *Bijdragen tot de Taal-, Land- en Volkenkunde* 145, no. 2/3: 235–64.
Comrie, Bernard. 1976. "Linguistic Politeness Axes: Speaker-Addressee, Speaker-Referent, Speaker-Bystander." *Pragmatics Microfiche* 1, no. 7: 1–12.
Conners, Thomas J., Claudia M. Brugman and Nikki B. Adams. 2016. "Reference Tracking and Non-Canonical Referring Expressions in Indonesian." In *Studies in Language Typology and Change*, ed. Yanti and Timothy McKinnon. *NUSA* 60: 59–88.
Cooke, Joseph R. 1968. *Pronominal Reference in Thai, Burmese, and Vietnamese.* Berkeley: University of California Press.

Court, C. 1998. Untitled posting on the SEALTEACH list, 30 April 1998.
Cysouw, Michael. 2005. "A Typology of Honorific Uses of Clusivity." In *Clusivity: Typology and Case Studies of the Inclusive-Exclusive Distinction*, ed. Elena Filimonova, 213–30. Philadelphia: John Benjamins.
Daniels, Timothy. 2005. *Building Cultural Nationalism in Malaysia: Identity, Representation and Citizenship*. London: Routledge.
Davies, Herbert John. 1991. "Marked Pronouns and Verbs for Marked Social Relationships in a Chadic and a Papuan Language." In *Man and a Half: Essays in Pacific Anthropology and Ethnobiology in Honour of Ralph Bulmer*, ed. Andrew Pawley, 397–405. Auckland: Polynesian Society.
De Young, John E. 1955. *Village Life in Modern Thailand*. Berkeley: University of California Press. https://doi.org/10.1525/9780520325975
DeFillipo, Cassie. 2020. "'Men Have the Power': Male Peer Groups as the Building Blocks of Political Masculinities in Northern Thailand." In *Masculine Power and Gender Equality: Masculinities as Change Agents*, ed. Russell Luyt and Kathleen Starck, 119–31. Cham: Springer Nature Switzerland.
Derrida, Jacques. 1997. *The Politics of Friendship*, translated by George Collins. London and New York: Verso.
Dewi, Kurniawati Hastuti. 2020. "Motherhood Identity in the 2019 Indonesian Presidential Elections: Populism and Political Division in the National Women's Movement." *Contemporary Southeast Asia* 42, no. 2: 224–50.
Dickey, Eleanor. 1997. "Forms of Address and Terms of Reference." *Journal of Linguistics* 33: 255–74.
Diller, Tony. 2006. "Polylectal Grammar and Royal Thai." In *Catching Language: The Standing Challenge of Grammar Writing*, ed. Felix Ameka, Nicholas Evans, Alan Dench, 565–608. New York: Mouton de Gruyter.
Djenar, Dwi Noverini. 2008. "Which Self? Pronominal Choice, Modernity, and Self-Categorizations." *International Journal of the Sociology of Language* 189, no. 1: 31–54.
———. 2015. "Pronouns and Sociospatial Ordering in Conversation and Fiction." In *The Pragmatics of Personal Pronouns*, ed. Laure Gardelle and Sandrine Sorlin, 195–213. Amsterdam: John Benjamins.
Djenar, Dwi Noverini, Michael C. Ewing and Howard Manns. 2018. *Style and Intersubjectivity in Youth Interaction*. Berlin: De Gruyter. https://doi.org/10.1515/9781614516439
Donohue, M. and J.C. Smith. 1998. "What's Happened to Us? Some Developments in the Malay Pronoun System." *Oceanic Linguistics* 37: 65–84.
Du Bois, John W. 2007. "The Stance Triangle." In *Stancetaking in Discourse: Subjectivity, Evaluation, Interaction*, ed. Robert Englebretson, 139–82. Amsterdam: John Benjamins.

Du Bois, John W. and Elise Kärkkäinen. 2012. "Taking a Stance on Emotion: Affect, Sequence, and Intersubjectivity in Dialogic Interaction." *Text & Talk* 32, no. 4: 433–51.
Du Bois, John W., Stephen Schuetze-Coburn, Danae Paolino and Susanna Cumming. 1993. "Outline of Discourse Transcription." In *Talking Data: Transcription and Coding Methods for Language Research*, ed. J.A. Edwards and M.D. Lampert, 45–89. Hillsdale NJ: Lawrence Erlbaum.
Du Bois, John W. and Rachel Giora. 2014. "From Cognitive-Functional Linguistics to Dialogic Syntax." *Cognitive Linguistics* 25, no. 3: 351–7.
Du Bois, John W., Wallace L. Chafe, Charles Meyer and Sandra A. Thompson. 2000. *Santa Barbara Corpus of Spoken American English, Part 1*. Philadelphia: Linguistic Data Consortium.
Du Bois, John, Stephan Schuetze-Coburn, Danae Paolino and Susanna Cumming. 1993. "Discourse Transcription." Santa Barbara Papers in Linguistics, vol. 4. Department of Linguistics, University of California, Santa Barbara.
Dutton, George, Jayne Werner and John K. Whitmore, eds. 2012. *Sources of Vietnamese Tradition*. New York: Columbia University Press.
Eades, Domenyk. 2005. *A Grammar of Gayo: A Language of Aceh, Sumatra*. Pacific Linguistics: Canberra.
Ekström, Mats. 2011. "Hybridity as a Resource and Challenge in a Talk Show Political Interview." In *Talking Politics in Broadcast Media: Cross-Cultural Perspectives on Political Interviewing*, ed. Mats Ekström and Marianna Patrona, 135–55. Amsterdam: John Benjamins.
Embree, John F. 1950. "Thailand—A Loosely Structured Social System." *American Anthropologist* 52, no. 2: 181–93.
Enfield, N.J. 2007a. *A Grammar of Lao*. Berlin and New York: De Gruyter. https://doi.org/10.1515/9783110207538
———. 2007b. "Meanings of the Unmarked: How 'default' Person Reference Does More Than Just Refer." In *Person Reference in Interaction: Linguistic, Cultural and Social Perspectives*, ed. N.J. Enfield and Tanya Stivers, 97–120. Cambridge, UK: Cambridge University Press.
———. 2009. "Everyday Ritual in the Residential World." In *Ritual Communication*, ed. Gunter Senft and Ellen B. Basso, 51–80. Oxford: Berg.
———. 2013. *Relationship Thinking: Agency, Enchrony, and Human Sociality*. New York: Oxford University Press.
———. 2014. *The Utility of Meaning: What Words Mean and Why*. Oxford: Oxford University Press.
———. 2017. "Distribution of Agency." In *Distributed Agency*, ed. N.J. Enfield and Paul Kockelman, 9–14. New York: Oxford University Press.

―――――. 2018. "Social Change in the Nam Theun 2 Catchment: The Kri Experience." In *Dead in the Water: Global Lessons from the World Bank's Model Hydropower Project in Laos*, ed. Shoemaker Bruce and Robichaud William, 141–55. Madison, Wisconsin: University of Wisconsin Press.

―――――. 2019. *Mainland Southeast Asian Languages: A Concise Typological Introduction*. Cambridge, UK: Cambridge University Press.

Enfield, N.J. and Gérard Diffloth. 2009. "Phonology and Sketch Grammar of Kri, a Vietic Language of Laos." *Cahiers de Linguistique - Asie Orientale* 38, no. 1: 3–69.

Enfield, N.J. and Jack Sidnell. 2019. "The Normative Nature of Language." In *The Normative Animal? On the Anthropological Significance of Social, Moral and Linguistic Norms*, ed. Neil Roughley and Kurt Bayertz, 265–78. New York: Oxford University Press.

Enfield, N.J. and Tanya Stivers, eds. 2007. *Person Reference in Interaction: Linguistic, Cultural and Social Perspectives*. Cambridge, UK: Cambridge University Press.

Englebretson, Robert. 2007. "Grammatical Resources for Social Purposes: Some Aspects of Stancetaking in Colloquial Indonesian Conversation." In *Stancetaking in Discourse: Subjectivity, Evaluation, Interaction*, ed. Robert Englebretson, 69–110. Amsterdam: John Benjamins.

Engelenhoven, Aone van and Juliette Huber. 2020. "East Fataluku." In *The Papuan Languages of Timor, Alor and Pantar: Volume 3, Sketch Grammars*, ed. Antoinette Schapper, 347–426. Berlin/Boston: De Gruyter Mouton. https://doi.org/10.1515/9781501511158-006

Errington, Joseph. 1982. "Speech in the Royal Presence: Javanese Palace Language." *Indonesia* 34: 89–101.

―――――. 1985a. *Language and Social Change in Java: Linguistic Reflexes of Modernization in a Traditional Royal Polity*. Athens, Ohio: Ohio University Press.

―――――. 1985b. "On the Nature of the Linguistic Sign: Describing the Javanese Speech Levels." In *Semiotic Mediation: Sociocultural and Psychological Perspectives*, ed. Elizabeth Mertz and Richard J. Parmentier, 287–310. Orlando, FL: Academic Press.

―――――. 1988. *Structure and Style in Javanese: A Semiotic View of Linguistic Etiquette*. Philadelphia: University of Pennsylvania Press.

―――――. 1998. *Shifting Languages: Interaction and Identity in Javanese Indonesia*. Cambridge, UK.: Cambridge University Press.

―――――. 2022. *Other Indonesians: Nationalism in an Unnative Language*. New York: Oxford University Press.

Ervin-Tripp, Susan M. 1972. "Sociolinguistic Rules of Address." In *Sociolinguistics: Selected Readings*, ed. J.B. Pride and Janet Holmes, 225–40. Harmondsworth: Penguin Books.

Evers, Han-Dieter. 1969. *Loosely Structured Social Systems: Thailand in Comparative Perspective*. New Haven: Yale University Southeast Asia Studies.

Ewing, Michael C. 2001. "Reference and Recovery in Cirebon Javanese Conversation." *Australian Journal of Linguistics* 21: 25–47.

―――. 2005a. "Colloquial Indonesian." In *The Austronesian Languages of Asia and Madagascar*, ed. Alexander Adelaar and Nikolaus P. Himmelmann, 227–58. New York: Routledge.

―――. 2005b. *Grammar and Inference in Conversation: Identifying Clause Structure in Spoken Javanese*. Amsterdam: John Benjamins.

―――. 2014. "Motivations for First and Second Person Subject Expression and Ellipsis in Javanese Conversation." *Journal of Pragmatics* 63: 48–62.

Ewing, Michael C. and Dwi Noverini Djenar. 2019. "Address, Reference and Sequentiality in Indonesian Conversation." In *The Social Dynamics of Pronominal Systems: A Comparative Approach*, ed. Paul Bouissac, 253–87. Amsterdam: John Benjamins.

Ferguson, Charles. 1964. "Baby Talk in Six Languages." *American Anthropologist* 66, no. 6, Part 2: 103–14. https://doi.org/10.1525/aa.1964.66.suppl_3.02a00060

Fleming, Luke. 2014. "Australian Exceptionalism in the Typology of Affinal Avoidance Registers." *Anthropological Linguistics* 56, no. 2: 115–58.

―――. 2016. "Of Referents and Recipients: Pohnpeian Humiliatives and the Functional Organization of Austronesian Honorific Registers." *Proceedings of the Annual Meeting of the Berkeley Linguistics Society* 42: 293–312.

―――. 2017. "Honorific Alignment and Pronominal Paradigm: Evidence from Mixtec, Santali, and Dhimal." *Proceedings of the Annual Meeting of the Berkeley Linguistics Society* 43: 95–120.

―――. 2018. "Undecontextualizable: Performativity and the Conditions of Possibility of Linguistic Symbolism." *Signs in Society* 6, no. 3: 558–606.

―――. 2022. "On Speaking Terms: Avoidance Registers and the Sociolinguistics of Kinship." Unpublished Manuscript.

Fleming, Luke and Jack Sidnell. 2020. "The Typology and Social Pragmatics of Interlocutor Reference in Southeast Asia." *The Journal of Asian Linguistic Anthropology* 1, no. 1: 1–20.

Fleming, Luke and James Slotta. 2018. "The Pragmatics of Kin Address: A Sociolinguistic Universal and its Semantic Affordances." *Journal of Sociolinguistics* 22, no. 4: 375–405.

Foster, Brian L. 1976. "Friendship in Rural Thailand." *Ethnology* 15, no. 3: 251–67.

Fox, James J. 2005. "Ritual Languages, Special Registers and Speech Decorum in Austronesian Languages." In *The Austronesian Languages of Asia and Madagascar*, ed. Alexander Adelaar and Nikolaus P. Himmelmann, 87–109. New York: Routledge.

Friedl, Ernestine. 1964. "Lagging Emulation in Post-Peasant Society." *American Anthropologist* 66, no. 3: 569–86.

Friedrich, Paul. 1979. "Structural Implications of Russian Pronominal Usage." In *Language, Context, and the Imagination: Essays by Paul Friedrich*, ed. Anwar S. Dil, 63–125. Stanford: Stanford University Press.

Gal, Susan and Judith T. Irvine. 2019. *Signs of Difference: Language and Ideology in Social Life*. Cambridge, UK: Cambridge University Press. https://doi.org/10.1017/9781108649209

Gammeltoft, Tine. 1999. *Women's Bodies, Women's Worries: Health and Family Planning in a Vietnamese Rural Community*. Richmond: Curzon.

Garde, Murray. 2013. *Culture, Interaction and Person Reference in an Australian Language: An Ethnography of Bininj Gunwok Communication*. Philadelphia: John Benjamins. https://doi.org/10.1075/clu.11

Geertz, Clifford. 1973. *The Interpretation of Cultures: Selected Essays*. New York: Basic Books.

_____. 1976 [1960]. *The Religion of Java*. Chicago: The University of Chicago Press.

Ghosh, Arun. 2008. "Santali." In *The Munda Languages*, ed. Gregory D.S. Anderson, 11–98. Oxford/New York: Routledge.

Goddard, Cliff. 2000. "'Cultural Scripts' and Communicative Style in Malay (Bahasa Melayu)." *Anthropological Linguistics* 42, no. 1: 81–106.

Goebel, Zane. 2010. *Language, Migration, and Identity: Neighborhood Talk in Indonesia*. New York: Cambridge University Press. https://doi.org/10.1017/CBO9780511778247

_____. 2017. "Infrastructures for Ethnicity: Understanding the Diversification of Contemporary Indonesia." *Asian Ethnicity* 18, no. 3: 263–76.

_____. 2019. "Contact Discourse." *Language in Society* 48, no. 3: 331–51.

_____. 2020. *Global Leadership Talk: Constructing Good Governance in Indonesia*. New York: Oxford University Press.

Goebel, Zane, Deborah Cole and Howard Manns. 2019. "Theorizing the Semiotic Complexity of Contact Talk." In *Contact Talk*, ed. Zane Goebel, Deborah Cole and Howard Manns, 1–28. London: Routledge.

Goffman, Erving. 1956. "The Nature of Deference and Demeanor." *American Anthropologist* 58: 473–502.

_____. 1974. *Frame Analysis: An Essay on the Organization of Experience*. Boston: Northeastern University Press.

_____. 1981. "Footing." In *Forms of Talk*, 124–57. Philadelphia: University of Pennsylvania Press.

Gonda, Jan. 1948. "The Javanese Vocabulary of Courtesy." *Lingua* 1: 333–76.

_____. 1973. *Sanskrit in Indonesia*. 2nd ed. New Dehli: International Academy of Indian Culture.

Greatbatch, David. 1992. "On the Management of Disagreement between News Interviewees." In *Talk at Work: Interaction in Institutional Settings*, ed. Paul Drew and John Heritage, 268–301. Cambridge, UK: Cambridge University Press.

Grijns, C.D. 1981. "Jakartan Speech and Takdir Alisjahbana's Plea for the Simple Indonesian Word-Form." In *Papers on Indonesian Languages and Literatures*, ed. Khaidir Anwar and Nigel Philips, 1–34. Paris: Association Archipel.

Gumperz, John. 2008. "Interactional Sociolinguistics: A Personal Perspective." In *The Handbook of Discourse Analysis*, ed. Deborah Schiffrin, Deborah Tannen and Heidi E. Hamilton, *215–28*. Malden, MA: Blackwell.

Haas, Mary R. 1969. "Sibling Terms as Used by Marriage Partners." *Southwestern Journal of Anthropology* 25, no. 3: 228–35.

Hafford, James. 2014. "Wuvulu Grammar and Vocabulary." PhD diss., University of Hawai'i at Manoa.

Hamid, Z. and N.Z. Abu. 2013. *Memupuk perpaduan di Malaysia — santun bahasa dalam kalanganmurid pelbagai etnik dari aspek penggunaan kata ganti nama diri.*

Hanitzch, Thomas, Tim P. Vos, Olivier Standaert, Folker Hanusch, Jan Fredrik Hovden, Liesbeth Hermans and Jyotika Ramaprasad. 2019. "Role Orientations: Journalists' Views of Their Place in Society." In *Worlds of Journalism: Journalistic Cultures Around the Globe*, ed. Thomas Hanitzch, Folker Hanusch, Jyotika Ramaprasad and A.S. (Arrie) De Beer, 161–97. New York: Columbia University Press. https://doi.org/10.7312/hani18642-008

Hanks, Lucien M. 1972. *Rice and Man: Agricultural Ecology in Southeast Asia*. Chicago: Aldine-Atherton. https://doi.org/10.1515/9780824843588

Harms, Erik. 2011. *Saigon's Edge: On the Margins of Ho Chi Minh City*. University of Minnesota Press. https://doi.org/10.5749/minnesota/9780816656059.001.0001

———. 2016. *Luxury and Rubble: Civility and Dispossession in the New Saigon*. Berkeley: University of California Press.

Harsojo. 1983. "Kedubayaan Sunda." In *Manusia dan kebudayaan di Indonesia*, ed. R. Koentjaraningrat, 300–26. Jakarta: Djambatan.

Hastings, Adi and Paul Manning. 2004. "Acts of Alterity." *Language & Communication* 24, no. 4: 291–311.

Hattori, Ryoko. 2012. "Preverbal Particles in Pingelapese: A Language of Micronesia." PhD diss., University of Hawai'i at Manoa.

Hattori, Shirō. 1964. "A Special Language of the Older Generations Among the Ainu." *Linguistics* 6: 43–58.

Haugevik, Kristin and Iver B. Neumann, eds. 2019. *Kinship in International Relations*. Abingdon, Oxon: Routledge.

Haugh, Michael. 2016. "'Just Kidding': Teasing and Claims to Non-Serious Intent." *Journal of Pragmatics* 95: 120–36.

Haugh, Michael and Derek Bousfield. 2012. "Mock Impoliteness, Jocular Mockery and Jocular Abuse in Australian and British English." *Journal of Pragmatics* 44, no. 9: 1099–114.

Head, Brian F. 1978. "Respect Degrees in Pronominal Reference." In *Universals of Human Language Vol. 3: Word Structure*, ed. Joseph H. Greenberg, 151–211. Stanford: Stanford University Press.

Heine, Bernd and Kyung-An Song. 2011. "On the Grammaticalization of Personal Pronouns." *Journal of Linguistics* 47, no. 3: 587–630.

Heritage, John. 1985. "Analyzing News Interviews: Aspects of the Production of Talk for an 'Overhearing' Audience." In *Handbook of Discourse Analysis, Vol. III: Discourse and Dialogue*, ed. Teun van Dijk, 95–119. London: Academic Press.

Heritage, John and Steven Clayman. 2010. *Talk in Action: Interactions, Identities, and Institutions*. Chichester: Wiley-Blackwell. https://doi.org/10.1002/9781444318135

High, Holly. 2011. "Melancholia and Anthropology." *American Ethnologist* 38, no. 2: 217–33.

Himmelmann, Nikolaus P. 2005. "The Austronesian Languages of Asia and Madagascar: Typological Characteristics." In *The Austronesian Languages of Asia and Madagascar*, ed. Alexander Adelaar and Nikolaus P. Himmelmann, 110–81. Abingdon, Oxon: Routledge.

Hoogervorst, Tom. Forthcoming. "Non-areal contact." In *The Oxford Guide to the Malayo-Polynesian Languages of South East Asia*, ed. Alexander Adelaar and Antoinette Schapper. Oxford, UK: Oxford University Press.

———. 2021. "South Asian Influence on the Languages of Southeast Asia." In *The Languages and Linguistics of Mainland Southeast Asia*, ed. Paul Sidwell and Mathias Jenny, 623–47. Berlin/Boston: De Gruyter Mouton.

Hook, Donald D. 1984. "First Names and Titles as Solidarity and Power semantics in English." *International Review of Applied Linguistics* 22, no. 3: 183–90.

Houtzagers, Peter. 2018. "The Honorific Third Person Plural in Slavic." *Russian Linguistics* 42: 1–26.

Howard, Kathryn. 2007. "Kinterm Usage and Hierarchy in Thai Children's Peer Groups." *Journal of Linguistic Anthropology* 17: 204–30.

Humphrey, Caroline 1993. "Women, Taboo, and the Suppression of Attention." In *Defining Females: The Nature of Women in Society*, ed. Shirley Ardener, 73–92. Oxford: Berg Press.

Irvine, Judith T. 1992. "Ideologies of Honorific Language." *Pragmatics* 2, no. 3: 251–62.

———. 1998. "Ideologies of Honorific Language." In *Language Ideologies: Practice and Theory*, ed. Bambi B. Schieffelin, Kathryn A. Woolard, and Paul V. Kroskrity, 51–67. New York: Oxford University Press.

Irvine, Judith T. 2011. "Leaky Registers and Eight-Hundred-Pound Gorillas." *Anthropological Quarterly* 84, no. 1: 15–39.
Ishiyama, Osamu. 2010. "Toward a Typology of Person Shift." *LSO Working Papers in Linguistics* 8: 23–32.
Jaworski, Adam. 1992. "The Vocative, First Name and the Pronoun *ty* in the Polish System of Address." *Biuletyn Polskiego Towarzystwa Językoznawczego* 47–48: 95–104.
Jaworski, Adam and Dariusz Galasiński. 2000. "Vocative Address Forms and Ideological Legitimization in Political Debates." *Discourse Studies* 2, no. 1: 35–53.
Jørgensen, Annette Myre. 2013. "Spanish Teenage Language and the COLAm-corpus." *Bergen Language and Linguistics Studies* 3, no. 1: 151–66.
Kádár, Dániel Zoltán. 2005. "The Powerful and the Powerless: On the Classification of the Chinese Polite Denigrating/Elevating Addressing Terminology." *Acta Orientalia Academiae Scientiarum Hungaricae* 58, no. 4: 421–43.
Kartomihardjo, Soeseno. 1981. *Ethnography of Communicative Codes in East Java*. Canberra: Pacific Linguistics.
Kaufman, Daniel. 2014. "The Syntax of Indonesian Imposters." In *Cross-Linguistic Studies of Imposters and Pronominal Agreement*, ed. Chris Collins, 89–120. New York: Oxford University Press.
Keane, Webb. 1997. *Signs of Recognition: Powers and Hazards of Representation in an Indonesian Society*. Berkeley: University of California Press. https://doi.org/10.1525/9780520917637
Keeler, Ward. 1975. "Musical Encounter in Java and Bali." *Indonesia* 19: 85–126.
———. 1984. *Javanese: A Cultural Approach*. Athens OH: Ohio University Center for International Studies.
Kendall, Martha. 1981. "Toward a Semantic Approach to Terms of Address: A Critique of Deterministic Models in Sociolinguistics." *Language & Communication* 1, no. 2/3: 237–54.
Keyes, Charles F. 1984. "Mother or Mistress but Never a Monk: Buddhist Notions of Female Gender in Rural Thailand." *American Ethnologist* 11, no. 2: 223–41.
Kiesling, Scott F. 2004. "Dude." *American Speech* 79, no. 3: 281–305.
Kim, Alan Hyun-Oak. 2011. "Politeness in Korea." In *Politeness in East Asia*, ed. Déaniel Kádár and Sarah Mills, 176–207. Cambridge, UK: Cambridge University Press.
Kitiarsa, Pattana. 2005. "'Lives of Hunting Dogs': Muai Thai and the Politics of Thai Masculinities." *South East Asia Research* 13, no. 1: 57–90.
Klamer, Marian. 2017. "The Alor-Pantar Languages: Linguistic Context, History and Typology." In *The Alor-Pantar Languages: History and Typology*, 2nd ed., ed. Marian Klamer, 1–48. Berlin: Language Science Press.

Kleinknecht, Friederike. 2013. "Mexican *güey*—From Vocative to Discourse Marker: A Case of Grammaticalization?" In *Vocative!: Addressing Between System and Performance*, ed. Barbara Sonnenhauser and Patrizia Noel Aziz Hanna, 235–68. Berlin: De Gruyter.

Kleinknecht, Friederike and Miguel Souza. 2017. "Vocatives as a Source Category for Pragmatic Markers." In *Pragmatic Markers, Discourse Markers and Modal Particles: New Perspectives*, ed. Chiara Fedriani and Andrea Sansò, 257–87. Amsterdam: John Benjamins.

Kockelman, Paul. 2007. "Agency: The Relation Between Meaning, Power, and Knowledge." *Current Anthropology* 48, no. 3: 375–401.

Koshal, Sanyukta. 1987. "Honorific Systems of the Ladakhi Language." *Multilingua* 6, no. 2: 149–68.

Kozok, Ulrich. 2006. "Indonesian Native Speakers-Myth and Reality." https://indonesian-online.com/wp-content/uploads/2016/08/Native-Speakers.pdf

Kridalaksana, Harimurti. 1974. "Second Participant in Indonesian Address." *Language Sciences* 31: 17–20.

Kruspe, Nicole. 2004. *A Grammar of Semelai*. New York: Cambridge University Press. https://doi.org/10.1017/CBO9780511550713

Kruspe, Nicole and Niclas Burenhult. 2019. "Pronouns in Affinal Avoidance: Evidence from the Aslian languages (Austroasiatic, Malay Peninsula)." In *The Social Dynamics of Pronominal Systems: A Comparative Approach*, ed. Paul Bouissac, 289–317. Amsterdam: John Benjamins.

Lauerbach, Greta. 2007. "Argumentation in Political Talk Show Interviews." *Journal of Pragmatics* 39: 1388–1419.

Laughren, Mary. 2001. "What Warlpiri 'Avoidance' Registers Do with Grammar." In *Forty Years On: Ken Hale and Australian Languages*, ed. David Nash, Mary Laughren and Barry Alpher, 199–225. Canberra: Australian National University.

Leach, Edmund 1964 [1954]. *Anthropological Aspects of Language: Animal Categories and Verbal Abuse*. Cambridge, Mass: MIT Press.

Lee, Kwang-Kyu and Youngsook Kim Harvey. 1973. "Teknonymy and Geononymy in Korean Kinship Terminology." *Ethnology* 12, no. 1: 31–46.

Lee, Sarah and Thila Shanmuganathan. 2019. "Reconceptualizing *Aunty* as an Address Term in Urban Multilingual Malaysia." *World Englishes* 39, no. 1: 198–213.

Leech, Geoffrey. 1999. "The Distribution and Function of Vocatives in American and British English Conversation." In *Out of Corpora: Studies in Honour of Stig Johansson*, ed. H. Hasselgård and S. Oksefjell, 107–20. Amsterdam: Rodopi.

Leow, Rachel. 2015. *Taming Babel: Language in the Making of Malaysia*. Cambridge, UK: Cambridge University Press

Lerner, Gene H. 1996. "On the Place of Linguistic Resources in the Organization of Talk-in-Interaction: 'Second Person' Reference in Multi-Party Conversation." *Pragmatics* 6, no. 3: 281–94.
Lerner, Gene H. 2003. "Selecting Next Speaker: The Context-Sensitive Operation of a Context-Free Organization." *Language in Society* 32, no. 2: 177–201.
Lévi-Strauss, Claude. 1966. *The Savage Mind*. Chicago: The University of Chicago Press.
Levinson, Stephen. 1983 [1979]. *Pragmatics*. Cambridge, UK: Cambridge University Press. https://doi.org/10.1017/CBO9780511813313
Linell, Per. 2009. *Rethinking Language, Mind and World Dialogically: Interactional and Contextual Theories of Human Sense-Making*. Greenwich, CT: Information Age Publishing.
Liu, Amy H. 2015. *Standardizing Diversity: The Political Economy of Language Regimes*. Philadelphia: University of Pennsylvania Press. https://doi.org/10.9783/9780812292107
Luong, Hy Van. 1984. "'Brother' and 'uncle': An Analysis of Rules, Structural Contradictions, and Meaning in Vietnamese Kinship." *American Anthropologist* 86, no. 2: 290–315.
―――. 1988. "Discursive Practices and Power Structure: Person-Referring Forms and Sociopolitical Struggles in Colonial Vietnam." *American Ethnologist* 15, no. 2: 239–53.
―――. 1990. *Discursive Practices and Linguistic Meanings: The Vietnamese System of Person Reference*. Amsterdam: John Benjamins.
Luong, Hy Van and Jack Sidnell. 2020. "Shifting Referential Perspective in Vietnamese Speech Interaction." In *Studies in the Anthropology of Language in Mainland Southeast Asia.*, ed. N.J. Enfield, Jack Sidnell and Charles H.P. Zuckerman, 11–22. *Journal of the Southeast Asian Linguistics Society*: Special Publication No. 6. Honolulu: University of Hawai'i Press.
Ma, Seng Mai. 2012. "A Descriptive Grammar of Wa." Master's thesis. Payap University, Chiang Mai.
Mahdi, Waruno. 2001. "Personal Nominal Words in Indonesian: An Anomaly in Morphological Classification." In *Issues in Austronesian Morphology: A Focusschrift for Byron W. Bender*, ed. Joel Bradshaw and Kenneth L. Rehg, 163–92. Canberra: Pacific Linguistics.
Manns, Howard. 2015. "Address Terms, Framing and Identity in Indonesian Youth Interaction." *NUSA Linguistic Studies of Languages in and around Indonesia* 58: 73–93.
Manosuthikit, Aree. 2013. "Language Ideologies and Practices of a Burmese Community in the US: A Critical Perspective on Multilingualism." PhD diss., University of Wisconsin-Madison.

Mansor, Nor Shahila. 2019. "How Women Address Their Spouses: A Current Trend in Pronoun Usage." *Lenguas Modernas* 54: 49–62.

Mansor, Nor Shahila, Normaliza Abd Rahim, Roslina Mamat and Hazlina Abdul Halim. 2018. "Understanding the Choices of Terms of Address: A Sociolinguistic Study of Malay Cultural Practices." *Indonesian Journal of EFL and Linguistics* 3, no. 2: 129–47.

Marr, David. 1981. *Vietnamese Tradition on Trial, 1920–1945*. Berkeley: University of California Press.

———. 2000. "Concepts of 'Individual' and 'Self' in Twentieth-Century Vietnam." *Modern Asian Studies* 34, no. 4: 769–96.

McCarthy, Michael J. and Anne O'Keeffe. 2003. "'What's in a Name?': Vocatives in Casual Conversations and Radio Phone-in Calls." In *Corpus Analysis: Language Structure and Language Use*, ed. Pepi Leistyna and. Charles F. Meyer, 153–85. Amsterdam: Rodopi.

McGinn, Richard. 1991. "Pronouns, Politeness and Hierarchy in Malay." In *Currents in Pacific Linguistics: Papers on Austronesian Languages and Ethnolinguistics in Honour of George W. Grace*, ed. Robert Blust, 197–221. Canberra: Pacific Linguistics.

McPhail, R.M. 1953. *Introduction to Santali*. Calcutta: Firma KLM Private Ltd.

Merlan, Francesca. 1982. *Mangarayi*. North-Holland: Amsterdam.

Mills, Mary Beth. 1997. "Contesting the Margins of Modernity: Women, Migration, and Consumption in Thailand." *American Ethnologist* 24, no. 1: 37–61.

Milner, G.B. 1961. "The Samoan Vocabulary of Respect." *Journal of the Royal Anthropological Institute of Great Britain and Ireland* 91, no. 2: 296–317.

Moerman. Michael. 1988. *Talking Culture: Ethnography and Conversation Analysis*. Philadelphia: University of Pennsylvania Press.

Moertono, Soemarsaid. 1968. *State and Statecraft in Old Java: A Study of the Later Mataram Period, 16th to 19th century*. Ithaca: Modern Indonesia Project, Southeast Asia Program, Cornell University.

Mohamad, Goenawan. 2008. "Gado-Gado." In *Bahasa! Kumpulan Tulisan di Majalah Tempo* [Language! Collected writings from *Tempo* magazine], ed. Bambang Bujono and Leila S. Chudori, 3–6. Jakarta: Pusat Data dan Analisa TEMPO.

Montgomery, Martin. 2008. "The Discourse of the Broadcast News Interview." *Journalism Studies* 9, no. 2: 260–77.

———. 2010. "Rituals of Personal Experience in Television News Interviews." *Discourse & Communication* 4, no. 2: 185–211.

Morford, Janet. 1997. "Social Indexicality in French Pronominal Address." *Journal of Linguistic Anthropology* 7, no. 1: 3–37.

Moussay, Gérard. 1981. *La langue minangkabau*. Paris: Association Archipel.

Müller-Gotama, Franz. 2001. *Sundanese*. Munich: Lincom Europa.

Müller, André and Rachel Weymouth. 2017. "How Society Shapes Language: Personal Pronouns in the Greater Burma Zone." *Asia* 71, no. 1: 409–32.

Murphy, Gregory L. 1988. "Personal Reference in English." *Language in Society* 17, no. 3: 317–49.
Murray, Thomas. 2002. "A New Look at Address in American English: The Rules Have Changed." *Names* 50: 43–61.
Newman, Stanley. 1944. *Yokuts Language of California*. New York: Viking Fund.
Nietzsche, Friedrich. 1996. *Human, All Too Human: A Book for Free Spirits*. Translated by R.J. Hollingdale. Cambridge: Cambridge University Press. https://doi.org/10.1017/CBO9780511812057
Normala Othman. 2006. "Current Trends in Pronoun Usage Among Malay Speakers." Paper presented at the *Tenth International Conference on Austronesian Linguistics*. Puerto Princesa City, Palawan, Philippines.
Norwanto. 2016. "Gender and Politeness in Javanese Language." PhD diss., University of Huddersfield.
Nothofer, Bernd. 2003. "A Preliminary Analysis of the History of Sasak Language Levels." In *Working Papers in Sasak*, vol. 2, ed. Peter K. Austin, 57–84. Melbourne: University of Melbourne.
Nur Salawati Mohd Nadzria and Hanita Hassan. 2013. "The Language Identities of Malaysians as Portrayed in Upin and Ipin." *Jurnal Teknologi* 65, no. 2: 109–14.
Ochs, Elinor and Bambi Schieffelin. 2011. "The Theory of Language Socialization." In *The Handbook of Language Socialization*, ed. Alessandro Duranti, Elinor Ochs and Bambi Schieffelin, 1–21. Malden, MA: Wiley-Blackwell.
Ockey, James. 1999. "God Mothers, Good Mothers, Good Lovers, Godmothers: Gender Images in Thailand." *The Journal of Asian Studies* 58, no. 4: 1033–58.
Oh, Sun-Young. 2007. "Overt Reference to Speaker and Recipient in Korean." *Discourse Studies* 9, no. 4: 462–92.
Pakir, Anne Geok-in Sim. 1986. "A Linguistic Investigation of Baba Malay." PhD diss., Department of Linguistics, University of Hawai'i.
Palacios Martínez, Ignacio M. 2018. "'Help me move to that, blood': A Corpus-Based Study of the Syntax and Pragmatics of Vocatives in the Language of British Teenagers." *Pragmatics* 130: 33–50.
Palmer, Bill. 2018. "Language Families of the New Guinea Area." In *The Languages and Linguistics of the New Guinea Area: A Comprehensive Guide*, ed. Bill Palmer, 1–19. Berlin: De Gruyter Mouton.
Patrona, Marianna. 2011. "Neutralism Revisited: When Journalists Set New Rules in Political News Discourse." In *Talking Politics in Broadcast Media: Cross-Cultural Perspectives on Political Interviewing*, ed. Mats Ekström and Marianna Patrona, 157–176. Amsterdam: John Benjamins.
Paulston, Christina Bratt. 1976. "Pronouns of Address in Swedish: Social Class Semantics and a Changing System." *Language in Society* 5, no. 3: 359–86.

Pennycook, Alistair. 2007. *Global Englishes and Transcultural Flows*. London: Routledge.
Peterson, John. 2014. "Figuratively Speaking: Number in Kharia." In *Number – Constructions and Semantics: Case Studies from Africa, Amazonia, India and Oceania*, ed. Anne Storch and Gerrit J. Dimmendaal, 77–110. Amsterdam: John Benjamins.
Petit, Pierre. 2015. "Mobility and Stability in a Tai Vat Village (Laos)." *The Asia Pacific Journal of Anthropology* 16, no. 4: 410–23.
Pham, Hoa Andrea. 2002. "Gender in Addressing and Self-Reference in Vietnamese: Variation and Change." In *Gender across Languages. The Linguistic Representation of Men and Women*, vol. 2, ed. M. Hellinger, M. and H. Bußmann, 281–312. Amsterdam: John Benjamins. https://doi.org/10.1075/impact.10.17pha
Phan Khôi. ca. 1930. "Cách đặt đợi danh từ (Ways of using pronouns)." *Phụ Nữ Tân Văn*, số 73: 13–14.
Philips, Susan U. 2010. "Semantic and Interactional Indirectness in Tongan Lexical Honorification." *Pragmatics* 42: 317–36.
Phillips, Herbert Phineas. 1963. "Relationships between Personality and Social Structure in a Siamese Peasant Community." *Human Organization* 22, no. 2: 105–8.
_____. 1966. *Thai Peasant Personality: The Patterning of Interpresonal Behavior in the Village of Bang Chan*. Berkeley: University of California Press.
Piker, Steven. 1968. "Friendship to the Death in Rural Thai Society." *Human Organization* 27, no. 3: 200–4.
Pisani, Elizabeth. 2014. *Indonesia Etc.: Exploring the Improbable Nation*. New York: Norton.
Pittman, Richard S. 1948. "Nahuatl Honorifics." *International Journal of American Linguistics* 14, no. 4: 236–39.
Platt, Maria, Sharyn Graham Davies and Linda Rae Bennett. 2018. "Contestations of Gender, Sexuality and Morality in Contemporary Indonesia." *Asian Studies Review* 42, no. 1: 1–15.
Poedjosoedarmo, Soepomo. 1968. "Javanese Speech Levels." *Indonesia* 6: 54–81.
Pressman, Jon F. 1998. "Classification and Counter-Classification of Language on Saint Barthélemy." *Language in Society* 27, no. 4: 459–94.
Purwo, Bambang Kaswanti. 1984. "The Categorial System in Contemporary Indonesian: Pronouns." *NUSA Linguistic Studies in Indonesian and Languages of Indonesia* 19: 55–74.
_____. 1993. "Factors Influencing Comparison of Sundanese, Javanese, Madurese, and Balinese." In *Topics in Descriptive Austronesian Linguistics*, ed. Ger P. Reesink, 245–91. Leiden: University of Leiden.
Quaglio, Paulo. 2009. *Television Dialogue the Sitcom Friends vs. Natural Conversation*. Amsterdam: John Benjamins. https://doi.org/10.1075/scl.36

Raja Rozina Raja Suleiman. 2017. *Impoliteness On-line among Users of Bahasa Melayu.* Paper presented at the 6th Universiti Malaya Discourse and Society International Conference, 5 and 6 December.

Ratliffe, Martha. 2010. *Hmong-Mien Language History.* Canberra: Pacific Linguistics.

Raymond, Chase Wesley. 2016. "Linguistic Reference in the Negotiation of Identity and Action: Revisiting the T/V Distinction." *Language* 92, no. 3: 636–70.

Reid, Anthony. 2015. *A History of Southeast Asia: Critical Crossroads.* Chichester: Wiley Blackwell.

Rendle-Short, Johanna. 2007. "'Catherine, you're wasting your time': Address Terms within the Australian Political Interview." *Journal of Pragmatics* 39: 1503–25.

―――. 2010. "'Mate' as a Term of Address in Ordinary Interaction." *Journal of Pragmatics* 42, no. 5: 1201–18.

―――. 2011. "Address Terms in the Australian Political News Interview." In *Talking Politics in Broadcast Media: Cross-Cultural Perspectives on Political Interviewing, Journalism and Accountability,* ed. Mats Ekström and Marianna Patrona, 93–111. Amsterdam: John Benjamins.

Rijkhoff, Jan. 1998. "Bystander Deixis." In *The Romani Element in Non-Standard Speech,* ed. Yaron Matras, 51–67. Wiesbaden: Harrassowitz.

Robbins, Joel. 1994. "Equality as a Value: Ideology in Dumont, Melanesia and the West." *Social Analysis* 36: 21–70.

Robson, Stuart O. 1992. *Javanese Grammar for Students.* Clayton VIC: Centre of Southeast Asian Studies, Monash University.

Roth, Andrew and David Olsher. 1997. "Some Standard Uses of 'What About': Prefaced Interrogatives in the Broadcast News Interview." *Issues in Applied Linguistics* 8, no. 1: 3–25.

Rydström, Helle. 2003. *Embodying Morality: Growing Up in Rural Northern Vietnam.* Honolulu: University of Hawai'i Press. https://doi.org/10.1515/9780824862336

Sabirin. 1957. "Anda, Kata Baru dalam Bahasa Indonesia." *Bahasa dan Budaja* 5, no. 5: 44.

Sack, Robert. 1986. *Human Territoriality: Its Theory and History.* New York: Cambridge University Press.

Saengtienchai, Chanpen, John Knodel, Mark Van Landingham and Anthony Pramualratan. 1999. "Prostitutes Are Better than Lovers: Wives' Views on the Extramarital Sexual Behavior of Thai Men." In *Genders and Sexualities in Modern Thailand,* ed. Peter A. Jackson and Nerida M. Cook, 78–92. Chiang Mai, Thailand: Silkworm Books.

Schapper, Antoinette. 2017. "Introduction." In *The Papuan Languages of Timor, Alor and Pantar,* vol. 2, ed. Antoinette Schapper, 1–54. Berlin: De Gruyter Mouton.

Schegloff, Emmanuel A. 1996. "Some Practices for Referring to Persons in Talk-in-Interaction: A Partial Sketch of a Systematics." In *Studies in Anaphora,* ed. Barbara Fox, 437–85. Amsterdam: John Benjamins.

_____. 2007. *Sequence Organization in Interaction: A Primer in Conversation Analysis*. Cambridge: Cambridge University Press.
Scott, James C. 2009. *The Art of Not Being Governed: An Anarchist History of Upland Southeast Asia*. New Haven: Yale University Press.
Scupin, Raymond. 1988. "Language, Hierarchy and Hegemony: Thai Muslim Discourse Strategies." *Language Sciences* 10, no. 2: 331–51.
Shamsul, Amri Baharuddin. 2005 [1999]. "From Orang Kaya Baru to Melayu Baru: Cultural Construction of the Malay 'New Rich'." In *Culture and Privilege in Capitalist Asia*, ed. Michael Pinches, 87–111. London: Routledge.
Shiohara, Asako. 2014. "Numerals in Sumbawa." In *Number and Quantity in East Nusantara*, ed. Marian Klamer and František Kratochvíl, 15–26. Canberra: Asia-Pacific Linguistics.
Shiraishi, Saya Sasaki. 1992. "Young Heroes: The Family and School in New Order Indonesia." PhD diss., Cornell University.
Shohet, Merav. 2010. "Silence and Sacrifice: Intergenerational Displays of Virtue and Devotion in Central Vietnam." PhD diss., University of California, Los Angeles.
_____. 2021. *Silence and Sacrifice: Family Stories of Care and the Limits of Love in Vietnam*. Oakland: University of California Press.
Sidnell, Jack. 2009. "Participation." In *Pragmatics of Interaction*, ed. Sigurd D'hondt, Jan-Ola Östman and Jef Verschueren, 125–56. Amsterdam: John Benjamins.
_____. 2019. "Vietnamese Interlocutor Reference, Linguistic Diversity and Semiotic Mediation." *Paradigmi: Rivista di critica filosofica* 37, no. 3: 467–90.
Sidnell, Jack and Merav Shohet. 2013. "The problem of Peers in Vietnamese Interaction." *The Journal of Royal Anthropological Institute (N.S.)* 19: 618–38.
Sidnell, Jack, Tùy An Trần and Thị Thanh Hương Vũ. 2020. "On the Division of Intersubjective Labor in Interaction: A Preliminary Study of Other-Initiated Repair in Vietnamese Conversation." In *Studies in the Anthropology of Language in Mainland Southeast Asia*, ed. N.J. Enfield, Jack Sidnell and Charles H.P. Zuckerman, 65–84. *Journal of the Southeast Asian Linguistics Society*: Special Publication No. 6. Honolulu: University of Hawai'i Press.
Siegel, James. 1993 [1986]. *Solo in the New Order: Language and Hierarchy in an Indonesian City*. Princeton: Princeton University Press.
Siewierska, Anna. 2004. *Person*. Cambridge, UK: Cambridge University Press. https://doi.org/10.1017/CBO9780511812729
Silverman, M.G. 1972. "Some Current Theoretical Problem and the 'Loose Structure' Debate." Review of *Loosely Structured Social Systems: Thailand in Comparative Perspective*, ed. Hans-Dieter Evers. *The Journal of the Polynesian Society* 81, no. 2: 256–67.

Silverstein, Michael. 1976. "Shifters, Linguistics Categories, and Cultural Description." In *Meaning in Anthropology*, ed. Keith H. Basso and Henry A. Selby, 11–55. Albuquerque: University of New Mexico Press.

———. 1979. "Language Structure and Linguistic Ideology." In *The Elements: A Parasession on Linguistic Units and Levels*, ed. Paul R. Clyne, William F. Hanks and Carol L. Hofbauer, 193–247. Chicago: Chicago Linguistic Society, University of Chicago.

———. 1981. *The Limits of Awareness*. Sociolinguistic Working Paper, 84. Austin, Texas: Southwest Educational Development Laboratory.

———. 1995. "Kiksht 'Impersonals' as Anaphors and the Predictiveness of Grammatical-Categorial Universals." *Proceedings of the Annual Meeting of the Berkeley Linguistics Society* 21: 262–86.

———. 2003. "Indexical Order and the Dialectics of Sociolinguistic Life." *Language & Communication* 23: 193–229.

Simpson, Rita. 1997. "Metapragmatic Discourse and the Ideology of Impolite Pronouns in Thai." *Journal of Linguistic Anthropology* 7, no. 1: 38–62.

Smith-Hefner, Nancy J. 1988. "The Linguistic Socialization of Javanese Children in Two Communities." *Anthropological Linguistics* 30, no. 2: 166–98.

Sneddon, James N. 2006. *Colloquial Jakartan Indonesian*. Canberra: Pacific Linguistics.

Sneddon, James N., Alexander Adelaar, Dwi Noverini Djenar and Michael C. Ewing. 2010. *Indonesian: A Comprehensive Grammar*, 2nd ed. London: Routledge.

Stasch, Rupert. 2008. "Referent-Wrecking in Korowai: A New Guinea Abuse Register as Ethnosemiotic Protest." *Language in Society* 37: 1–25.

———. 2009. *Society of Others: Kinship and Mourning in a West Papuan Place*. Berkeley: University of California Press.

Statham, Paul. 2007. "Journalists as Commentators on European Politics: Educators, Partisans or Ideologues?" *European Journal of Communication* 22, no. 4: 461–77.

Stivers, Tanya. 2007. "Alternative Recognitionals in Person Reference." In *Person Reference in Interaction: Linguistic, Cultural and Social Perspectives*, ed. N.J. Enfield and Tanya Stivers, 73–96. New York: Cambridge University Press. https://doi.org/10.1017/CBO9780511486746.005

Stivers, Tanya, N.J. Enfield, and Stephen C. Levinson. 2007. "Person Reference in Interaction." In *Person Reference in Interaction: Linguistic, Cultural, and Social Perspectives*, ed. N.J. Enfield and Tanya Stivers, 1–20. Cambridge: Cambridge University Press.

Storch, Anne. 2011. *Secret Manipulations: Language and Context in Africa*. Oxford: Oxford University Press. https://doi.org/10.1093/acprof:oso/9780199768974.001.0001

Sugamoto, Nobuko. 1989. "Pronominality: A Noun-Pronoun Continuum." In *Linguistic Categorization*, ed. Roberta Corrigan, Fred Eckman and Michael Noonan, 267–91. Amsterdam: John Benjamins.

Suharno, Ignatius. 1982. *A Descriptive Study of Javanese*. Canberra: Pacific Linguistics.

Surjaman, Ukun. 1968. "The Problem of Personal Pronouns in Bahasa Indonesia and the Presentation of the Words: nia, dia and ia." *Asian Studies* 6, no. 1: 90–7.

Sutton, Peter John. 1978. "Wik: Aboriginal Society, Territory and Language at Cape Keerweer, Cape York Peninsula, Australia." PhD diss., University of Queensland.

Taguchi, Yoshihisa. 2021. "Historiography of Hmong-Mien Linguistics." In *The Languages and Linguistics of Mainland Southeast Asia*, ed. Paul Sidwell and Mathias Jenny, 139–47. Berlin/Boston: De Gruyter Mouton.

Tai, Hue-Tam Ho. 1992. "Radicalism and the Origins of the Vietnamese Revolution." Cambridge, MA: Harvard University Press.

Tamtomo, Kristian. 2016. "The Push and Pull of Language Ideologies: Multilingual Communicative Practices of Youths in an Indonesian City." PhD diss., State University of New York at Albany.

_____. 2017. "The Creation of Monolanguaging Space in a Krámá Javanese Language Performance." *Language in Society* 48: 95–124.

_____. 2018. "The Compartmentalization of Languages and Identities among Nationalist Youth in Semarang." *Wacana* 19, no. 1: 168–190.

Tannen, Deborah. 1993. "The Relativity of Linguistic Strategies: Rethinking Power and Solidarity in Gender and Dominance." In *Gender and Conversational Interaction*, ed. Deborah Tannen, 165–88. Oxford, UK: Oxford University Press.

_____. 1995. "Waiting for the Mouse: Constructed Dialogue in Conversation." In *The Dialogic Emergence of Culture*, ed. Dennis Tadlock and Bruce Mannheim, 198–216. Champaign: University of Illinois Press.

Tham Seong Chee. 1970. "Tradition, Values and Society Among the Malays." *Review of Southeast Asian Studies* 4: 4050.

_____. 1982. "Rural and Urban as Categories in Malay life: An Interpretation." *Archipel* 24: 189–203.

Thompson, Laurence C. 1988. *A Vietnamese Reference Grammar*. Seattle: University of Washington Press.

Thomason, Sarah G. and Daniel L. Everett. 2005. "Pronoun Borrowing." *Proceedings of the Twenty Seventh Annual Meeting of the Berkeley Linguistics Society*. no. 1: 301–16. Berkeley: University of California at Berkeley Department of Linguistics.

Thurgood, Ela. 1998. "A Description of Nineteenth Century Baba Malay: A Malay Variety Influenced by Language Shift." PhD diss., University of Hawai'i.

Thurgood, Graham. 1999. *From Ancient Cham to Modern Dialects: Two Thousand Years of Language Contact and Change*. Honolulu: University of Hawai'i Press.

Thurgood, Graham and Randy J. LaPolla, eds. 2016. *Sino-Tibetan Languages*, 2nd ed. Abingdon, Oxon: Routledge.
Tran, Allen. 2018. "The Anxiety of Romantic Love in Ho Chi Minh City, Vietnam." *Journal of the Royal Anthropological Institute* 24: 512–31.
Tran, Ben. 2017. *Post-Mandarin: Masculinity and Aesthetic Modernity in Colonial Vietnam*. New York: Fordham University Press.
Trinh T. Minh-Ha.1992. *Framer Framed*. New York and London: Routledge.
Truitt, Allison. 2008. "On the Back of a Motorbike: Middle-Class Mobility in Ho Chi Minh City." *American Ethnologist* 35: 3–19.
Tsunoda, Tasaku. 1981. *The Djaru language of Kimberley, Western Australia*. Canberra: Pacific Linguistics.
Uehara, Satoshi. 2011. "The Socio-Cultural Motivation of Referent Honorifics in Korean and Japanese." In *Motivation in Grammar and the Lexicon*, ed. Klaus-Uwe Panther and Günther Radden, 191–212. Philadelphia: John Benjamins.
Uhlenbeck, Eugenius M. 1978. *Studies in Javanese Morphology*. The Hague: Martinus Nijhoff.
Urichuk, Matthew and Verónica Loureiro-Rodríguez. 2019. "Brocatives: Self-Reported Use of Masculine Nominal Vocatives in Manitoba (Canada)." In *It's Not All About You: New Perspectives on Address Research*, ed. Bettina Kluge and María Irene Moyna, 355–72. Amsterdam: John Benjamins.
Van Dalen, Arjen, Rosa Berganza, Thomas Hanitzsch, Adriana Amado, Beatriz Herrero, Beate Josephi, Sonja Seizova, Morten Skovsgaard and Nina Steindl. 2019. "Trust: Journalists' Confidence in Public Institutions." In *Worlds of Journalism: Journalistic Cultures Around the Globe*, ed. Thomas Hanitzch, Folker Hanusch, Jyotika Ramaprasad and A.S. (Arrie) De Beer, 233–57. New York: Columbia University Press. https://doi.org/10.7312/hani18642-010
Van Esterik, Penny. 1996. "Nurturance and Reciprocity in Thai Studies." In *State Power and Culture in Thailand*, ed. E. Paul Durrenberger, 22–46. New Haven: Yale University Southeast Asia Studies.
Vanlandingham, Mark, John Knodel, Chanpen Saengtienchai, and Anthony Pramualratana. 1998. "In the Company of Friends: Peer Influence on Thai Male Extramarital Sex." *Social Science & Medicine* 47, no. 12: 1993–2011.
Vientiane Times, Staff. 2004. "Greedy Thieves Are the Leeches of Society." *Vientiane Times*, 30 January.
———. 2009. "Sport Healthy in Moderation." *Vientiane Times*, 4 June.
Weintraub, Andrew N. 2010. *Dangdut Stories: A Social and Musical History of Indonesia's Most Popular Music*. Oxford: Oxford University Press. https://doi.org/10.1093/acprof:oso/9780195395662.001.0001

Winichakul, Thongchai. 2000. "The Others Within: Travels and Ethno-spatial Differentiation of Siamese Subjects, 1885–1910." In *Civility and Savagery: Social Identity in Tai States*, ed. Andrew Turton, 38–63. London: Curzon.

Wiryomartono, Bagoes. 2020. *Livability and Sustainability of Urbanism: An Interdisciplinary Study on History and Theory of Urban Settlement*. London: Palgrave Macmillan. https://doi.org/10.1007/978-981-13-8972-6

Wolff, John U. and Soepomo Poejosoedarmo. 1982. *Communicative Codes in Central Java* (Linguistic Series VIII, Data Paper no. 116). Ithaca, NY: Cornell University Southeast Asia Program.

Wolfowitz, Clare. 1991. *Language Style and Social Space: Stylistic Choice in Suriname Javanese*. Urbana: University of Illinois Press.

Wood, Linda A. and Rolf O. Kroger. 1991. "Politeness and Forms of Address." *Journal of Language and Social Psychology* 10, no. 3: 145–68.

Woolard, Kathryn. 1998. "Language Ideology as a Field of Inquiry." in *Language Ideologies: Practice and Theory*, ed. Bambi B. Schieffelin, Kathryn Woolard and Paul V. Kroskrity, 3–47. New York and Oxford: Oxford University Press.

Wortham, Stanton. 2006. *Learning Identity: The Joint Emergence of Social Identification and Academic Learning*. Cambridge: Cambridge University Press.

Wu, Xiao An. 2009. "China Meets Southeast Asia: A Long-Term Historical Review." In *Connecting and Distancing: Southeast Asia and China*, ed. Ho Khai Leong, 3–30. Singapore: ISEAS Publishing.

Yoong, David. *2011*. "Orderly and Disorderly Practices of Personal *Pronouns* during Question Time in the *Malaysian* House of Representatives." *Journal of Modern Languages* 21, no. 1: 33–47.

Yun, Sung-kyu. 1993. "Honorific Agreement." PhD diss., University of Hawai'i at Manoa.

Zainal, Abidin bin Ahmad. 1950. "Malay Manners and Etiquette." *Journal of the Malayan Branch of the Royal Asiatic Society* XXIII, Part III, Aug. Kuala Lumpur.

Zentz, Lauren. 2014. "'Love' the Local, 'use' the National, 'study' the Foreign: Shifting Javanese Language Ecologies in (Post)modernity, Postcoloniality, and Globalization." *Journal of Linguistic Anthropology* 24, no. 3: 339–59.

⸻. *Statehood, Scale and Hierarchy: History, Language and Identity in Indonesia*. Bristol: Multilingual Matters.

Zuckerman, Charles H.P. 2016. "Phatic Violence? Gambling and the Arts of Distraction in Laos." *The Journal of Linguistic Anthropology* 26, no. 3: 294–314.

⸻. 2018. "Good Gambling: Meaning and Moral Economy in Late-Socialist, Laos." PhD diss., University of Michigan.

⸻. 2020. "'Don't Gamble for Money with Friends': Moral-Economic Types and Their Uses." *American Ethnologist* 47, no. 4: 432–46.

_____. 2021a. "Introduction to the Generic Special Issue." *Language in Society* 50, no. 4: 509–15.

_____. 2021b. "On the Unity of Types: Lao Gambling, Ethno-Metapragmatics, and Generic and Specific Modes of Typification." *Language in Society* 50, no. 4: 557–82.

_____. 2022. "When Ethics Can't Be Found: Evaluative Gaps in Ordinary Life." *Cultural Anthropology* 37, no. 3: 450–85.

Zuckerman, Charles H.P. and N.J. Enfield. 2020. "Heavy Sound Light Sound: a Nam Noi Metalinguistic Trope." *Journal of the Southeast Asia Linguistic Society* Special Publication 6: 85–92.

_____. 2021. "The Unbearable Heaviness of Being Kri: House Construction and Ethnolinguistic Transformation in Upland Laos." *The Journal of the Royal Anthropological Institute* 28, no 1: 178–203.

Index

addressee-honorifics
  attested in East and Southeast Asia, 198–200
  first-person pronouns, 201
  form of, 198
  markedness of, 199
addressee-reference, 4, 163, 168, 184, 190, 200–2, 206, 209
  in Indonesian and deferential acts, 165–8
  open-class nouns employed in, 204
  sociolinguistics of, 3–6
addressee-targeting
  development of, 200
  first-person pronouns in Indonesian languages, 210–12
  honorific pronouns in addressee and speaker-reference, 211
  speech levels, 210
address systems, 190
address terms, 4, 64, 67–8, 70, 72, 76, 86, 95, 146–7
alerter (attention getting device), 74
alluding, practice of, 85
anticolonial movement, 49
anti-honorific pronominals, 206
Arendt, Hannah, 161, 185
Austroasiatic languages, 27
Austronesian languages, 7, 17, 194, 198, 203
Austronesians (stateless sea peoples), 16

baby-talk, 4
Balinese honorific repertoires, 199

Balinese system, of kinship terminology, 5
básá, 1
Cerbon/basa Cerbon-Dermayu. *See* Cirebon Javanese
kedhaton (palace language), characteristic of, 192, 213n4
Bourdieu, Pierre, 16, 46
Brown, Radcliffe, 14–15
Brown, Roger, 2–3, 9–11, 15, 55–6
Bru language, 27
bystander honorifics, 212n1

cascading questions, 176–8
"chiefly languages" of Western Polynesia, 194
Chinese linguistic influence in Southeast Asia, 16
chronotopes, 91
Cirebon Javanese, 20, 66
  choice of address terms, 68
  first- and second-person subjects, 70
  pronominal forms, 71
  vocatives in, 68–72
    addressee reference, 70–2
    forms of, 68–70
    importance of, 68
    used for "metaphoric kin", 69
Civilization of New Learning, A (1904), 133
Classical Chinese language, 17
collision, metaphor of, 85
confrontation talk, 99
Confucian teachings, influence on Vietnamese language, 14

contact talk analysis, 91
conversation analysis, techniques of, 10–11

deference and demeanour
  collaborative construction of, 163, 176–8
  differentiating degrees of, 178–80
  to enact alignment and opposition, 178
  focus of, 192
  indexing through
    question design, 172–80
    self-reference, 168–72
  interrelationship between, 2, 14–16
  markers of, 19
  origo of, 192
  in political interviews, 168
  target of, 166
deference-to-addressee, ideological function of, 16
Dewantara, Ki Hadjar, 49, 52, 53
Đoàn, Đinh, 14
"dominated" class, 47

East Asian honorifics, 197
elliptical grammatical constructions, 57
English-Malay contact register, 90
English pronouns
  egalitarian-type participant relations, 108
  neutrality of, 100
  regulation through Malay address conventions, 102
Errington, Joseph, 5, 16, 19, 68, 190, 208, 209
ethnic identities, 58, 92
European T/V systems, 200–1, 211, 213n6

face-to-face interaction, 2, 12, 63
face-to-face talk, in contact situations, 91

Fataluku (non-Austronesian language), 22n6
Ferguson, Charles, 4
first-person plural, 13, 104, 211

Geertz, Clifford, 5, 148
generation-graded hierarchical system, 111
Geoghegan decision-trees, 11
Gilman, Albert, 2, 4, 9–11, 15, 55, 56
gimana interrogatives, 163, 173–7
Goffman, Erving, 14–15, 41, 112, 163
grammaticalised honorifics, 189
Greater Burma Zone, 18

Hamid, Zulkifley, 89, 97
Harms, Erik, 134
Hmong-Mien language, 17
honorific alignment, 201, 203, 208
honorific language
  emergence of, 189
  functional instantiation of, 199
  norms of, 199
  social hierarchy and, 189
honorific pronouns, 191, 200, 202
  addressee-targeting, 210–11
honorific registers, 189
  characteristic of, 212n1
  dual metapragmatic-pragmatic structure, 193
  in East and Southeast Asian languages, 196
  indexical focus and honorification, 191–2
  Korowai anti-honorific lexical register *xoxulop*, 193
  of person deixis, 200
    indexical focus in, 200–3
  properties of, 196
  speaker-addressee lexical honorifics, 193–6
honorific vocabularies, 189, 191, 195–6, 199, 213n3

identity politics, 164
indexing of agency, 86
indexing social relations, strategy for, 90, 95, 108
Indo-European languages, 2
Indonesian language
  addressee-targeting first-person pronouns in, 210–12
  propagation of, 17, 49, 180, 197, 210
  use of non-singular first-person pronouns in, 211
  institutional framework, neutralism "breach" and reworking of, 180–4
integrative struggles
  class-based, 46–7
  in Javanese Indonesia, 54
interactional engagement, Javanese modes of, 55
interactional role-inhabitancy, 205
interaction, vocatives in, 73–84
  alignment, 79–80
  in narrated conversation, 77–8
  as structure of address, 73
  summons and offer, 78–9
  topic shift, 75–7
interethnic communication, 107
interlocutor reference systems. *See also* speaker-reference
  acts of, 12
  delimiting the domain of, 1–3
  formal and functional attributes of, 203
  of languages of East and Southeast Asia, 203
  meaning of, 2
  pragmatic salience of, 208–10
interpersonal relations, 42
  ethics of, 20
intersubjectivity in language, role of, 66
intimate interpersonal hierarchy, ethics of, 111
Islamic revivalism, 93
I/you usage, 89–91
  hierarchical reciprocal use, 101–7

to index values associated with modernity, 106
in Kuala Lumpur Malay, 98–9

Javanese language
  Cirebon variety of, 66
  differentiation of personal pronouns, 45–6
  influence on the national language, 54
  kin terms, ethnicity, and nationality, 49–52
  krama andhap, 197–8
  linguistic hierarchies in, 44
  personal pronouns, use of, 55
  programmatic redundancy in, 86
  sociopolitical dynamics of, 44
  system of interlocutor reference, 19
  use in an exemplary centre, 45–9
  use of kin terms and personal pronouns in, 44
  vocabularies of politesse, 45
Javanese linguistic etiquette, 148
Javanese *priyayi* conceptions of self, 21n2
journalistic adversarialness and deference, 172
journalistic deference, notion of, 163, 172, 178

Kendall, Martha, 9–11
kin-based title forms, 28
kinship relations in Vietnam, male-oriented model for, 124
kin terms
  interactional significance of, 47, 49–52
  links with modes of social stratification, 51
Kobon (Papuan language), 40
Korowai anti-honorific lexical register *xoxulop*, 193
krama, 1, 189, 192, 195, 197, 198
Kri (Vietic language)
  axes of asymmetry

hierarchy (up-down), 28
inclusion (inside-outside), 28
dialect of, 27
kin relation categories, 42
kin relations and terms, 32
matrilocality, practice of, 35
mree relation, 36–7
practice of *pato'oj* in, 42
practices for referring to persons
   consanguineal relations, 30
   in-laws, 35–6
   parents, 30
   parents of married couples, 41
   parents' siblings, 30–1
   second cousins, 31
   siblings, 31
prefixes to personal names in, 28
pronouns, 29
teknonymy, use of, 28, 38
words for an in-law, 37–8
Kuala Lumpur Malay, 20, 90, 93, 108
I/you in, 98–9, 107

language reform, metadiscourse of, 12
language use
   in exemplary centre, 45–9
   semiotic theory of, 2
langue, 10
Leach, Edmund, 5
lexical alternations, 193, 197
lexical honorific registers, 193, 196, 202
   addressee-targeting, 194–6
   in Austronesian languages, 194
   avoidance relations, 195
   "chiefly languages" of Western Polynesia, 194
   in Indonesian languages, 197
   krama inggil vocabulary, 197
   referent-targeting, 194
lexical noun, 89, 165, 172
   as pronoun substitutes, 165
linguistically encoded hierarchy, 140
linguistic etiquette, elements of, 47

linguistic hierarchies, in south-central Java, 44
linguistic mediation, of self-other relations, 5
Liu, Amy, 54
loakaeiah wahu (language of respect), 213n6
loose structure literature, 145

Malay-English bilinguals, 89, 93
   in confrontation talk, 99
   English norms for indexing social hierarchy, 108
   I/you usage, 98–107
   Malay norms for indexing social hierarchy, 108
   medium of exchange, 102
   negotiations of suitable address forms, 106
   social indexicality to modernity, 99–101
Malay ethnolinguistic identity, 91
Malay language modernisation, 93
Malay pronouns, strategy for adapting, 97
matrilocality, practice of, 35
"Me" and "You"
   senses of relationality between, 57–8
metalinguistic reflections, 193
metaphoric kinship, act of, 185
metapragmatic awareness, biasing of, 193
metasigns, 3, 11–14, 112, 135
modernity-affiliated address strategies, 96
modern Malay, concept of, 105
Mohamad, Goenawan, 58
"mother-in-law languages" of Aboriginal Australia, 195

nationalist movement, language of, 49, 54
national language agency, 89
ndiká, 46
neutrality, idea of, 94
"neutral" nouns, 194
New Order regime, 49–50, 54, 58, 185
   regime of the standard, 54–5

news interview
  forms of self- and addressee-reference, 163
  in Indonesian and deferential acts, 165–8
  indexing deference through self-reference, 168–72
  Indonesian panel interviews and the 2019 general elections, 164–5
  neutralism norms, 163
  norms of neutralism and adversariality, 162
  question cascade, 163
  symmetrical deference, 163
  third-party reference, 166, 168
ngoko vocabulary, 209
non-referential indexicality, 205, 209
nonrestraint evidence relations, pronouns of, 158
nouns
  grammaticalised, 17–18
  lexical, 6–9, 11–12, 15

object honorifics, 198
object signs, 3, 11–14, 180
  of interlocutor reference, 135, 161
  reflexive semiotic model of conduct, 112, 135
  social significance of, 20, 135
Omar, Asmah Haji, 89
open class interlocutor reference (OCIR), 165, 204
  characteristics of, 17
  deictic selectivity and indexical focus in, 205–8
  Vietnamese, 17
open-class noun reference, 205
organisational vocatives, 65
origo of deference, 192

panel or debate agenda interviews, 160
panjenengan, 1, 46, 55–6

Papuan (non-Austronesian) languages, 17
parole, 10
participant deixis, registers of, 15
partisan advocate, role of, 184
peers, problem of, 140
personal identity, index of, 9, 168, 171
personal pronoun, use of, 46, 55–6, 93, 189
person deixis
  honorific registers of, 200
  mapping of, 205
  social indexicality in, 190
Phan Khôi, 12–13
Pingelapese (Austronesian) lexical honorifics, 213n6
plural terms, reciprocal use of, 55
politeness
  norms of, 89
  theory of, 9
political interviews, indexing deference in, 168
pragmatic salience
  of interlocutor reference, 190, 208–10
  of morphemes, 208
  of person, 191
priyayi traditions, 45–6, 49
pronominal complexity, 18
pronominal imposters, 6
pronominal mutation, 18
pronouns, 6–9, 11. *See also* personal pronoun, use of
  borrowing, 9
  dual pronouns for lower in-laws, 38–41
  English, 99–100
  European, 55
  first-person, 7, 55, 201
  honorific, 200
  I and *you*, 20
  Indonesian, 12, 89
  judicial use of, 82
  in Kri (Vietic language), 29
  of nonrestraint evidence relations, 158
  second-person, 7, 55–6, 65

substitutes, 6
substitution, 71
   in Thai language, 13
   third person, 7
   T/V pronouns, 9
   in Vietnamese language, 12
pronoun substitutes, 6, 165, 191

question cascade, 163, 176–8
question design, indexing deference through, 172–80
   "bare" *gimana* construction, 173–6
   cascading question, 176–8
   collaborative accomplishment of deference, 176–8
   differentiating degrees of deference, 178–80
   juxtaposing perspectives, 172

Raymond, Chase, 10–11
referential indexicality, 205, 209
referent-targeting honorific repertoires, 198
Reid, Anthony, 16
"relativity" of discourse strategies, 9

Saek (Tai language), 27
Saigon urban development project, ethnography of, 134
sampéyan, 46
Sanskrit language, influence on western Indonesian, 17
Santali (Austroasiatic) dialect, 40, 201–2
self-humbling repertoires, 198–200
self-raising speaker-reference, 201
self-reference
   indexing deference through, 168–72
   Indonesian forms for, 168
semantic derogation, principle of, 197
semantics, 56
   characterisation of, 10

difference with ground-level pragmatic significance, 10
   for interactional relations, 55
Sidnell, Jack, 190
Silverstein, Michael, 2, 10, 11, 209
Sino-Tibetan language, 17
Slavic languages, 201
small talk, 162
social deixis, 96, 101
social hierarchies, 17, 53, 189, 199
   discursive interaction and ideologies of, 190
social identities, 12, 91, 92, 101–2, 107, 108n7
social indexical functions, mapping of, 198
social indexicality, 65, 190
   of English forms, 96
   to modernity, 99–101
social pragmatics
   in East and Southeast Asian languages, 210
   of interlocutor reference, 190
   of speaker-reference, 210
   typology of, 209
social registers, use of, 66–7
social relationships, 7, 30, 63, 65, 68, 85–7, 101, 191
social relations, linguistic mediators of, 208
social stratification, 190, 199
   modes of, 51
sociocultural ideologies of hierarchy, 190
sociolinguistic change, "macro" and "micro" aspects of, 58
solidarity
   semantic, 3
Southeast Asian languages, 7
   history of, 16–17
   pronominal systems of, 18
   sociolinguistic typology of, 16–18
speaker-reference
   addressee-honouring nouns, 213n5
   sociopragmatic activation of, 211

Index

use of open-class nouns in, 211
speech level systems, development of, 211
symmetrical deference, 163

Tai-Kadai language, 17
Taman Siswa school, 49–50
"target" of deference, 166
Thai language
   open class interlocutor reference (OCIR), 17
   use of pronominals in reference to a monk, 22
Tibetan *zhesa* (respect language), 193
titles, used as prefixes to personal names, 28
T/V pronouns, 3, 9, 201
   alternation in European languages, 200, 211
   alternations in various dialects of Spanish, 10
   properties of, 200
   S-A alignment in, 201

universality of person, as a grammatical category, 22n7
urban social identities, creation of, 101
utterances
   grammatical constituent of, 65
   grammatical structure of, 86

verbal agreement, 22n6
   patterns of, 7
Vietnamese kinship system, 124, 136n12
Vietnamese language, 2, 12
   comparison with French and modern Chinese language, 12
   influence of Confucian teachings on, 14
   intergenerational hierarchy, 121
   intimate interpersonal hierarchy, ethics of, 111
   lexical nouns, use of, 12

"neutral" and "unanimous" pronouns, 12
notion of *văn minh* (civility), 134
practices of interlocutor reference, 112
   bi-directional bonds, 122
   for egalitarian solidarity, 122
   model of social relations, 126
   object signs of, 135
   sibling terms in interlocutor reference
      alternative arrangements for usage of, 122–33
      differences from English "brother" and "sister", 112–17
      reported and imagined, 122–33
   use of
      pronouns between husband and wife, 23n17
      sibling terms, 112–17
      tôi in the 1930s, 18
vocative expressions, in Javanese conversations
   interpersonal, 65
   for marking solidarity and intimacy, 65
   motivations of choosing one form over another, 72
   pragmatic functions associated with, 65
   repetition of, 75
   syntactic constructions of, 64
   variation in usage in terms of frequency, 72–3

Wa (Palaungic language of northern Myanmar), 40
WhatsApp (messenging program), 138
   "bare" friendships, 146–52
   lasting friendships, 155–6
   "loose" friendships, 144–6
   substance of *Siaw1*, 140–4
   thrown away friendships, 153–5
Whorfian social pragmatics, 190

Zomia, 16